ANSELM AND A
NEW GENERATION

ANSELM AND A NEW GENERATION

BY

G. R. EVANS

CLARENDON PRESS · OXFORD
1980

Oxford University Press, Walton Street, Oxford OX2 6DP

OXFORD LONDON GLASGOW
NEW YORK TORONTO MELBOURNE WELLINGTON
KUALA LUMPUR SINGAPORE JAKARTA HONG KONG TOKYO
DELHI BOMBAY CALCUTTA MADRAS KARACHI
NAIROBI DAR ES SALAAM CAPE TOWN

Published in the United States by
Oxford University Press, New York

British Library Cataloguing in Publication Data
Evans, Gillian Rosemary
    Anselm and new generation.
    1. Anselm, *Saint*
    2. Theology, Catholic
    I. Title
    230'.2'0924   BX4700.A58   79-41121
    ISBN 0-19-826651-0

Phototypeset in V.I.P. Baskerville by
Western Printing Services Ltd, Bristol
Printed in Great Britain at
The Pitman Press, Bath

M. H.

PREFACE

The haze of questions and opinions in my head began to disperse, and its place was taken by three or four great questions: What is God? What does Jesus mean for us? What is the purpose of our life? How will we achieve this purpose? . . . I made a rule for myself: the simpler the better. I did not lose my delight in learning; indeed I studied more zealously and with more pleasure than before, but what I now looked for in books and from my professors was the true knowledge of simplicity. My aim now was to become more profound, clearer, more definite in this knowledge.[1]

THESE are words which, with some unimportant modifications, might have been spoken by St. Anselm. They could not have come from any of his twelfth-century successors in the schools; although there were in the monastic orders men of *simplicitas*, that is perhaps a *simplicitas* of another kind. It is not that twelfth-century thinkers did not reflect in this way about the direction of their lives, or about the best use to be made of their powers of mind. Of course they did; there is ample incidental evidence to that effect, if little in the way of coherent autobiographical statement. But Anselm's natural taste for profound simplicity had a freedom to develop in its own way which would not have been allowed to it if he had lived the life of a scholar such as Peter Abelard, moving from school to school with his reputation to make among men most readily impressed by a command of technical expertise.

A change in public expectations was already under way in Anselm's lifetime, and towards the end it influenced him considerably in his writing and even perhaps in his thought. But as it happened the circumstances of his life enabled him to remain outside its ambience until he was fully mature as a thinker. Abelard encountered its effects from his earliest youth and so far did he go to meet it that he himself became instrumental in making of it the kind of change it ultimately proved to be. Abelard could impress an audience with his quick-wittedness with ease. From his colleagues he sparked the most refreshingly challenging of responses, and he even refers to them as *aemuli*,

[1] E. Busch, *Karl Barth*, trans. J. Bowden (London, 1976), p. 35, quoted from a sermon of Karl Barth's given on 13 Oct. 1912.

those who were jealous of him. The powers of mind which were developed in the atmosphere of such schools as Abelard knew were those which made great use of a capacity for distinguishing differences in things but less use of a capacity for seeing straight to the heart of a question. The search for essential simplicity was replaced by a search for technical exactitude. Karl Barth's three or four questions—to which the bulk of Anselm's thought can be reduced—became three or four hundred, which not only proved irreducible, but proliferated in their turn until they became three or four thousand.

Anselm took the optimistic view that if a man who held a mistaken opinion had his error reasonably explained to him, and if he listened to the explanation with a receptive mind, he would be cured of his error. On the assumption that God would help the faithful soul to understanding, that was not a naïve view. Within the community of Bec and among the wider circle of Anselm's acquaintances in the monasteries of Normandy, it was, in practice, quite a workable view. Those who came to Anselm with questions often did so in the appropriate frame of mind. Like Boso when he first came to Anselm fresh from the schools of northern France and full of uncertainties, they were eager to have their doubts resolved. Anselm was always able to help such honestly worried young men and set their minds at rest.

The first purpose of this book is to look at what was happening to the theological certainties in which Anselm had such confidence, in his own day and in the generation or two after his death. It is clear from the events of the first half of the twelfth century that this was a time when a comparatively small number of men could shape an intellectual revolution. Perhaps there is nothing peculiar to the twelfth century in that. But here we can observe surprisingly closely a small group of dedicated people communicating with one another about what interests them most. These are not men carried about by great changes over which they have no control, but people engaged in one of the major pleasures of life: talking about something they want to understand better and which is important to them. They played an active part in bringing about the changes they experienced, and they draw the modern reader into their work because they are asking afresh many of the questions about fundamentals which almost everyone is likely to ask at some time in his life.

Even in his own day, Anselm was recognized as a quite outstanding figure, an exceptionally good and clever man. There has always been a difficulty in placing him in the context of his own times which does not arise in the same degree in the case of Peter Abelard or John of Salisbury; these were great men but they were not giants, while Anselm stood head and shoulders above his own contemporaries. Nevertheless, Anselm's thought, for all its profound independence, is in many ways a product of its time. A number of the topics he was prompted by his friends to talk and write about were matters of immediate contemporary interest. The habits of thought which directed his attempts at problem-solving were partly bred by his training in the liberal arts and the study of Scripture and the Fathers. The balance between his peculiar independence of mind on the one hand, and his debt to the training he received and to the ideas and interests of those around him, on the other, is not easy to determine. But it is important that we should try to understand it if we are to know what value to set upon his achievement.

It is important for another reason, too. The change which was taking place at the end of Anselm's life—and which was beginning to affect his own thinking in the last treatises—was to set the course for later medieval theology and for scholastic thought in general. This was to prove an alteration of such long-term consequence that it was to decide the character of medieval intellectual endeavour for several centuries. There are few streams of medieval and even Renaissance thought which do not draw upon the great river which began to flow at full flood in the twelfth century.

It is the second purpose of this study (and by no means its subordinate purpose) to try to distinguish that quality which marks Anselm's thought so distinctively and which, ironically enough, limited the range of his influence. Anselm saw theological truths with a directness compounded of spiritual and intellectual insight. He unites the virtues of the monastic and scholastic traditions which were increasingly to diverge in the twelfth century. There is often a visionary air about his thought which we shall not normally find in the work of the theologians of the twelfth-century schools. He seems a Mary to their Martha, and it is partly for this reason that he was of little help to them in the practical difficulties with which they were already busy. The reasons why they could not make greater use of what he had to say have a good deal to tell us about the differences between his vision and theirs.

I have argued in *Anselm and Talking about God*[2] that it is important that we should try to understand what Anselm himself thought he was saying. But it is also important that we should look at the community of thought in which he wrote. His language is the language of his time; his time was a period of vigorous development in the technical language of theology and philosophy. To read him out of context is to risk misunderstanding what he is saying, and it is also to leave out of account the views of contemporaries, and of the next generation, which are of considerable interest in their own right.

I should like to acknowledge the help and encouragement, over a number of years, and at many points in the writing of this book, of Mr A. K. Bate, the Revd Professor H. Chadwick, Mr D. H. Farmer, Dr M. T. Gibson, Dr D. P. Henry, Professor J. C. Holt, Dr R. W. Hunt, Dr B. R. Kemp, Miss P. McNulty, Professor J. Norton-Smith, Dr M. Reeves, Dr B. Smalley, Sir Richard Southern, Sister Benedicta Ward.

[2] *Anselm and Talking about God* (Oxford, 1978).

CONTENTS

ABBREVIATIONS

AB	R. W. Southern, *St. Anselm and his Biographer* (Cambridge, 1963).
Abelard, *Dialectica*	*Petrus Abaelardus Dialectica*, ed. L. M. de Rijk (Assen, 1956).
Archives	*Archives d'histoire doctrinale et littéraire du moyen âge.*
Beiträge	*Beiträge zur Geschichte der Philosophie und Theologie des Mittelalters.*
Cahiers	*Cahiers de l'institut du moyen-âge grec et latin*, Copenhagen.
CCCM	*Corpus Christianorum Continuatio Medievalis.*
Garlandus, *Dialectica*	Garlandus Compotista, *Dialectica*, ed. L. M. de Rijk (Assen, 1959).
Gilbert on Boethius	Gilbert of Poitiers, *Commentaries on Boethius*, ed. N. M. Häring (Toronto, 1966).
JTS	*Journal of Theological Studies.*
LM	*Logica Modernorum*, ed. L. M. de Rijk (Assen, 1967), 2 vols.
Lottin	O. Lottin, *Psychologie et morale aux xiie et xiiie siècles*, V (Gembloux, 1959).
MARS	*Mediaeval and Renaissance Studies.*
Memorials	*Memorials of St. Anselm*, ed. R. W. Southern and F. S. Schmitt (London, 1969).
MGH	*Monumenta Germaniae Historica.*
PL	*Patrologia Latina*, ed. J. P. Migne.
RTAM	*Recherches de théologie ancienne et médiévale.*
S	*Anselmi Opera Omnia*, ed. F. S. Schmitt (Rome/Edinburgh, 1938–68), 6 vols.
SSL	*Spicilegium Sacrum Lovaniense.*
Theol. Chr.	Peter Abelard, *Theologia Christiana*, ed. M. Buytaert, *CCCM* XII (Turnholt, 1969).
Theol. Tractates	Boethius, *Theological Tractates*, ed. H. F. Stewart and E. K. Rand (London, 1973, reprint).

Thierry on Boethius   *Commentaries on Boethius by Thierry of Chartres and his School*, ed. N. M. Häring (Toronto, 1971).

VA   *Eadmer's Life of St. Anselm*, ed. R. W. Southern (London, 1962).

SCHOOLS AND SCHOLARS:
A WHO'S WHO

SOME of the thinkers of the generation after Anselm failed to make a name for themselves at all; a band of anonymous *magistri* make their presence felt only in references to their opinions by other writers, perhaps with an initial which would have served to identify them for contemporaries. Even the better-known are not easily grouped. An able young man was likely to make an effort to hear several masters, and to draw upon a variety of sources in his own work. For very few is it possible to reconstruct a biography in any detail. The picture which emerges is of an academic society on the move, exchanging books and pupils and ideas remarkably freely in the absence of any fixed institutional framework which might have imposed a stricter order on the proceedings.

For that very reason, despite the difficulty of doing so at all satisfactorily, it may be helpful to say something by way of preliminary about the complex of relationships which existed among the scholars who appear in the text. Some of them were close friends; some were enemies, some merely colleagues, or master and pupil for a time. But they knew one another in many instances, and the scholars of the day rarely worked in the comparatively isolated circumstances of earlier times. We can speak of a community of thought amongst them.

Of the Benedictine monks, **Anselm** himself (born *c.* 1033), Prior of Bec from 1063, Abbot from 1078, Archbishop of Canterbury from 1093 to 1109, had friends and pupils in the next generation of scholars, both in the monasteries and outside them. **Gilbert Crispin** entered Bec as a boy and grew up there during the years when Anselm was Prior. About 1078 or 1079 he was taken to Canterbury by Lanfranc, and about 1085 he became Abbot of Westminster. He and Anselm met again when Anselm came to England, and their talks were useful to Anselm while he was working on the *De Incarnatione Verbi* and the *Cur Deus Homo*. **Eadmer** was one of the Canterbury monks, who became devoted to Anselm during the years of his Archbishopric, and who subsequently wrote Anselm's biography. **Guibert of Nogent** knew Anselm as a visitor to the monastery at Fly, and he speaks of him as a spiritual director in his own autobiography, the *De Vita Sua*.

In Germany, **Rupert of Deutz** (*c.* 1070–1129 or later) became Abbot of Deutz, near Cologne, about 1120, after teaching at Liège and Sigeberg. He is the author of a massive work on Holy Scripture, highly original in its conception, but belonging to the monastic tradition of exegesis rather than using the new dialectical methods of the schools. He was instrumental in the conversion of **Hermannus Judaeus**, whose account of his experience of conversion preserves a rare Jewish view of the new, more open intercourse between Jews and Christians.

Of the **Victorine Canons** of the house of St. Victor at Paris, **Hugh of St. Victor** (*c.* 1096–1141) was perhaps the most influential. He wrote both mystical works, and textbooks designed to help the beginner in his study of the Bible: elementary manuals, encyclopedias, and the comprehensive handbook to Bible study and doctrine, the *De Sacramentis Christianae Fidei*. He studied at St. Victor under **William of Champeaux** (*c.* 1070–1121), who had retired there in order to escape the embarrassment he had been suffering in the schools as a result of Abelard's assaults upon his teaching. **Richard** and **Adam of St. Victor** are heirs to the double tradition of sound scholarship in the study of Holy Scripture and mystical theology which marks the St. Victor scholars distinctively. **Walter of St. Victor** (d. after 1180), later a Prior of the house, is the author of a polemic against Peter Abelard, Peter Lombard, Peter of Poitiers, and Gilbert of Poitiers, whom he believed to be abusing dialectic in their theological arguments.

The Schools

Laon

The brothers **Anselm and Ralph of Laon** ran a school at Laon which, in the last decade of the eleventh century and the first decades of the twelfth, attracted most of the coming young men. William of Champeaux studied there, as did Peter Abelard. Anselm of Laon (d. 1117) had been trained at Bec under St. Anselm. He taught biblical exegesis by methods in which there was an element of the new emphasis, on expertise in grammar in particular, but which belonged, in spirit, to the monastic tradition.

Chartres

Bernard of Chartres (d. 1130) taught a number of thinkers who were to make use of Calcidius' commentary on Plato's *Timaeus* and the *Theological Tractates* of Boethius in their own work. Among them was **William of Conches** (c. 1080–c. 1145), and **Gilbert of Poitiers** (1076–1154), Bishop of Poitiers from 1142 to 1154, who was condemned for his opinions at the Synod of Reims of 1148. Bernard's younger brother **Thierry** shared these special interests, as well as possessing a full command of the technical skills of the liberal arts of the day. He taught at Chartres about 1121, went to Paris in the 1120s, became Archdeacon of Dreux in 1136, and succeeded Gilbert as Archdeacon and Chancellor of Chartres in 1141. He, too, was present at the Synod of Reims in 1148. None of these scholars spent his whole working life at Chartres, and they may be called 'Chartrians' only in the loosest sense. They belong to Paris and other schools, too.

Paris

Peter Abelard (1079–1142) was first the pupil of **Roscelin of Compiègne** (died about 1125), the dialectician who challenged the orthodoxy of St. Anselm's teaching. Then he studied under William of Champeaux and Anselm of Laon, before setting up as a teacher at Paris. There he stayed until his career was interrupted by his love affair with Héloise, and he retired to monastic life at St. Denys. At the Council of Soissons of 1121 he was condemned for his teaching on the Trinity. He became Abbot of St. Gildas in 1125, but came back to Paris about 1136, to begin teaching again. At the Council of Sens of 1141 he was condemned again, on certain propositions attributed to him; he retired again, this time to Cluny, where he was made welcome by the Abbot, **Peter the Venerable**. He was succeeded at Paris by **Robert of Melun** (d. 1167), an Englishman who had studied at Paris, and who had run a school at Melun from 1142 to 1148. He, too, was present at the condemnation of Gilbert of Poitiers in 1148. From 1163 to 1167 he was Bishop of Hereford. Robert of Melun continued Abelard's work as a theologian, while **Adam of Petit Pont (Adam of Balsham)** inherited his mantle as a dialectician at Paris. With Adam, we might group the enigmatic **Garlandus**, whose *Dialectica* appears to belong to the late eleventh or perhaps the early twelfth century, but about whose career only the most fragmentary evidences can be pieced together.

(Quite unclassifiable is **Honorius Augustodunensis**, a wanderer about whose life very little can be established, but who certainly knew Anselm of Canterbury's work, and whose eclecticism attests to the curiosity which made him a traveller in search of knowledge in the last years of the eleventh century and the early twelfth.)

Peter Lombard (*c.* 1100–60) is the author of the massive compilation of extracts from the Fathers, arranged in an orderly manner for reference, which became the definitive sentence-collection; it was still the principal textbook of its kind in Aquinas's day and after. He taught at Paris from about 1139, and was among those who condemned Gilbert of Poitiers in 1148. **Peter of Poitiers** and **Peter Comestor, Simon of Tournai**, and others, all working at Paris, glossed or commented upon the *Sentences*, or wrote similar works of their own, in the second half of the century. Among the Paris theologians of the later twelfth century we might number **Alan of Lille** (d. 1202), who studied at Paris, and whose works reflect a comprehensive knowledge of the liberal arts, of the *Timaeus*, and Boethius' *Theological Tractates*, of the Sentence-literature and the Fathers themselves—in whom, in short, all these related areas of study came together.

John of Salisbury stands a little apart (*c.* 1110–80). He, too, studied in the schools of importance and under the outstanding masters, at Paris, under Abelard, William of Conches, Gilbert of Poitiers, and probably at Chartres. Unlike Alan of Lille, who made use of his learning to write more works of a theological or philosophical kind, he was primarily an observer of the scene, whose *Metalogicon* contains an account of his experiences in the schools, his *Memoirs of the Papal Court* (*Historia Pontificalis*) and *Policraticus* a certain amount of political and social commentary. But like Alan of Lille, John was an all-round scholar, a literary man as well as a political and philosophical thinker.

INTRODUCTION

First Principles Revisited

WHEN a twelfth-century schoolmaster introduced his pupils to the study of a new author he frequently provided them with a short formal introduction, or *accessus*. Among other things, this explained what was the subject-matter of the work, what was the author's intention in writing it, what branch of study it belonged to, and what was the *utilitas* or profitableness of studying it.[1] We find ourselves on familiar ground here, among students of a generation in the habit of asking why it is that something is worth studying and whether they are going about their investigations in the right way. Something like this has been happening in our own day, with no less intellectually unsettling a result. The processes of reassessment of established assumptions and the questioning of first principles which went on in twelfth-century schools engage a strong fellow-feeling. Nowhere is this process more evident—and nowhere does it touch more deeply on the roots of the assumptions which underlie the thought of the age—than in the study of theology. Theological studies were for twelfth-century scholars rather what the sciences are for modern man, in their concern with method and purpose and appropriate choice of subject-matter. They carried the same unquestioned intellectual respectability; they aspired to a similar exactness of discipline; they were regarded as being of the first importance for the long-term welfare of mankind, and they were felt to carry a considerable weight of responsibility in that connection.

At the beginning of his *Summa Theologica* Aquinas asks what kind of study theology is. Is it a science? Is it a single science or many? Is it a practical science? Is rational argument an appropriate method for use in connection with theology?[2] This is a question—or rather a series of questions—which it would not have occurred to Anselm to ask in quite this way, and which he

[1] On the *accessus* see R. B. C. Huygens, *Accessus ad Auctores* (Leiden, 1970). The *accessus* has a long history before the twelfth century, but it had not been so widely used before.
[2] *Summa Theologica*, Q. 1.

would certainly not have been equipped to answer in the terms
Aquinas chooses.

Aquinas is writing for beginners, as he says in his *Prologue*,
but even at the most elementary stage of their formal study of
theology he clearly expects his thirteenth-century students to
come to the task equipped with a good deal of learning in the
liberal arts, especially in the field of dialectic.[3] He assumes, too,
that their early training will have given them the habit of
questioning first principles, and accordingly he tries systematically to meet every objection he can envisage. Anselm writes for
beginners, too, but he expects to be able to satisfy them with
only occasional reference to the techniques of the *artes*. Above
all, he does not anticipate, at least in his earlier works, that
what he says will be subjected to criticisms of a hostile kind.[4]

The habit of questioning first principles, which is beginning
to be in evidence among the theologians and dialecticians of
Anselm's later years, became an integral part of theological
method during the course of the twelfth century. Still less could
be taken for granted in Aquinas's day than had been left
unquestioned at the end of Anselm's life, and that is partly a
result of new technical developments which seemed to under-
mine old certainties. But it is at least in part a result of a change
in outlook, a reflection of new public expectations. When educated men require to have things scientifically demonstrated to
them, a popular critical—even sceptical—attitude has the
effect of obliging the guardians of a contemporary body of
established knowledge to rethink the grounds of their own
assumptions. The result may be a shifting of certainties and a
periodical taking up of attitudes where the ground seems for the
moment to be firm. It is easy for things to get out of hand in such
circumstances. The habit of asking questions of this order had
in the twelfth century, as in any other age, a sometimes destructive character, but often it is merely exploratory; it reflects an

---

[3] For the pattern of study in the University of Paris at the time see G. Leff, *Paris and Oxford Universities in the Thirteenth and Fourteenth Centuries* (New York, 1967), pp. 116–82. Between Anselm's day and Aquinas's day a good deal of Aristotle had become available to the scholars of the West.

[4] The *De Incarnatione Verbi* is the first of Anselm's treatises to be written in answer to someone's objections to the orthodox view. The *Cur Deus Homo* incorporates *objectiones infidelium*. The last treatises contain a high proportion of arguments designed to refute errors.

attitude of mind, a willingness to take risks with fundamentals, not far removed from that of our own century. And it set up remarkably similar tensions of thought and belief.

One result of searching for sureties in a climate of uncertainty is the temptation it creates to take refuge in attempts to decide at least what may be denied. It may be partly for his reason that the influence of Pseudo-Dionysian 'negative theology' makes itself felt with increasing force in the course of the twelfth century. When Nicholas of Amiens says in his *De Arte Catholicae Fidei* that God is *immensus, incomprehensibilis, ineffabilis, innominabilis*[5] (immeasurable, incomprehensible, beyond speaking of, beyond naming), he is expressing a quite commonly held contemporary view that all we can safely say of God refers to what he is not. The principle finds its way down to the level of detailed textual commentary. (We are almost never in the twelfth century dealing with generalizations; every idea has been tested meticulously in specific applications.) Among the commentaries on Boethius' *De Trinitate* we find this thought: '"Infinite" is the word for something negative, while "eternal" is the word for something positive.'[6] Infinite is not-finite, in other words, and it seems that the best approximation we can make to describing the boundlessness of God is to say that he is unbounded, without limit, in-finite—all negations of the positive idea which is conveyed when we speak of something as being limited or finite. Human language does not always let us down here. 'Eternal' describes God in more positive terms. But the need to resort to negatives, or at best to inadequate human expression, was consciously felt as a failing in the language available to theologians.[7]

There is no question of an entire 'negative theology' taking the place of more positive approaches. But it seems that the Pseudo-Dionysian material which was beginning to awaken more general interest from the beginning of the twelfth century if not earlier,[8] may have met a particular contemporary need. Negative statements about what God is not can be asserted with confidence even when the climate of thought makes it

---

[5] *PL* 210.601, I, Art. xvi.   [6] Thierry on Boethius, p. 501.63–5.
[7] Ibid., p. 501.66–7.
[8] It is difficult to trace any influence on Anselm himself, but within a decade of his death the material was being quite widely studied.

increasingly difficult to make unchallengeable propositions of a positive kind. When we make such statements we set aside some of the problems which arise when we try to speak of God. Our commentator points out that when we say that something is not true of God, we may be said to deny the applicability of the words we use to the special case of God: *negat a deo vocabulorum proprietatem.*[9] The very terms *affirmatio* and *negatio* would have been familiar to any student of dialectic.[10] The growing body of technical skills which constituted the arts of language, the increasingly scientific method applied to the study of language, made it difficult for technical reasons for twelfth-century thinkers to make statements about God in the confidence that they could not be challenged.

Pseudo-Dionysius[11] also provided a means of meeting another difficulty which was increasingly hard felt as the twelfth century wore on; this again was a need which presented itself forcibly only from the middle of the century. He spoke of a *theologia* divided, where different considerations apply in different branches of the subject, a theology of heaven, a theology of earth, a theology of God himself, who is above the heavens, a *theologia coelestis, subcoelestis, supercoelestis.* There are references, too, to a *naturalis theologia*, a *civilis theologia*,[12] a *theologia hypothetica*, and a *theologia apothetica.*[13] We can see twelfth-century scholars responding to the pressure of hard questioning of the applicability of their methods by subdividing the subject-matter and looking for principles which would be generally acceptable, albeit within a smaller area of thought. This is an understandable reaction to a state of uncertainty about first principles. Subdivisions of the subject proliferated to the point where Aquinas felt that there was a need for an introductory textbook; it would help the beginner over the difficulties caused by the multiplication of questions, not all of them helpful, and the general disorderliness of treatment occasioned by the attempt to settle individual differences in separate

---

[9] Thierry on Boethius, p. 502.91.   [10] *PL* 64.370–8 and *passim.*

[11] John Scotus Erigena's renderings of Pseudo-Dionysius' works are in *PL* 111. For some of Alan of Lille's borrowings of his terminology see M. T. d'Alverny, *Textes inédits d'Alain de Lille* (Paris, 1965), pp. 223–6.

[12] Augustine discusses this division of theology, together with the theology of fables, in *The City of God* VIII. 5.

[13] *Textes inédits*, p. 195.

works.[14] This was the result, for the most part, of a single century's new work upon the foundations of the study of theology.

The proliferation of branches of theology began slowly, and only gradually gained momentum. In Anselm's day and immediately after, the principal division which theologians perceived was that between the subject-matter which pagan philosophers and Christian thinkers had in common (the questions to do with the existence and nature of God) and the theology of the Redemption. It became something of a commonplace in the first half of the century to remark on the principle adumbrated in *Romans* I: 19–20: even pagans have no excuse for not worshipping God the *Creator* because they can learn of his existence and his nature from studying the created world. The work of God as *Redemptor* is another matter. The reasons why God redeemed the world in the way that he did are not to be found in creation. When they discuss the doctrine of the Trinity, or the attributes of the Godhead, twelfth-century thinkers commonly draw upon the technical skills and the principles of analysis with which the 'pagan philosophers' furnished them in the textbooks of the *artes*. Terminology and method both proved remarkably appropriate; even if they raised as many fresh difficulties as they resolved, they were helpful because they provided a system of thought well fitted for discussing the kinds of problem involved. When contemporary scholars examine the reasons why God became man and changed the course of history by redeeming mankind, they find that such procedures are of limited use. What is required is a method of argument which will accommodate change and its paradoxes, which will be able to explain not only how things are, but how that which immutably and eternally is may become something else and yet remain the same, how the course of events may change without altering the eternal plan. It was in this area that Anselm made the most outstanding contribution to the discussion of topics which were the subject of especial interest in his own day and immediately after. There is less that is entirely original in his perception of the problems raised by unity and Trinity and by the attributes of God. But it was not for another generation that it was clearly seen by a

[14] *Summa Theologica, Prologue.*

large number of thinkers that these two branches of theology required to be approached according to different habits of thought. And only in the later twelfth century did theology further subdivide itself according to a variety of principles of division, until it became a multiplicity of subjects.

It would be misleading to suggest that the tendency of twelfth-century theology was always to diverge, that it entered a state of disorder. On the contrary, it is marked by the increasingly close-knit integration of work across a broad front. But a part at least of its interest for the modern reader must lie in what it demonstrates of the workings of a process of re-evaluation, the reforming of the subject-matter, and procedures of an advanced and demanding intellectual discipline in an age when nothing less than the whole content of a culture was being re-examined. In many writers of the time, even if only intermittently, a note of freshness and surprise at what they discover makes their work attractive. Even at its most technical it is rarely incomprehensible to the layman. We can see the highest disciplines of the mind laid bare to their bones far more clearly than is likely to be possible in the case of the changes of our own day for that very reason.

The Direction of Change

It is rarely difficult to understand Anselm's arguments, or to see something of their force, even if we do not necessarily find them all still convincing. But it is not at all easy to enter into the untroubled certainty of his mind when he approaches a theological difficulty. It is inconceivable to him that if he applies his reason to the problem in a humble and devout frame of mind he can fail to solve it; even if a full solution does not present itself, at least as far as he is able to understand the matter he is sure that reason and truth must converge upon one another, and that they will never be found to be at odds. The perplexity of mind with which twelfth-century theologians often approach theological problems is much more familiar to us. The results of their discussions may lack the shining clarity of Anselm's explanations, but their way of going about things is frequently easier for us to understand. No modern scientist can share Anselm's confidence that all the laws of his subject will prove resistant to every attempt to question them or reassess them. He might, however, have some insight into the urge which led Abelard and his contemporaries to examine every move they made in their search even for a method of approach—let alone in their pursuit of the right answers. Anselm allows us to watch him at work; he is exceptionally open in his revelations of his own thought-processes. But to read one of his dialogues is to find oneself following in his footsteps, waiting to be shown the next departure. Abelard and his contemporaries are far less explicit about their means of access to their arguments in many cases; they rarely lead their readers by such easy stages through the process of argument as Anselm does. And yet they give their readers a sense of being present in the workshop. Many mid-twelfth-century resolutions of theological problems lack that finish which in Anselm's writings was intended to put an end to uncertainty about the issue in question for good. They present us rather with a well-made working scheme for solving a difficulty.

Anselm's very sureness of touch sets him a little apart. His sheer stature as a thinker makes it impossible to join him in his explorations as anything but a pupil-companion. It would often have been possible to share more fully in the work of the twelfth-century theologians, not only because they were lesser men, but also because their uncertainties are familiar and acceptable to us, their process of finding out more recognizably an exploration.

Despite the considerable appeal which Anselm's thought about some of the most important topics of theology had for thinkers of the thirteenth century and later, he appears to have had remarkably little influence upon the theological scholars of the century after his death, with a few exceptions among those who had come under his personal influence or who worked mainly within the monastic ambit. It is easy to see that the flavour of the work of later twelfth-century theologians is different from his. It is not so easy to determine the exact nature of the change which makes it so much less difficult for us to understand their bafflement and their habit of asking awkward questions than to enter into the calmer waters of Anselm's certainty about the nature of the truth.

It is possible to discover fragmentary borrowings taken directly from Anselm's treatises in the work of a few scholars, or collected together for reference by a monastic compiler,[15] and such an exercise has the value of showing that Anselm's work was not entirely neglected. But the discovery of the precise limits of his direct influence will not quite meet the difficulty. The central preoccupations of Anselm's theology: the nature of God, the mystery of the Trinity, the Incarnation, and the Redemption, are also the chief concerns of his successors. The methods he uses are, technically speaking, largely their methods, too, although their technical expertise is more developed and often more obviously in evidence. Yet a change of fashion in theological writing has taken place, which has left Anselm's work temporarily without appeal to a generation of scholars. There are good practical reasons why his works were not more widely read; those he influenced most strongly in his own day worked within the monastic ambience and not in the schools where they might have brought his ideas to the notice of other working masters and so helped to give them a place in the syllabus of studies as it slowly evolved. But the interest of the matter perhaps lies chiefly in this: the neglect of Anselm's writings by scholars of the next generation demonstrates as no comparison with the work of any other writer can hope to do, the nature and direction of that crucial shift of emphasis which made the style of his theology incompatible with theirs.

What Anselm has to say about the central problems of the Christian faith has, for the most part, been framed in answer to other people's questions. That is true of every treatise except the *Proslogion*. Left to himself he was a thinker remarkably free from doubts and uncertainties, since, as far as we know, reflection always showed him a reasonable way round them. In the second half of the twelfth century, Alan of Lille remarks at the opening of his commentaries upon the Apostle's Creed[16] and the Nicene Creed[17] that theology, like every other branch of knowledge, consists in two things: positive instruction and negative aspects which have to do with defending the truth

---

[15] Among the MSS which contain Anselmian borrowings and collections of Anselm's sayings which are not listed in the *Memorials* are items in Hereford Cathedral Library MS O.i.vi., Bodl. MS Bodl. 839, BL MSS Royal 4.B. x, and Egerton 3323.

[16] N. M. Häring, 'A Commentary on the Apostle's Creed by Alan of Lille', *Analecta Cisterciensia*, 30 (1974), 7–45.

[17] N. M. Häring, 'A Commentary on the Creed of the Mass by Alan of Lille', *Analecta Cisterciensia*, 30 (1974), 281–303.

against its antagonists. Anselm would, at least in his middle years, have seen its purpose as entirely positive, a building-up of faith.[18] The settling of other men's doubts would have seemed to him an unfortunate but necessary concomitant, but no part of the task of theology in that ideal world whose right order[19] was so clear to him. Whether he dealt with the difficulties raised by able men with trained minds—such as Roscelin —or with the simple questions of simple men (Simon of Tournai's *rudes et ydiote*)[20] he dealt conscientiously with everything which was put to him.[21] But he saw no need at all to try to envisage the further difficulties which might be raised. In Anselm's view the normal state of a reasonable man's mind was a condition of orthodox faith. It was necessary to expunge specific doubts and uncertainties, and then he would be restored to that natural state.

The contrast is startling. The tendency of Anselm's theology is always to try to put things back as they were before the improper question was asked, by showing either its theological or its dialectical impropriety.[22] The contemporaries of Abelard frequently felt, like Anselm, that there were questions which it might be illuminating to ask; but their assumption is that theology is a subject open to development and growth in directions which Anselm would not readily have countenanced. When he says that men should use their reason to help them understand their faith he intends them to do so only in order to understand what they ought already to believe, and not to seek out new items of faith so as to extend the range of their beliefs. His successors could not, however, expect to go back to first principles and find them undisturbed. There is no brushing of flies off an immaculate surface about twelfth-century theology. The structure is visibly in process of rebuilding from its foundations up.

The twelfth-century recognition that doubts and uncertainties might really have sufficient basis for it to be necessary to

---

[18] That is the drift of what he has to say in the short homily with which the *De Incarnatione Verbi* begins.

[19] *Rectus ordo* is a major theme of Anselm's in the *Cur Deus Homo*.

[20] 'Simon of Tournai's *Commentary on the so-called Athanasian Creed*', ed. N. M. Häring, *Archives*, xliii (1976), p. 150, II.4.   [21] See for example S, 2.147.10–11.

[22] *Proprietas* has a clearly-defined dialectical usage in Anselm's day. See D. P. Henry, *The Logic of St. Anselm* (Oxford, 1967), p. 255 for a list of references.

rebuild the body of doctrine was not the product of mere
intellectual insecurity on the part of twelfth-century thinkers. It
was, after all, only because they were asking questions with
more confidence that the difficulty arose. Anselm's pupils often
come to him with a difficulty which they want cleared out of the
way for them. Roscelin, on the other hand, approaches with a
challenge. Anselm, he says, must either revise his opinions, or
concede that the view he holds makes nonsense of the doctrine
of the Trinity. In the last decades of Anselm's life and throughout the twelfth century, a good deal of inventiveness on the part
of some of the best minds of the day was being devoted to the
discovery of fresh items for belief, to the posing of questions
which, it was anticipated, might change things, or add to the
body of doctrine.[23]

It seems probable that student demand had a good deal to do
with this. Just as Anselm had to attempt to iron out his pupils'
difficulties, so in the 1160s Simon of Tournai had to settle
matters of dispute in his *Disputationes*, in order to preserve the
standing of what he regarded as the right view in the light of the
evidence he could bring to bear. We need not conclude that
Simon would have wished to give such prominence to the
wrong as to the right view. Nevertheless, throughout the *Disputationes* and also in his *Expositio Symboli*, the commentary on
the Athanasian Creed, he systematically lists the heretical
items (*articuli hereses*).[24] Only once does Anselm do anything like
this, at the beginning of the *Cur Deus Homo*,[25] and there the
material is slight enough in compass for him to list his *respon-
siones* briefly, and move on to the main argument of the treatise
after a few chapters.

That option was not open to Simon of Tournai partly
because there were so many more *articuli hereses* to be considered, but also because it was the habit of the masters of his
generation to take them seriously and to give them space. Each
problem is followed through until its full implications are clear.
Question XVII of the *Disputationes* for example begins by asking a question with a long history in patristic thought:
'Whether Christ assumed a particular man'. This is a difficulty
implicit in the Latin. *Assumpsit hominem* may mean either, 'He

---

[23] Some of these questions, and something of this process, are considered in Part II.
[24] Simon of Tournai on the Athanasian Creed, p. 183, VII.1.   [25] S,2.50.15.

assumed manhood', or, 'He assumed a particular man.' If we adopt the latter interpretation, does it follow, asks the second part of this *quaestio*, that a particular man was predestined to be the Son of God? And if, for the sake of argument, Christ assumed from the race of men one man called Peter, would that Peter be Christ?[26] This is the sort of question we can imagine Anselm settling immediately in discussion if one of his pupils at Bec had raised it, by pointing out that such a view cannot be right because it leads to unnecessary difficulties about the identity of Person in Christ when he became Man.

Simon and his contemporaries did not enjoy Anselm's prolonged intimacy with his pupils in the gentler atmosphere of a monastic school. Their pupils were insistent and combative. They could and did marshal arguments from grammar and dialectic to support their case. And so such issues became the subject of serious debate. So did a number of matters not directly concerned with the central issues of theology. Are we, for example, to hate the Devil as much as we are to love Christ?[27] The intention of whoever raised the question was to have it settled so as to create a new article of faith. Anselm has no time for what he would perhaps have seen as essentially artificial exercises in expanding the scope of belief.

It will be clear that we are not in most cases dealing with men whose minds were in a state of distressing uncertainty, but with thinkers who found the raising of difficulties stimulating and instructive, both for themselves and for their pupils. There is something very positive even about the apparently more destructive aspects of twelfth-century theological inquiry, at least in terms of the attitudes of mind they reveal. More: it does not follow from the presence of a spirit of questioning which attacks even fundamentals and leaves everything open to debate that no one will be able to take up a position on the intellectual battlefield. Each writer puts forward a viewpoint which he believes to be correct. The products of these schools are not open-ended explorations of possibilities, but exercises in the purposeful application of new methods to new areas of uncer-

[26] Simon of Tournai, *Disputationes*, ed. J. Warichez, *SSL* 12 (1932), *Quaestio* XVII, 1-3, pp. 58-61.
[27] O. Lottin 'Alain de Lille, une des sources des *Disputationes* de Simon de Tournai', *RTAM* 17 (1950), 176.

tainty, with a view to finding solutions. One of the most significant differences from the works of Anselm lies in the general
recognition that no solution can be expected to go unchallenged
for long.

It is not then that twelfth-century scholars confronted a
philosophically more difficult task in their speculative theology
than Anselm did, but rather that they were increasingly hard
put to it to make headway against a mass of detail of which
Anselm knew nothing (or sometimes simply failed to acknowledge as fit matter for theological reflection). This is a
problem which has tended to confront modern scholars in a
variety of disciplines. The attempt to encompass more and
more material stretches existing categories to the point where it
becomes necessary to consider whether they will stand any
longer as adequate principles of division. A rethinking of
methods and purposes follows and sometimes the subject as a
whole undergoes radical change as a result.

Anselm's especial gift was that he was able to preserve a
sense of direction and an over-all clarity of vision in thinking
about complex problems. The skill he possessed enabled him to
tackle profound philosophical issues, while much of the time of
twelfth-century thinkers is taken up with technical *minutiae*. But
it is doubtful whether even Anselm could have achieved what
he did if the field of his studies had been so cluttered with the
debris of other men's petty doubts and uncertainties as Alan of
Lille found his to be when, in the later twelfth century, he tried
to find some principle of organization in his *Regulae Theologicae*[28]
and to set out the axioms on which Christian doctrine
depended. The desire to discover a means of ordering—or at
least cutting through—a mass of new material is sometimes a
response to a sense of incipient confusion. It is, in the twelfth
century, recognizably sometimes an attempt to hold at bay
what might otherwise overwhelm. But it is also a sign of great
mental energy and a lively intellectual curiosity.

[28] *PL* 210.617–84.

I

THE CHANGE OF SCENE

THE FIELD OF STUDY

IT may be that the absence of a well-defined and generally-accepted technical term to describe it is not in itself any substantial hindrance to the development of a field of study. But it is an indication perhaps that that field of study has not yet been mapped out very far. When Anselm and his immediate successors speak of the *studium sacrae scripturae* (the study of Holy Scripture), *lectio divina* (holy reading), *sacra doctrina* (holy learning), *divinitas* (divinity), their terms of reference are often a little uncertain even to themselves. Hugh of St. Victor entitled his most comprehensive theological work the *De Sacramentis Christianae Fidei*, 'On the Mysteries of the Christian Faith', for lack of a widely-accepted term sufficiently comprehensive in its signification to embrace all the topics he wished to consider. *Theologia* was used by Abelard in the title of his *Theologia Christiana*, but there he restricts himself principally to Trinitarian theology; it was not yet usual to employ the term 'theology' for the full range of aspects of Christian doctrine covered by Hugh.

For scholars of the first half of the twelfth century theology was first of all concerned with the study of the Bible, and it was by no means clear as yet where the dividing line between speculative theology and Scriptural commentary lay, or even whether any such line existed. This view of the scope of theology was partly a matter of terminology. The writers of the later twelfth century were confident enough about the meaning of the term *theologia* to be able to adapt it to new purposes, and to speak of natural theology, hypothetical theology (the study of created spirits), a theology of heaven, a theology of earth, a theology of him who is above the heavens, and so on. But when Abelard says in his *Historia Calamitatum* (ix) that he wrote 'a certain work on theology' (*quemdam theologiae tractatum*) he has not departed from the sense of the term which Boethius defines in his treatise *On the Trinity*. Boethius says that theology deals with things which do not change, that is with the nature of God, his unity, and his Trinity. The subject of the book to which

Abelard refers was *The Divine Unity and Trinity*. In the thirteenth
century, Aquinas' *Summa Theologica* leaves nothing out which it
had seemed to later twelfth-century scholars proper to include
in the study of theology in its broadest sense.

Peter Abelard once remarked that he found it surprising that
educated men who could read the Bible for themselves with
informed understanding should find it necessary to have a
master expound it to them.[1] The fellow pupils of Anselm of
Laon to whom he put this point of view challenged him to
lecture on Ezekiel, which was renowned for its difficulty and
obscurity. He did so without hesitation, for, as he told his
listeners, he was accustomed to rely on his wits rather than
upon careful preparation.[2] As evidence of his success, he says
that his lectures soon attracted large numbers of hearers, all
anxious to take down what he said and to write out his glosses
for themselves.[3] Perhaps this was indeed a victory for native wit
over solid scholarship, but it was certainly not a victory for
untutored wit. Whatever Abelard said about Ezekiel, it must
certainly have measured up to the highest standards of technical skill in the analysis of the written word. It struck his
listeners as new and exciting because, as pupils of Anselm of
Laon, they were not accustomed to hear Scripture expounded
according to the procedures of the *artes* in such a thoroughgoing
manner. For all his own mastery of grammar, Anselm preferred
on the whole to attribute the foundation of his arguments to
Scriptural and patristic authority.[4]

Abelard lived at a time in the course of development of the
medieval study of the Bible when a freedom was allowed to him
which he could not so easily have made use of later. The late
eleventh and early twelfth century was an age of rapid and fluid
change in attitudes to the study of Scripture. Modern scholarship has concentrated for the most part on distinguishing the
early signs of those trends in Scriptural interpretation which
were to give rise to the procedures of the later twelfth and
thirteenth centuries, to a tried and established method of Bible

[1] Peter Abelard, *Historia Calamitatum*, ed. J. Monfrin (Paris, 1967), p. 68.193–5.
[2] Ibid., p. 69.207–9.
[3] Ibid., p. 69.217–21.
[4] The surviving Sentences of the school of Laon are printed in Lottin. On Anselm's
prowess as a master of grammar see R. W. Hunt, 'Studies on Priscian in the eleventh
and twelfth centuries', *MARS* 1 (1941–3), 194–231 and 2(1950), 1–56.

study and the *Glossa Ordinaria*.[5] But the experiments of
Abelard's day and earlier perhaps have a further interest. They
demonstrate how fresh and original an approach some scholars
were able to make to an old task—perhaps always the
theologian's principal task—that of making the meaning of
Scripture clear to others.[6] Some of their ideas soon faded into
obscurity. But the urge to think about the Bible afresh was
strong enough and common enough to indicate something of
importance about the nature and direction of the changes
which were taking place in the climate of thought.

Anselm comes closer than any other scholar of the day to
achieving a Christian theology built entirely upon the use of
reason, and couched in the form of independent treatises which
deal with more or less separate issues. But he has his eye on
Scripture as he writes, so that he can claim with untroubled
confidence that nothing he has to say is out of keeping with its
teaching.[7] For all speculative theologians of the day, and not
only for the commentators, the Bible was the starting-point for
theological reflections; constant recourse is made to Scripture
for corroboration. The difficulty lay in the fact that it was now
seen that the secular arts and the 'philosophers'[8] also raised
theological questions. The more clearly the range of derivation
and application of these philosophically-inspired issues was
worked out, the harder it became to find a form of words in
which to write about theology which would seem neither technically inaccurate nor theologically unsound. One result of
such explorations was a gradual improvement in precision of
expression and a greater awareness of the dangers inherent in
loosely-framed statements.[9]

Some scholars retreated in discomfort or dismay from these
developments. William of St. Thierry says at the beginning of

---

[5] B. Smalley, *The Study of the Bible in the Middle Ages* (Oxford, 1952), esp. Ch. 2, and on
early experiments see B. Smalley, 'Quelques prédécesseurs d'Anselme de Laon',
RTAM 9(1937), 365–401.

[6] B. Smalley, op. cit., is the classic study of the rise of the *Glossa Ordinaria*.

[7] S, 3.199.18–19, *Letter* 72, to Lanfranc.

[8] In *De Civitate Dei* Books VII–VIII, Augustine had examined the theological views
of the schools of philosophy known to him. The late 11th century saw a revival of
interest in the topic.

[9] See my article, '*Inopes verborum sunt Latini*: technical language and technical terms in
the writings of St Anselm and some commentators of the mid-twelfth century', *Archives*,
xliii (1976), 113–34.

his *Commentary on Romans* that the book poses many very difficult questions. He has examined them, not with a view to settling them himself, for that is beyond him, but so as to find among the sayings of the Fathers material for a continuous exposition (*continua explanatio*) which will be, in its substance, not his but theirs. The greater the standing of the 'author', he feels, the greater will be the authority of his words. Besides, the work will be *gratior*, more acceptable, to its readers if it contains no novelty and no hint of vanity (*non novitatis seu vanitatis praesumptio*).[10] The monastic commentator Rupert of Deutz displays rather more boldness, but a similar reserve. He points out that in commenting upon the Gospel of John he has presumed to follow in the footsteps of a great Father, Augustine. But he is sure that he has been guided aright by the Holy Spirit: *Ego autem testem me habere confidi Deum in animam meam.* He has been inspired by sheer delight in what he reads in the Gospel to write about it: *illa me causa impulit, quia 'memor fui Dei et delectatus sum'.*[11] Although it would not be true to say that every Scriptural commentator of the period between Anselm and Abelard was whole-heartedly involved in the new work which was afoot, it is clear that even those who had little to contribute from the fields of the *artes* were being moved by a general sense that the study of the Bible was important and exciting, to write new commentaries or to refurbish old ones. Among them were men who were thinking with considerable originality about the purpose of Bible study. But even those who were conservative in their approach seem to have been infected by an enthusiasm which gave rise to great productivity in work on the Bible.

Attitudes

Rupert of Deutz wrote a commentary on the Bible which he regarded as an account of the work of the Holy Trinity upon the course of human history. He says in his introductory letter to Cuno, Abbot of Sigeberg, that he has planned the work in three parts, which are to deal with the Creation and with all subsequent events up to the end of the world. The first part runs from the Creation to the Fall of Adam, the second from the Fall of Adam to the Passion of Christ, the third from the Passion to the

[10] William of St. Thierry, *Commentary on the Epistle to the Romans*, PL 180.547.
[11] *Epistola Nuncupatoria* at the beginning of the *Commentary on John*, PL 169.201–2.

end of the world. The first age belongs to the Father, the second to the Son, the third to the Holy Spirit.[12] There is nothing revolutionary in this scheme in itself. It was to become something of a commonplace in twelfth-century interpretations of history to speak of ages or *status*;[13] the scheme of history put forward by Joachim of Fiore perhaps represents the flowering of this system of interpretation of sacred and human history.[14] But Rupert of Deutz is saying rather more than that he envisages the Bible as an account of the working out of God's purposes in history. He sees the three ages as in some sense an image of the Trinity. We are to seek God in the mirror of his works: *quaerentes operum ipsius speculum*.[15] This notion, too, is common enough in Rupert's day and after. Romans 1: 19–20 is frequently cited as Scriptural evidence for the view that the created world serves the purpose of showing us as much of God's glory as we are able to bear. But again, Rupert's view goes a little further. Like Augustine in the *De Trinitate*,[16] he looks in his 'mirror' for a threefold image. Augustine speaks of the 'trinity' in the mind of man, where memory represents the Father, and so on. (Anselm has borrowed the idea in the Monologion.)[17] Rupert's mirror, on the other hand, is an outwardly visible one, a mirror held up to God by events in the created world. The work of the Persons of the Trinity at each stage of history is reflected in the mirror of history in a threefold image. Rupert has conceived a novel addition to the range of 'images of Trinity' which were in circulation in the late eleventh and early twelfth century,[18] not by an exercise of new philosophical insight, but simply by taking a fresh look at old material and refashioning old habits of thought.

This image has pronounced limitations. It is a device of the same type as the familiar 'Nile' image which Anselm took from Augustine and adapted, used in the *De Incarnatione Verbi*, and

[12] *De Sancta Trinitate*, ed. H. Haacke, *CCCM*. 21, p. 122.111.

[13] See, for example, Anselm of Havelberg, *Dialogus*, ed. G. Salet (Paris, 1966).

[14] On Joachim see M. Reeves, *The Influence of Prophecy in the Later Middle Ages* (Oxford, 1969), and M. Reeves and B. Hirsch-Reich, *The Figurae of Joachim of Fiore* (Oxford, 1972), and M. Reeves, *Joachim of Fiore and the Prophetic Future* (London, 1976).

[15]. *De Sancta Trinitate*, p. 126.46.

[16] Augustine, *De Trinitate* X, 11–12, XIV.8.   [17] S, 1.77–8.

[18] I have looked at some of these in 'St. Anselm's Images of Trinity', *JTS* xxvii (1976), 46–57.

found himself obliged to defend against the questioning of the
'Greeks' in the *De Processione Spiritus Sancti*.[19] That is to say, it
has a 'linear' character. In the Nile, the spring, river, and pool
succeed one another in sequence. So, in Rupert's historical
image of the Trinity, the ages of the Father, Son, and Holy
Spirit succeed one another in order. The objections to any
image which suggests that there is any sequence in the Trinity,
or that the Procession of the Spirit takes place from the Father
through the Son are obvious. But Rupert is not a philosopher.
He intends his image to be visually pleasing, interesting, and
vivid for his readers: *Igitur adorandum sanctae Trinitatis gloriam in
hac peregrinatione quaerentes operum ipsius speculum sensibus nostris
admoveamus*.[20] ('Therefore let us fix our senses in adoration upon
the mirror of his works as we seek the glory of the Holy Trinity
in this exile.') Rupert's exhortation is to wonder and admiration, not to hard analysis. He emphasizes the glory and mystery
of the words of the Bible. Moses' face, he reminds his readers,
was shining when he had been talking to God: *ex collocutione Dei
splendida sit*. It was necessary for his face to be veiled. In just the
same way, the meaning of what God had said to him had to be
veiled in figurative terms (*figurativis cum vocibus*) because it was
too great for men to bear.[21] In his *De Victoria Verbi Dei* Rupert
speaks of the responsibility which weighs upon any interpreter
of the Word of God, since the Word of God is Christ himself: *Sed
quoniam propositio est de ipso Verbo, verba mihi nascitura esse non
incongrua spero*.[22] ('But since our subject is that Word himself, I
hope that the words which will occur to me will not be unfitting.') Rupert cannot be said to be a technical innovator; the
emphasis of his thought is upon clear restatement of established
principles. But he has evidently been excited by his reading to a
point where he has achieved a largeness of view about the
purposes of Scriptural commentary; a strong sense of the gran-
deur of his task pervades his writings. The sheer vigour of the
new interest in the study of the Bible is impressive, not least
among those who cannot be reckoned to be leaders in the field
of technical developments.

Rupert mentions the veiling of Moses' face. One of the most

[19] Augustine, *De Fide et Symbolo* 8, S, 2.31–3, S, 2.203–6.
[20] *De Sancta Trinitate*, p. 126.46.   [21] Ibid., p. 125.3.
[22] *De Victoria Verbi Dei*, PL 169.1221, Book I, iv.

frequently-expressed concerns of our writers is with the question of the extent to which Scriptural mysteries should be made plain. Honorius suggests that God intends something of the mystery of Holy Scripture to remain opaque: 'The mysteries of this book are hidden beneath images and allegories, lest they become commonplace because they are obvious to everyone.'[23] Elsewhere, he takes the view that what is obscure to the idle (*desidiosis obscurum*) becomes clear to those who make an effort to understand, by the illumination of the Holy Spirit.[24] He is speaking for a considerable body of contemporary opinion here. If there is one characteristic which distinguishes the scholars of his day more decisively than any other, it is the breadth of their curiosity. Mysteries tempted investigation. Honorius has found a form of words which allows him to suggest that it is right for a scholar to be curious about the secrets of Scripture, so long as he awaits the illumination of the Holy Spirit upon his researches. That is Anselm's view, too. In the hands of a master of the secular arts it is developed further. Abelard explains to Héloise that the function of a parable is to indicate the truth obliquely: *Sciendum vero in omni parabola non tam rei veritatem expressam esse quam ex parte aliqua rei similitudinem inductam esse, et saepe historiae veritati similitudinem quasi rem gestam adiungi.*[25] ('We must be aware that it is not so much that the truth of the thing is expressed in a parable, as that an analogy is introduced, so as to match some aspect of the thing, and often the analogy takes the form of a story which represents the literal truth.') He looks for the technical procedures involved (the *similitudo*), but he, like Honorius, sees no reason for hesitation before Scriptural mysteries. His instinct is to try to understand their implications. Not all his contemporaries would have agreed with him by any means. But none of them could fail to be aware of the existence of mysteries and of the need to consider afresh how they should be approached.

A further common concern is with orderliness of exposition. The gloss or commentary which follows the sequence of the text has a structure imposed upon it by that very order. For the first time scholars were beginning to consider how helpful such a treatment might be. Honorius points out that David wrote the

[23] *PL* 172.269.   [24] *PL* 172.347.   [25] *Heloissae Problemata*, 12, *PL* 178.693.

Psalms not as a continuous sequence, but *sparsim*; they are accordingly not orderly (*ordinatim*) in the same way as other books of the Bible.[26] Odo of Asti, who wrote on the Psalms for St. Bruno of Segni, prefaced his work with a letter in which he explains that he has avoided mixing the order of the *versus* so that he will not interrupt the continuity of the sense: *ut sententiārūm nusquam interrumperem perpetuitatem*.[27] Abelard keeps to the order of Romans in his commentary, but he finds it necessary to break off the sequence at intervals so as to insert a longer treatment of a *quaestio*. It is easy to see how such *quaestiones* might be felt to be more conveniently presented in collections than left in their places in the course of continuous commentary. This brings us to the question of literary form, which is not our immediate concern here. But those very changes of form which we shall be looking at in due course reflect a general questioning of the helpfulness of a strictly orderly treatment of biblical texts. Again, this questioning indicates a widespread willingness to look at first principles and familiar assumptions.

Not unrelated to this concern with order is an interest in the proper level of detail in exposition. Odo of Asti evidently had some sympathy with the view that genius is an infinite capacity for taking pains. 'For I knew that the heavier the labour the more acceptable the result', he says: *sciebam enim quia quanto labor gravior, tanto actus gratior*.[28] He sees that it is best if a commentary contains neither an excess of detail, nor an inadequate amount of material,[29] but nevertheless he has written a full account: *compendiose scripserim*.[30] The length of the commentaries of the day varies a good deal; there can be little doubt that the matter was of practical interest to many writers. Just as they were asking themselves how helpful it was to discuss each passage in order, so they were reconsidering the amount of detail it was proper to include.

Methods

Again, when we look at the place technical skills of the *artes* were coming to hold in Scriptural commentary, we find the bolder thinkers of this generation proposing the adoption of a

---

[26] *PL* 172.271. [27] *PL* 165.1141. [28] Ibid. [29] Ibid. [30] Ibid.

larger view, while almost no one remains unaffected by the new methods.[31] In his *Prologue* to the *Commentary on Job* Rupert of Deutz reminds his readers of the conventional view that philosophy has three branches: *ethica, physica, logica*.[32] He suggests that in the Book of Job readers will find matters of ethics and of physics, and of *theorica*, 'which in Holy Scripture takes the place of logic' (*quae in sacris Scripturis habetur pro logica*).[33] The idea is not restricted to Rupert. Honorius has borrowed it in the *Prologue* to his selection from the Psalms. He suggests that Genesis is the place to look for *physica*, which deals with natural laws (*quae de naturis loquitur*); the Pauline Epistles contain treatments of ethical issues (*quae de moribus tractant*), and the Psalter deals with logic or *theorica*.[34] He feels that different parts of the Bible have different philosophical characters. But both he and Rupert have had in mind the idea of looking for branches of philosophy in the Bible.

Honorius approaches Bible study as he would the study of any other book, with the conventional questions of the *accessus* in his mind.[35] Its purpose (*intentio*) is to exhort us to strive to imitate Christ. The subject-matter (*materia*) of the Psalms, he says, is Christ and the Church. The book belongs to that branch of philosophy (*cui parte philosophiae supponitur*) which is known as *theorica*, that is the *divina scientia*. Its profitableness (*utilitas*) is that we learn from it to avoid sin, to do good, and to hope for eternal life.[36] Whether or not a scholar intended to press the application of the technical skills of the *artes* further and further into service in Scriptural commentary it was difficult for him to avoid coming to the study of the Bible with a series of questions already in his mind, simply because in whatever school he had got his early training, the mere acquisition of literacy coloured his attitude to the reading of any book with habits learned at the most elementary stage of study. The *accessus*, or introduction to the authors, was used with young schoolboys, to help them understand what kind of book they

---

[31] On the first instances of systematic use of techniques drawn from the *artes* in Scriptural commentary see M. Gibson, 'Lanfranc's Commentary on the Pauline Epistles', *JTS* xxii (1971), 86–112.

[32] Isidore, *Etymologiae*, ed. W. M. Lindsay (Oxford, 1911), 2 vols., II.xxiv.3–4.

[33] *PL* 168.961–2.   [34] *PL* 172.270.

[35] On the *accessus*, or introductions to the authors, see R. B. C. Huygens (Leiden, 1971).   [36] *PL* 172.271.

were studying and to tell them a little about the author and his works. It was not a sophisticated device for introducing mature scholars to advanced studies. There may have been schoolboys who did not learn the procedure, but Honorius is certainly applying no obscure or erudite technical device here. It is largely the freshness of the contemporary approach to the problems of writing about the Bible which enabled these familiar assumptions to find a natural place in Honorius' foreword.

But Honorius himself is conscious that there is another level of technical interest for the learned: *multa sunt indoctis de Psalterio dicenda; sed pauca doctis summatim stylo perstringenda.*[37] (The unlettered need to be told many things about the Psalms but for the learned only a few things need to be briefly stated.) Later in the century Alan of Lille seems to have had rather the same distinction between the requirements of the learned and the less well-educated in mind in composing his *Distinctiones Dictionum Theologicarum*. It is, he says, dangerous to be unsure of the force of theological words in reading the Bible (*periculosum est theologicorum nominum ignorare virtutes*).[38] He elaborates. We may be unfamiliar with the words, or the words may differ in their meaning from their usual sense. Nouns may be treated as pronouns, adjectives as substantives (*nomina pronominantur . . . adiectiva substantivantur*).[39] Anselm would have been entirely in sympathy with Alan of Lille's view that it is important for every reader of the Bible to understand clearly how words are being used there. Although he composed neither formal commentary nor dictionary of biblical language, Anselm did try to meet the difficulties of understanding his students might encounter in reading Scripture, in the 'three treatises pertaining to the study of Holy Scripture',[40] the *De Veritate*, the *De Libertate Arbitrii*, the *De Casu Diaboli*, and he did so in terms which took account of the special language difficulties which were likely to arise. The exercise is altogether less mechanical than Alan's, but Anselm's experiment has about it something of the same concern for the avoidance of those dangers which attend upon reading the Bible without an understanding of the 'force of

[37] *PL* 172.269.   [38] *PL* 210.687.
[39] Ibid. On the genre to which this piece belongs see R. H. and M. A. Rouse, 'Biblical Distinctions in the Thirteenth century', *Archives*, xli (1974), 27–37.   [40] S, 1.173.2.

theological words'. Abelard, too, made highly conscious of grammatical difficulties by the nature of his early training, introduces straightforward aids to understanding such as paraphrases of obscure phrases. Technicalities of grammar appear occasionally in the *Commentary on Romans: subiecit proprium nomen eius quod est Iesus, ut hunc videlicet Christum a ceteris tam singularitate personae quam dignitate distingueret.*[41] ('He makes the proper name of him who is Jesus the subject, so as to distinguish this man, that is Christ, from others, as much in his singularity of person as in His dignity.') There are grammatical issues among the Bible study problems Héloise put to them.[42] There is nothing unique to Abelard in this. His contemporaries display similar preoccupations[43] which had, after all, been put forward by Augustine in the *De Doctrina Christiana*. Anselm's approach to the solution of such grammatical problems in the 'three treatises' is peculiar to himself, however, because of the philosophically more large-minded form it takes.

It differs from Abelard's view of the matter in another respect too. In the preface to the *Sic et Non* Abelard allows for the possibility that writers of old may have made mistakes. Much of what he has to say is plain common sense, and he cannot be said to have impugned the authority of patristic writers directly. He merely points out that errors of copying and errors of judgement (later corrected, in the case of Augustine, in his *Retractationes*),[44] should be watched for in reading.[45] But Anselm does not refer directly to patristic authority, with one or two minor exceptions. When he approaches an apparent anomaly of a grammatical kind in a Scriptural text he assumes that the Bible cannot be in error, and that he must look for a means of understanding it as it is. This is particularly noticeable in the case of those passages in the *De Concordia* where Anselm tries to reconcile St. Paul's use of the past tense in speaking of God's choice of those he will save, with the fact that in God there is no time, and therefore a present tense would seem a more logical choice.[46] Anselm's instinct is to explain the grammatical point

---

[41] Peter Abelard, *Commentary on Romans*, ed. E. M. Buytaert, *CCCM* 11 (Turnholt, 1969), p. 54.234–7.   [42] *PL* 178.680.

[43] Rupert of Deutz, for example, introduces rather simpler stuff, *PL* 168.961–2.

[44] *PL* 178.1341–2.   [45] *PL* 178.1339–49.

[46] S, 2.253–5, *De Concordia* I,5; cf. Romans 8:28–9.

away rather than to question the sense of Scripture or Paul's accuracy. There is an undeniable difference in attitude here. Anselm protested to Lanfranc that there was nothing in the *Monologion* which went against the authority of Scripture or the Fathers.[47] His desire to find both fully authoritative never leads him to question their ultimate correctness, although he is ready to find their surface appearance improper. Abelard is prepared to do so.

Neither Alan of Lille, in his *Distinctiones*, nor Anselm, in the 'three treatises', takes as his subject-matter actual passages of Scripture. Alan selects specific words and gives some guidance as to their meaning in Scripture. Sometimes he cites an example; sometimes he quotes directly, but the biblical passages he chooses are designed to illustrate what he is saying; he does not attempt to study them in their own right. Much the same is true for Anselm's use of biblical quotations in the three treatises. He never sets a passage of Scripture directly before him as a subject for discussion. He writes instead about truth, free will, and the Fall of Satan, and makes the use of Scripture incidental.

But Anselm says that the treatises pertain to the study of Holy Scripture (*pertinentes ad studium sacrae scripturae*).[48] In what sense are we to take this? The Preface to the *De Veritate* which opens with this statement was written after all three treatises had been completed, and Anselm must have thought that the finished works did serve exactly this purpose. He knew that they would not be of value as straightforward commentary material. It is probable that he saw the study of the Bible and what we should now call speculative theology as all of a piece, and not as two distinct branches of *divinitas*.

His method is this: firstly he poses a philosophical problem, in the *De Veritate* that of the nature of truth. He suggests a means of approach to the solving of the problem, and some aspects of truth are reviewed: truth of signification, truth of thought, truth of will. Once all this is clear, the *discipulus* who accompanies Anselm in the dialogue begins to understand that truth in anything consists, not in the thing itself but in a common truth in which all true things participate, Anselm begins to introduce Scriptural examples. When we are told that Satan did not

[47] S, 3.199.18–19.   [48] S, 1.173.2.

remain in the truth, he says, what are we to conclude but that he abandoned the truth by an act of will?[49] He therefore ceased to have truth of will. Christ says that he who does wrong hates the light and he who does truth comes to the light.[50] What truth does this refer to, Anselm asks his pupil? The pupil readily supplies the answer: 'Unless I am mistaken, by the same rule by which we recognised truth in other things before, this refers to truth in action.'[51] Anselm helps the pupil to work over these two examples carefully in the course of Chapter 5, until he reaches a point where the philosophical discussion of the nature of truth can proceed. The pupil has learnt to apply a general principle of argument to a specific term or theme when he meets it in his reading of the Bible. Later in the *De Veritate*, just before they arrive at a final definition of righteousness, Anselm does much the same.[52] It must be conceded that direct Scriptural references are few in the *De Veritate*, but there Anselm is primarily concerned with establishing the method to be used, in this technique of interpretation by argument about the general problems raised by specific passages.

In the *De Libertate Arbitrii* Anselm confines himself largely to the discussion of one central Scriptural text: *qui facit peccatum servus est peccati*[53] ('he who commits a sin is a slave to sin'). Master and pupil examine the sense of the word *servus* until the pupil, who has been shown how slavery consists in the impossibility of recovering the condition of rightness which has been abandoned by the exercise of free will,[54] is able to say. 'Truly I see clearly what you are saying about slavery, in which "he who commits sin" is made a "slave" to sin.'[55] The discussion has come full circle and the Scriptural passage in question has been methodically made plain. Anselm takes this farther still. In Chapter 12 he arrives at a point where the pupil can say that he now sees that a man always has freedom of will, but that he is not always 'a slave to sin'; that is the case only when he does not have a right will.[56] In this treatise Anselm has been able to make a single Scriptural quotation serve his purpose throughout. The argument here might almost be said to amount to a detailed exposition of this single text, although the pupil is still

[49] S, 1.180.22, John 8:44.   [50] S, 1.181.13–14, John 3:20–1.   [51] S, 1.181.17–18.
[52] S, 1.196.19–25.   [53] John 8:34.   [54] S, 1.209–22.
[55] S, 1.222.20.   [56] S, 1.224.20–1.

consistently being encouraged to take a broader view, and to learn from this exercise how to approach the analysis of other texts.

It is not surprising to find that in the *De Casu Diaboli* Anselm returns to the text with which he had been concerned in the *De Veritate*, which says that Satan fell because he did not remain in the truth.[57] He had already shown there that Satan fell because of an act of will, and it is this interaction between will and righteousness which he wishes to explore further in the *De Casu Diaboli*. A few incidental biblical citations appear, but the drift of the treatise depends upon the interpretation of this text in particular. Again the pupil is learning to employ a methodical approach. Again, he is being encouraged to see that procedures which will illuminate one passage will help him to understand others. But the help Anselm gives him in understanding Scripture by this means is of a high level of philosophical abstraction, for all the simplicity of its presentation. Alan of Lille's students, who needed a dictionary of biblical language, are being helped to avoid misconstruing the meanings and usages of the words of the Bible. Anselm's pupil is being taught to think systematically about what it is assumed he already understands quite adequately in a general way.

The difference partly reflects differences in mental make-up between the two masters. For all his impressive grasp of a wide range of skills Alan of Lille is not a philosopher of the same order as Anselm. But the contrast also reflects a change of emphasis between the schools of Anselm's day and those of Alan's time. Anselm could omit systematic treatments of his subject-matter in mechanical terms but Alan could not, if he was to work as a professional teacher in the schools.

Forms of Exposition

For the would-be writer on Scripture it increasingly became a matter, as the twelfth century wore on, of choosing between an orderly exposition by gloss or commentary and the method of the question (or choosing perhaps to work by compiling a collection of authorities, or the writing of Sentences, or some other form which was to prove more strictly useful for theological speculation or as an aid to the writing of sermons than for

[57] S, 1.235.23, John 8:44, S, 1.266.16.

Bible study).[58] Anselm wrote no Scriptural commentaries. His preference was for a more sustained treatment of theological issues than close textual analysis permitted. But there was no tradition of formal procedure as yet which insisted that the handling of questions in commentary must be kept short and that the extended *quaestio* was best treated as a separate exercise. Anselm chose to write no commentary at all; Abelard chose to compose a form of commentary which includes *quaestiones*. Both thinkers are exercising a freedom of their time. The 'two fairly distinct elements' which Beryl Smalley thus isolates, *quaestio* and systematic exposition which keeps close to the text, were, as she demonstrates, jostling one another for a place in commentaries of the early and middle years of the twelfth century. Abelard's compromise is not unique. The outcome was a separation of one thing from the other, and the gradual development of distinct genres of theological composition.[59]

Anselm does not appear to have been much attracted by the possibilities suggested by the nascent tradition of the Sentences, where extracts from Scripture and the Fathers bearing on a particular question were collected together for reference and discussion. His last work, the *De Concordia*, takes the form of three *quaestiones*, topical treatments of the relation between free will and predestination, foreknowledge and grace respectively. Into the last of these he packs as many Scriptural passages as his contemporary Anselm of Laon could have desired. But there is really no similarity of approach between Anselm of Laon's workmanlike assembling of points and St. Anselm's treatment of the philosophical and theological issues involved.[60] The pattern of such works demanded that each topic should be treated in brief and separately. Anselm's remarks about the discussion of will, power, and necessity in the *Cur Deus Homo* might be applied more broadly to his view of many other topics: *sic se habent, ut earum nulla possit plene sine aliis considerari*.[61] ('They are so related to one another that none of them can be fully considered without the others.') Anselm

---

[58] On the development of new forms see B. Smalley, op. cit., Ch. 2; P. Glorieux, 'La Somme "Quoniam homines" d'Alain de Lille', *Archives*, xxviii (1953), 112–364, esp. 114.   [59] Smalley, op. cit., p. 73.

[60] The briefest comparison of the Laon Sentences with Anselm's writings will make the point plain.   [61] S, 2.49.10.

preferred to write treatises in which he could explore the ramifications of a few issues at some length until he had, as he thought, exhausted them. In this he stands apart from the majority of his successors among the theologians of the twelfth century. It became their custom to give unity to their collections of separate Sentences by putting them together in an orderly arrangement. Something of this exercise in building a theological system was attempted by Honorius in his *Elucidarium* in Anselm's time. The work owes something in its content but not in its over-all shape to Honorius' borrowings from St. Anselm.[62] Honorius does not include extended Sentences, only brief questions and answers. But the tendency is to strive for theological unity of treatment by making compilations of various kinds grew stronger during the twelfth century and almost no one followed Anselm of Canterbury in his preference for a more leisurely treatment of a narrower range of issues.

Abelard, too, avoided the writing of Sentences. We must not confuse the view he took of Anselm of Laon's personal shortcomings as a master with his attitude to the Sentence-method to which his school seems to have given so much impetus.[63] But when Abelard says in the *Historia Calamitatum* that he has found Anselm's answers to questions cloud the issue rather than clarify it,[64] he is expressing a distaste not only for the man but also for the method. Abelard's chief quarrel with Anselm of Laon was that his explanations were all words and no matter. 'His tree seemed covered in leaves to those who saw it from a distance, but when they drew nearer and inspected it more closely, they found it barren of fruit.'[65] Abelard's qualities of mind made him hard to satisfy; the conventional material of the Laon gloss and the summary disposing of questions which took place in the Sentences which have come down to use left him intellectually dissatisfied. Setting aside the personal antipathy he felt for the wordy Anselm, that dissatisfaction can be attributed to two things: both the content and the form were limited in their possibilities. When he accuses Anselm of Laon of having little matter to impart, Abelard is clearly referring to the content of the teaching to be had at Laon. But there is some

[62] *AB*, pp. 210–13.
[64] *Historia Calamitatum*, p. 68.170–1.
[63] Smalley, op. cit., pp. 76–7.
[65] Ibid., p. 68.172–4.

evidence in the format of his own *Commentary on Romans* that he found the Sentence-form inadequate in itself. He often says that he will deal more fully with a *quaestio* which has arisen when he writes his *Theologia*. (Sometimes he did in fact do so, but not always.)[66] The *quaestio*-within-a-commentary did not allow him enough scope to develop his thoughts, except in instances where the problem was exceptionally easy to deal with briefly.[67] Still less would the extracting of 'Sentences' from the continuous sequence of exposition have satisfied him. Abelard always preferred to write at length and to set what he had to say within the context of a larger whole, whether commentary or treatise.

Perhaps the most important point to emerge from this sketch of the forms Abelard chose for his compositions, is that he was feeling his way towards an appropriate genre. In an age when theological writing and Scriptural commentary took many forms, none of them settled, Abelard looked about him for a scheme which would provide a good working vehicle for his own thought. It is doubtful whether he found it. Anselm seems to have been far more at home in composing his treatises. Not all of them take the form of a dialogue, although that is the most typical shape for him to choose. Even in those treatises where there is no pupil to ask questions directly, Anselm addresses himself to a hypothetical listener, anticipating objections and answering questions tacitly assumed to have been raised by him. Once only did Abelard choose the dialogue form—in the *Dialogus* between a Philosopher, a Christian, and a Jew, and there are no masters and pupils there. Elsewhere, even though the presence of pupils often makes itself felt, Abelard cannot be said to be holding a conversation with them. It is difficult to avoid the impression that *Notandum est* ('It should be noted') frequently introduces, not the answer to a question which has been actually put to him, but the settling of a common difficulty which, it appears, Abelard has grown impatient of dealing with every time it is raised, and wants now to remove once and for all. That interplay of minds which engages the reader's interest in Anselm's treatises as he is himself led through the process of unravelling with the *discipulus* or with Boso, is entirely absent from Abelard's works. Anselm was able to cast in a permanent

[66] Buytaert discusses the point fully in his introduction, op. cit., pp. 16–20.
[67] *Commentary on Romans*, p. 110.19–24, on the meaning of *lex*.

written form thoughts which he had actually worked out with his friends and pupils. The literary genre he chooses matches his needs exactly. The same cannot be said for Abelard, whose teaching evidently had a different flavour. We have an account of his lectures, certainly, but it lacks literary unity. The only literary wholeness the *Commentary on Romans* or the dialectical commentaries possess is that which they derive from their host, the parent work whose sequence they follow. Abelard's treatises, especially the theological treatises, are another matter. But even there he seems less at ease in the form he has chosen than Anselm. Both the novelty and the increasingly wide range of possible genres made Abelard's choice more difficult than Anselm's. Abelard's own less happy marriage of teaching with writing heightened the difficulty for him.

In this period of change and innovation in attitudes to the study of the Bible the spirit of experiment surprisingly rarely got out of hand. Innovations were cautiously made. Older scholars kept a tight rein as long as they could. Anselm of Laon forbade Abelard to lecture on Scripture, partly perhaps out of personal pique. But he seems, too, to have been anxious lest Abelard's experiments with method and procedure led him into error, and encouraged him to mislead others. Few scholars seem to have approached the Bible without a strong sense of its uniquely important place. As Rupert of Deutz says, 'the words we read in Holy Scripture' are set there by God through the Word himself (*a Deo per hoc Verbum effecta*).[68] Yet it is this strong contemporary awareness of the importance of the task which accounts in part for the upsurge of interest in the best way of carrying it out. At the beginning of his *Sententiae* Robert of Melun describes the different ways in which the lecturers of his day treat the text of Scripture. Some, he says, dwell on specific points, with a promise that in due course they will give a summary; the disadvantage of this method is that they are neither sufficiently careful over the details, nor full enough in their summarizing. Others are so intent on giving a general view that they leave out detailed explanations altogether. A well-judged, informative brevity is, he concedes, hard to achieve.[69] But he has evidently given a good deal of thought to

---

[68] *PL* 169.1219–20, *De Victoria Verbi Dei.*
[69] Robert of Melun, *Sententiae,* ed. R. Martin, *SSL* 21 (1947), p. 3.3–20.

the methods he has himself used, and tried to strike the right balance.

The same consciousness of the supreme importance of the task inspires the search for new methods of interpretation. God himself is to be sought for and found in the pages of the Bible. Only the peculiar liveliness and freshness of approach these scholars excited in one another during these decades could have encouraged Odo of Asti to see the study of the Bible as an exciting chase: 'So it came about that I hunted the deer, now fleeing, now slipping from my grasp. Now my grasp was utterly eluded by the speed of his flight; now, as deer are wont to do, he reappeared to his huntsman farther off. At last, captured and vanquished, he is still.'[70] Something of the quality of his enthusiasm, and that of his fellows, communicates itself still.

[70] *PL* 168.15.

THE CHALLENGE OF THE UNBELIEVERS

WHEN Anselm wrote the *Proslogion*, he made use, half in play, of the notion of the Fool in the Psalms, who said in his heart that there is no God. He set about making it clear to the Fool that he cannot think such a thought at all if he really understands what he is thinking. The Fool is not to be taken seriously precisely because he is too foolish to know what he is saying. Anselm found it inconceivable that anyone who gave serious thought to Christian doctrine could fail to be orthodox in his beliefs. Gaunilo, monk of Marmoutiers, took the Fool's part and pointed to a flaw which he thought he had found in the ontological argument. But he did so in a spirit of friendly challenge, and not because he seriously wanted to dispute the existence of God. The unbeliever in the fullest sense—the out-and-out atheist—is unlikely to have come Anselm's way.

In later years he did, however, encounter *infideles* of several kinds, in the form of dissidents from orthodox teaching. The *infideles* are allowed to have their say for several chapters at the beginning of the *Cur Deus Homo*. In the *De Incarnatione Verbi* and the *De Processione Spiritus Sancti* Anselm addressed himself to topics of considerable importance in Trinitarian theology: the paradox of unity and trinity in the Godhead; the way in which it was possible for only the Son to be incarnate; the Procession of the Holy Spirit. In each case he did so not because he had chosen freely to write on such matters, but because he had been obliged to do so by the vocal insistence of the *infideles* upon the correctness of their views. Anselm cannot be said to have taken the lead in the new missionary theology of the day, or to have exercised a conspicuous influence on its development. But he was drawn into it despite himself.

Gilbert Crispin, Abbot of Westminster, who had been a pupil of Anselm's at Bec, wrote a dialogue between a Christian and a Jew which was much read in the twelfth century, and which came to be perhaps the best known of the numerous examples of the genre which were composed from the end of the eleventh century. He seems to have worked on it for some years; during the time before he became Abbot of Westminster about 1085, and before he met Anselm again when Anselm came to England just before he was made Archbishop, he completed a draft which has survived.[1] The final version was ready only after Anselm's elevation to the See of Canterbury, and is addressed to him accordingly. This long period of gestation seems, to judge from Gilbert's other works, to have been characteristic. In this instance it is of especial interest because it suggests the possibility that Anselm and Gilbert may have talked over some of the problems which had been raised in Gilbert's conversations with the Jews. Anselm was not moved to write a dialogue of his own. But the topics Gilbert covers have some affinity with the subject-matter of the *Cur Deus Homo*. The Jews objected to the doctrine of the Incarnation on various grounds, both to its possibility and to its necessity, and the necessity for the Incarnation is one of Anselm's main concerns in the *Cur Deus Homo*. The coincidence of subject-matter brings Anselm at least into the ambit of the debates with the Jews, even if he cannot be shown to have taken any active part in them.

The reports of such debates which survive sometimes take the form of imaginary conversations. Peter Abelard describes a vision he has had, in which three men came towards him along different paths and, 'as one does in a dream' (*iuxta visionis modum*),[2] he challenged them at once and was invited to sit in judgement upon their debate. The three men were a Christian, a Philosopher, and a Jew. Other dialogues—including Gilbert's—may describe actual debates.[3] Gilbert says that he was in the habit of holding discussions with a certain Jew of Mainz. He sets his dialogue—and it should be emphasized that it was a public debate, with a sizeable audience—in a house in London.[4] But even this, like Gilbert's companion-piece, the *Dispute*

---

[1] BL MS Add. 8166. On this period of Gilbert's life see R. W. Southern, 'St. Anselm and Gilbert Crispin, Abbot of Westminster', *MARS* 3 (1954), 78–115.

[2] Peter Abelard, *Dialogus inter Philosophum, Christianum et Judaeum*, ed. R. Thomas (Stuttgart, 1966), p. 41.2–4, *PL* 178.1611, cf. Daniel 7:7.

[3] C. C. J. Webb, *Studies in the History of Natural Theology* (Oxford, 1915), pp. 94ff.; cf. C. C. J. Webb, 'Gilbert Crispin's *Dispute of a Christian with a Heathen*', *MARS* 3 (1954), p. 57, where a revised opinion is given.

[4] Ibid.; cf. *PL* 159.1005–6. Gilbert's *Disputatio Judei et Christiani* is edited by B. Blumenkranz (Antwerp, 1956), pp. 27–8.

of a Christian with a Heathen,[5] is, in one sense at least, a literary artefact. It may well have been the product of actual discussions, but it is too elegant to be a straightforward report, a verbatim account of a single debate; it has been made into a book.

It is unlikely that these dialogues would have been written if the presence of Jews in the community had not acted as a catalyst. The Jews of the twelfth century, in northern France at least, mixed comparatively freely with Christians of their own social class in town and country.[6] They were no uncommon spectacle and they did not live apart in separate communities. What is more, they had within their own tradition of learning a highly developed system of biblical exegesis—for the Old Testament at least—which was patently worthy to stand comparison with that of Christian scholars, if only on the level of literal interpretation; and they could offer help over the interpretation of the text because they had a knowledge of Hebrew. Andrew of St. Victor took serious account of their scholarship in his own work.[7]

The Jews to whom reference is made in the dialogues are often praised for their erudition, and for the trouble they have taken to familiarize themselves with Christian doctrine.[8] Hermannus Judaeus, the author of *A Little Book on his Conversion*, was himself converted by such discussions; in his case, it seems that Rupert of Deutz was instrumental in bringing about the change of heart. The conversion took some time because, as Hermann is anxious to make clear, he was not so easily converted as unbelievers often are: *non ea facilitate conversus sum, qua multos saepe infideles*.[9] He explains the process of his conversion in order from the beginning,[10] and he says that he found that the new insights he attained worked slowly in his mind as he thought over their implications. He likens himself to a cow chewing the cud: *in ventrem memoriae saepius mecum ruminanda transmisi*.[11] ('I often chewed the matter over in the stomach of my memory.') It was put to him that the Jews were like brute beasts because they were content with the chaff of the literal

---

[5] Ed. cit.   [6] B. Smalley, op. cit., pp. 149–56.

[7] Ibid., pp. 156–72.   [8] *PL* 159.1005; Blumenkranz, p. 27.

[9] *PL* 170.805–6. Hermann's treatise is also edited by G. Niemeyer, *MGH Quellen* 4 (Weimar, 1963), p. 69.11–12.

[10] Ibid.; *PL* 170.807; Niemeyer, p. 69.16.   [11] *PL* 170.808; Niemeyer, p. 74.16.

sense of Scripture, while the Christian, who is like a rational being, profits from the spiritual sense, the sweet heart of the grain (*dulcissima paleae medulla*).[12] This appeal to his intellectual pride he found most forceful. It is clear that Hermann was both a competent scholar in his own tradition of faith and a conscientious seeker after enlightenment about the Christian faith. Even if other discussions with Jews did not always bring about such striking conversions, it seems that they are likely to have been singularly well-informed discussions. In encounters where the participants on both sides had a strong interest in what their opponents had to say and a strong case to put themselves, there existed the conditions which could stimulate active discussions and give rise to the new interest in a genre of composition of which these dialogues are examples. The treatises are varied in their content partly at least because of the novelty and freshness of the discussions which have prompted their composition. Gilbert Crispin's became his most popular work[13] and Alan of Lille depended on it considerably when he wrote the part of his *Contra Hereticos* which deals with the opinions of the Jews.[14] But it did not fix the typical subject-matter for such dialogues in its own time. The emphasis of the discussions with the Jew in Peter Abelard's *Dialogus* is quite different.[15] Gilbert Crispin is interested in the problem posed for the Jew by the Christian contention that God became man and was subject to human weakness and death, when Christians also claim that God is immutable.[16] Abelard is concerned with the different concepts of morality, law, and ethics his speakers have, and with the pursuit of happiness (*beatitudo*) in which each is engaged. Peter Damian shows in his earlier *Dialogus contra Judaeos* that he is interested in the notion of 'law', too. He tries to satisfy the Jews who say that if Jesus came not to

---

[12] *PG* 170.808; Niemeyer, p. 74.9.

[13] Webb, *MARS* 3 (1954), p. 56. Blumenkranz lists 31 MSS of the 12th to 15th centuries, ed. cit., pp. 13–14.

[14] *PL* 210.315–430. On this work, see M. T. d'Alverny, *Textes inédits* (Paris, 1965), pp. 156–62.

[15] It should be noted that Abelard's Christian and Jew both argue with the Philosopher and not with one another. Although the dialogue is unfinished, sufficient indication is given of Abelard's intentions to make it clear that this was his plan.

[16] Cf. BL MS Royal 5 E xiv, fos. 70–3 and Bodl. MS Laud Misc. 264, fos. 122–5. The dialogue these MSS contain has a similar emphasis. It begins with a summary of what Christians believe which is intended to show its sheer absurdity to the Jew's mind.

destroy the law but to fulfil it, they cannot understand why he did certain things which seem to them to go against their law.[17]

These varied materials have found their way into the dialogues at the demand of particular Jews who wanted satisfaction from particular Christians, no doubt. But they have been chosen, too, in an attempt to find common ground of dispute, where the combatants might meet with equal interest. It was necessary not only to isolate the areas of belief where Christian differed from Jew or 'philosopher' and where they therefore had something in common to talk about, but also to examine the methods of proof or demonstration which would be acceptable to both. It is common for both matters to be raised early on the treatises. As we shall see, they were precisely the two points which it seemed to Anselm of Canterbury and Anselm of Havelberg quite essential to settle before they began on their discussions of the viewpoint of the Greeks concerning the Procession of the Holy Spirit.

Abelard's three combatants, he says, have in common principally the fact that they all worship one God.[18] Before he considers their differences, he makes it clear that they do not all find the same methods of demonstration acceptable. While the Philosopher is content with natural law (*naturali lege contentus*), the Jew and the Christian have Scriptures; the Jew accepts the Old Testament and the Christian the whole of the Bible.[19] Their respective positions on the matter of method are largely determined by these differences. The philosopher will, in principle, be willing to accept nothing which cannot be demonstrated by reason. He points out that this is the usual practice of his kind: to investigate the truth by reason (*rationibus veritatem investigare*) and to follow the lead of reason (*rationis sequi ducatum*).[20] Because he rests his case on first principles in this way, on natural law, *quae prima est*, it seems best for him to lead the discussion, so that the other two may, in turn, try to make their views acceptable to him. Gilbert Crispin's *Gentilis* of the *Dispute of a Christian with a Heathen* (who is no ignorant pagan,

[17] *PL* 145.57–68. Blumenkranz gives various examples of earlier models from patristic times to Fulbert of Chartres, ed.cit., p. 10, but these had not been inspired by discussions of quite the kind our scholars enjoyed.

[18] Thomas, ed. cit., pp. 41–4, *PL* 178.1611–12; Blumenkranz, p. 29.

[19] Cf. Gilbert Crispin, *PL* 159.1007.

[20] Thomas, ed. cit., p. 41. 16–18, *PL* 178.1611–12.

but a philosopher, too) takes the same line. He too demands to be convinced by reason, because, as he and the Christian agree, *veritas enim et ratio a nullo refutanda est*[21] ('truth and reason can be refuted by no one'). The Christian concedes the point: 'Let us leave out of account then the authority of our Scriptures.'[22] In thus setting aside authority (although authorities do have a place in the discussion) Gilbert is placing the discussion between Christian and Philosopher on one kind of footing, methodologically speaking, and that between Christian and Jew on another. The first is to be conducted on the basis of *ratiocinatio* and the second on a basis of *auctoritas* in addition. It remains for the Jew and the Christian to settle between them the extent of the authority they are both prepared to accept. Gilbert establishes that the Jew will accept only the authority of the Old Testament.[23]

The question of common method has rather more to it than that. The Jew approached the use of authority in a somewhat different spirit from that in which the Christian came to it. At one point Gilbert Crispin's Jew accuses the Christian of distorting Scriptural authority: *Violentiam Scripturae infers, et ad fidei vestrae assertionem Scripturas intorques.*[24] ('You do violence to Scripture and you twist the Scriptures to fit the assertions of your faith.') Jewish exegesis was normally confined to the literal sense. Although Hermann was vanquished by the argument that Jewish exegesis was more limited in its aspirations and that Christian scholarship had something of a higher order to offer, other Jews evidently persisted in the view that allegorical interpretation was unjustified, and that it represented a distortion of the meaning of the text.

These meetings of mind between Jews and Christians were fruitful because they gave rise to discussions of method and common subject-matter as well as creating a climate of thought in which the teachings of the 'philosophers' could be set beside that of Jew and Christian, and some orderly assessment of their respective claims attempted. As the twelfth century wore on and the Cathar and Waldensian heretics became the object of increasing concern among Churchmen, some missionaries

---

[21] Ed. Webb, *MARS* 3 (1954), p. 61.
[22] Ibid., p. 60.
[23] *PL* 159.1007; Blumenkranz, p. 29.
[24] *PL* 159.1024; Blumenkranz, p. 51.

made the effort to talk to the heretics personally. Egbert of Schönau says that he and a friend of his held discussions with the heretics: 'I and my friend Bertolph held debates with such believers and I paid close attention to their errors and defences',[25] he says. But Alan of Lille cannot be credited with having taken the trouble to talk to representatives of all his four types of 'heretic': Cathar, Waldensian, Jew, and Muslim, before he wrote his four-part defence of the faith late in the twelfth century.[26] The section on the Muslims in particular is thin and scrappy. It was the unique contribution of the encounters with the Jews at the end of the eleventh century and the beginning of the twelfth that they brought urgently to life the problems posed for orthodox Latin Christians by the existence of holders of other faiths.

The Jews had achieved a high level of scholarship without making use of the developing Christian schools. They brought in fresh air, and the challenge which Muslim scholarship also offered rather later—that of a living academic tradition which was quite independent of the tradition of Christian scholarship. It was one thing to try to make the ancient philosophers live again so as to rebut their views in the light of Christian scholarship. It was quite another to accept the challenge of a vigorous and contemporary non-Christian scholarship, especially where it touched, as it did in the case of the Jews, upon a part of Christian Holy Scripture. The debates with the Jews helped to shift polemical theology on to scholarly ground. When Latin translations of the Koran became available in the middle of the twelfth century they were made with scholarly questions in mind. One author says that not only the *philosophi graeci*, the Greek philosophers of ancient times, but also the *heretici Christiani*, the Christian heretics in their various sects, consider the technical difficulties posed by 'genera and species, difference and propriety and substance and accident and relation and quality and quantity and so on, and proposition and assumption and conclusion'[27]—by all the rules of elementary dialectic. If anyone wants to outwit them in argument he must, however reluctantly, prepare himself to meet them on their own ground

[25] *PL* 195.13–14.   [26] *PL* 210.315–430.

[27] M. T. d'Alverny, 'Deux traductions latines du Coran au moyen âge', *Archives*, xvi (1948), 93.

(*his et similibus verbis uti in suis disputationibus*) because they are
subtle and learned men, although they are heretics (*subtiles et
eruditos homines, licet hereticos*).[28] He has borne all this in mind in
rendering the Koran. Indeed, Muslim scholars proved themselves to be outstandingly well equipped in the technical skills
of the liberal arts, and to have a good deal to teach Western
Christians in this respect. The refuting and the conversion of
'heretics' and 'unbelievers' turned out to be an exercise which
stretched the best minds of the day to their limit, and even if the
influence of Muslim scholarship was not yet fully making itself
felt in the first half of the twelfth century, that of the Jews had
had a signal impact.

A general question arose for many thinkers in the face of the
new awareness of diversity of opinion. Why does God allow
other faiths to survive? It was, as R. W. Southern has suggested, 'the mystery of its existence' which first struck Western
observers of Islam, rather than its doctrinal content. The principal theological problem it presented was the mystery of why
God allowed it to come into being and to endure, what, in other
words, was its 'providential role' in history.[29] Anselm of
Havelberg gives a good deal of thought to the problem in the
first book of his *Dialogus*, before he goes on to look at the
particular case of the Greeks.[30] The question had always been
there for the asking, but at no time in the earlier Middle Ages
had it presented itself so forcefully as it did in these years when
Jew and Greek, Muslim and Latin Christian with a heretical
bent, all came forward to put a case against the orthodox view.

The Controversy with the Greeks

In October 1098 Urban II looked round the assembled
ecclesiastical dignitaries at the Council of Bari in search of
Anselm of Canterbury. When he had discovered where he was
sitting, he asked him to act as spokesman for the Latin Church
and to refute the view of Greek Christians that the Holy Spirit
proceeds from the Father only, and not from the Father and the
Son alike. Anselm gave a discourse which formed the basis of

[28] Ibid.
[29] R. W. Southern, *Western Views of Islam in the Middle Ages* (Harvard, 1961), p. 3.
[30] Anselm of Havelberg, *Dialogus*, Book I, ed. G. Salet (Paris, 1966), pp. 34ff.

the treatise *On the Procession of the Holy Spirit* which he wrote a few years later.

During the next half-century the matter became a topic of general interest in the schools, together with the question of whether leavened or unleavened bread should be used in the celebration of the Eucharist, on which Anselm also wrote a short answer at the request of Walram, Bishop of Naumburg, in the *Letters on the Sacraments*. The most notable work of the mid-twelfth century on these subjects was written by Anselm, Bishop of Havelberg, who had been for a time a student at Laon,[1] where Anselm of Canterbury's works were known.[2] He was also an intimate of the Papal Court, where again, copies of some of Anselm's works were available.[3] But he appears to have developed his views on the Procession of the Holy Spirit and on the sacraments quite independently, and when he wrote on these matters he showed himself no heir of St. Anselm, but a man of his own time.

Anselm of Havelberg held formal discussions with advocates of the Greek viewpoint most conscientiously and at some length, as Anselm of Canterbury almost certainly had no opportunity to do. Yet St. Anselm was called upon by Urban to refute the views of the Greeks at the Council of Bari and we must assume that he was the best spokesman the Pope had. Whether he encountered actual holders of the Greek doctrine there or whether he spoke on the basis of what he had read of their opinions is not clear from the *De Processione Spiritus Sancti*, which he completed some years later at the request of those who had heard him speak. The treatise does not take the form of a dialogue and the interpolations Anselm anticipates from those who disagree with him take the rather vague conventional form: *si quis tamen vult dicere*[4] ('But if anyone wishes to say'), or: *Quod si dicunt*[5] ('If they say'). Eadmer says in his *Life of Anselm* that he was 'persuaded by the Pope' to confute the Greeks in a

---

[1] Anselm of Havelberg, *Dialogus*, ed. G. Salet (Paris, 1966), p. 8. A bibliography for Anselm is given ibid., pp. 23–4. I should like to thank the editors of *Analecta Praemonstratensia* for permission to use material from my article, 'Anselm of Canterbury and Anselm of Havelberg: the controversy with the Greeks', *Analecta Praemonstratensia*, 53 (1977), 158–75.

[2] Lottin, p. 253, No. 322, for example, and see *AB*, pp. 357–62.

[3] The *De Incarnatione Verbi* and the *Cur Deus Homo* were both sent to Urban II when they were finished, S, 2.3.3 and S, 2.39–41.   [4] S, 2.204.13.   [5] S, 2.205.18.

rational and catholic disputation (*rationabili atque catholica disputatione*)[6] but the word *disputatio* did not at this time carry so clearly-defined a technical sense as it was to do later, and it appears more likely that Anselm gave an address, than that he conducted a public debate as Anselm of Havelberg later did.

The possibility that Anselm of Canterbury discussed the matter with holders of the opposing view cannot be dismissed; he begins his treatise with a clear statement of the two principles on which he intends to base what he has to say, because he knows that this is where the differences lie: the Greeks deny that the Holy Spirit proceeds from the Son, and they do not accept the Latin authorities (*doctores nostros Latinos*) whom Latin Christians follow in adopting their own standpoint. But the objections he anticipates do not, on the whole, have the flavour of matters raised in live argument, even though Eadmer says in the *Historia Novorum* that the Pope called upon him to address 'those Greeks whom you see trying to take away the Church's honour' (*suam integritatem vides Graecos istos conari adimere*) and there may well have been holders of the Greek opinion present: *mota est quaedam quaestio ex parte Graecorum* ('a question was put on behalf of the Greeks', 'who made many objections').[7]

By contrast, there can be no doubt at all of Anselm of Havelberg's opportunity to talk to holders of the Greek view. In 1135 he was sent as an ambassador to Constantinople.[8] In his *Dialogus* not only his opponent Nechites, Archbishop of Nicomedia, is named, but also the three learned Latins who understood both Greek and Latin and who were present as witnesses to what was said: James of Venice, Burgundius of Pisa, and Moses of Pergamum.[9] Anselm even gives the dates of the conversations.[10] He has done everything he can to give verisimilitude to his account and to show that here is no schoolroom dialogue, no discussion with a hypothetical opponent,[11] but the fruit of actual debate.

There is a second area of contrast in the spirit in which the two Anselms have approached their task. For Anselm of Can-

---

[6] The speech at the Council of Bari is described by Eadmer *VA*, pp. 112–13, and in the *Historia Novorum*, ed. M. Rule, Rolls Series, 81 (1884), pp. 104–10.

[7] *Historia Novorum*, pp. 104–5.   [8] *Dialogus*, p. 8.   [9] *PL* 188.1163.

[10] *PL* 188.1163; cf. *Dialogus*, p. 8.

[11] A number of the contemporary dialogues between Christians and 'unbelievers' name no actual protagonists.

terbury it was, almost certainly, not a very welcome task. He carried it out from a sense of duty. At the time when he was invited to speak at the Council of Bari he was still working on the subject-matter of the *Cur Deus Homo*, and he seems to have finished the appendix to that work, the *De Conceptu Virginali*, before he completed the treatise *De Processione Spiritus Sancti* which represents the polished version of his speech at Bari. He was, in other words, busy with other work. The treatise opens with the hope that his Greek opponents will be willing to be convinced, and not determined at all costs to win what can only be an empty victory (*pro inani victoria contendere*).[12] Throughout the work Anselm considers conscientiously all the possible objections the Greeks may raise, but there are only occasional indications that he himself derived pleasure from the task, where a novel method of demonstration has occurred to him. This was not, in other words, a subject Anselm had chosen for himself; nor was it one on which he would ever have needed to write had he not been made aware that a large body of Christians were in error, and that it was his duty to try to put them right.[13]

For Anselm of Havelberg the issue was of burning interest. Perhaps it had been brought alive for him by his encounters with Eastern Christians. Certainly he seems to have felt that although he was not qualified to write about it by a personal knowledge of the Greek language and the Greek Fathers, he was uniquely well equipped to convey to the Latin world what the Greeks believed because he had made a special study of their views, because he had consulted experts in both languages, and because he had himself had some success (according to the *Dialogus* account) in bringing about conversions. He was inspired by his achievement to write a preliminary book—which forms Book I of the *Dialogus*—in which he discusses the grand historical and theological issues raised by the existence of differences of opinion within the Church. St. Anselm's view had always been that where differences existed reflection would show that they were illusory, and that there was no difference in reality at all.[14] This was an attitude which

[12] S, 2.177.8.   [13] S, 2.212.3-4.
[14] See his discussions of the differences in usage between Greeks and Latins in talking about the substance and Persons of the Trinity: S, 1.8.14-8, S, 2.35.5-9, S, 4.96.23-97.47, *Letter* 204.

it became increasingly difficult for him to maintain in later years, as he was brought more forcibly into contact with men who did not agree with him, but it remained substantially his position to the end.[15]

For Anselm of Havelberg the existence of the Greek believers constituted an intellectual challenge; it also provided a stimulus to thought about what were in his day topical issues of historical theology: *Solent plerique mirari, et in quaestionem ponere, et interrogando non solum sibi, verum etiam aliis scandalum generare . . . Quare tot novitates in Ecclesia Dei fiunt?*[16] ('Many men are in the habit of wondering, and posing the question (and they cause not only themselves but others to meet a stumbling-block when they ask) . . . why so many novelties occur in the Church of God?') In attempting to answer this question he discourses on the working out of God's purposes in history. There is nothing like this to be found anywhere in St. Anselm's writings. That is not surprising. Anselm of Havelberg is responding to a convention of his own day in trying to interpret sacred history in this way, and to link it with contemporary events.[17] A preoccupation with what is 'new' is apparent already in the title of William of Malmesbury's *Historia Novella*, or in that of Eadmer's *Historia Novorum*, his 'history of recent events', but Eadmer does not try to construct a philosophy of history round his narrative. Yet Anselm of Havelberg has been prompted by his talks with the Greeks to think hard about the place of the phenomenon of doctrinal disagreement in the divine plan; he has written an original work of historical theology in the first book of the *Dialogus*, as well as a discussion of the actual doctrinal differences he has attempted to resolve.

The subject-matter of the debate with the Greeks was itself of greater interest in the middle years of the twelfth century than it had been in Anselm of Canterbury's day—at least as a topic for debate in the schools. J. de Ghellinck suggests that as a result of the debates over the *Filioque* clause a certain unease had crept into the schools about the use of Greek authorities and the

---

[15] From the time, just before he was made Archbishop of Canterbury, when Anselm drafted the *De Incarnatione Verbi* in response to Roscelin's accusations, he found himself more and more often obliged to encounter opponents as well as friends in the world of theological debate and ecclesiastical politics. [16] *Dialogus*, p. 34.

[17] B. Smalley, 'Ecclesiastical attitudes to novelty c. 1100–c. 125', *Studies in Church History*, 12 (1975), 113–33 has discussed some of the contemporary views of novelty.

interpretation and borrowing of Greek terms.[18] What was said by the Greeks was at best less authoritative (*minus authenticum*),[19] and at worst erroneous. In the absence of a common knowledge of Greek, it was difficult for any systematic study of the Greek Fathers to throw light on the strengths and weaknesses of their work. Robert of Melun professes himself ignorant of the Greek language,[20] and there were comparatively few men who could stand beside Anselm of Havelberg's Greek-speaking Latin scholars. A language-barrier existed, despite the active interest early and mid-twelfth-century scholars show in Greek terms. Thierry of Chartres and the commentators of his 'school' raise a number of points of technical terminology, where the Greek word is compared with the Latin.[21] In the climate of developing interest in language and in technical terms in which contemporary scholars worked, the slightest acquaintance with Greek usages was of fresh interest and value.

Behind these discussions, however, lay the shadow of the *Filioque* controversy. Thierry of Chartres remarks that the Greeks say that the Holy Spirit proceeds from the Father but not the Son: *quod falsum est*[22] ('but this is false'): *et alie plures auctoritates id consonant*[23] ('and many other authorities agree'). Not every occasion on which the Procession of the Holy Spirit is discussed provokes such a comment, but it is difficult for any contemporary to leave the Greek view out of account. Hugh of St. Victor mentions it, as does Abelard.[24] St. Anselm's treatise has not been effective in convincing the Greeks and bringing about a lasting change in their attitude. Anselm of Havelberg seriously hopes that he has achieved what Anselm has not,[25] and in any case he has brought back, in some triumph, a report of success from the battle front.

Anselm of Havelberg has chosen the dialogue-form for his *Dialogus* for the simple reason that he has an actual debate to

---

[18] J. de Ghellinck, *Le Mouvement théologique du xii*ᵉ *siècle* (Bruges, 1948), p. 402.

[19] Eberhard of Bamberg, *Letter* xvi, in a passage on the Greeks, *PL* 193.555.

[20] Robert of Melun, *Sententiae*, ed. R. Martin, *SSL* 21 (1947), p. 38.

[21] Thierry on Boethius, pp. 238, 240, 242, 247, 248 *et al.*

[22] Ibid., p. 494.26–30.   [23] Ibid., p. 494.32–3.

[24] *PL* 176.52; *Summa Sententiarum* I, 6.; Abelard, *Theologia Summi Boni*, ed. H. Ostlender, *Beitrage*, 35 (1939), p. 10 3; *Theologia Christiana*, ed. M. Buytaerti, *CCCM* 12 (Turnholt, 1969), IV.120, p. 325.; *Ysagoge* III, '*Ecrits théologiques de l'école d'Abelard*, ed. A. Landgraf, *SSL* 14 (1934), p. 254.   [25] *PL* 188.1209–10.

recount. When St. Anselm employs the dialogue in his earlier works, he makes the protagonists master and pupil; the exercise is one of teaching rather than argument. In the *Cur Deus Homo* the participants are Anselm himself and his friend and pupil Boso. Although Boso proposes to speak for the *infideles*[26] he does not in fact do so consistently throughout, and the discussion falls into a different pattern, where two friends explore the solution of various difficulties together. In Anselm of Havelberg's dialogue the two combatants speak in turn—although Anselm himself has taken the larger share of the space available—and far from exploring the issue together they retain their clearly-defined and distinct viewpoints throughout, until the Greek concedes defeat at each stage of the argument. Anselm of Havelberg is writing in the contemporary tradition of the dialogues between Christians and the holders of other faiths, after the fashion of Gilbert Crispin or Peter Abelard. His *Dialogus* (although it might be said to resemble Lanfranc's earlier dialogue with Berengar in the *De Corpore et Sanguine Domini* in some respects)[27] reveals early twelfth-century habits of scholarship. St. Anselm's dialogues have a far more Augustinian flavour. Neither in the *De Processione Spiritus Sancti* nor in the *De Incarnatione Verbi*, where he was arguing against specific opponents, did Anselm of Canterbury find the dialogue the most comfortable vehicle for his exposition. Up to a point, this is a reflection of his personal preference; but it indicates, too, that a change in attitude had taken place by Anselm of Havelberg's day, which made it natural for him to try to give immediacy and topicality to his dialogue by describing the debate he had had with the Greeks as graphically as possible.

In certain respects, the approach of the two writers to the solving of the problem of the difference of opinion with the Greeks is superficially similar. Anselm of Havelberg, like St. Anselm, begins by giving a summary of received doctrine. He points out that Greek and Latin Christians accept that God is three in one, that there are three Persons, Father, Son, and Holy Spirit, and that they share the whole of Trinitarian doctrine except the view that the Holy Spirit proceeds from the Father and the Son.[28] St. Anselm says very much the same.[29]

---

[26] S, 2.50.16.   [27] Printed in *PL* 150.407–47.
[28] *PL* 188.1164.   [29] S, 2.177.18–178.12.

This seems to have been the usual method of posing the problem, although sometimes it is done more briefly, as it is, for
example, by Abelard and Thierry of Chartres. Abelard simply
states the main point of difference, that on the basis of *Spiritus
qui a patre procedit* in John 15:26, the Greeks believe that the Holy
Spirit proceeds from the Father alone.[30] But while Anselm of
Havelberg and Abelard alike use this as a point of departure for
discussions which grow broader, and which range over the
whole field of implications of this view, for St. Anselm it is a
means of defining the issue in question as narrowly as possible.
He says that he is unwilling to go beyond what he has been
asked to do: *quod postulant aggrediar*[31] ('I shall attempt to do what
they ask'). From the beginning of his treatise he makes it plain
that it is not congenial to him to be forced to extend the scope of
his treatment of a matter which there would be no need to write
about at all, if no one held the heretical view. Anselm always
preferred to prove what orthodox doctrine asserted, to demonstrate by reason what he and his fellow Latin Christians already
held by faith, rather than to argue a case against an alternative
viewpoint. There is nothing in St. Anselm's treatise of the sheer
pleasure in controversy, the curiosity about other men's opinions, which is so marked a feature of the *Dialogus* of Anselm of
Havelberg.

Both Anselm of Havelberg and Abelard give a list of the
teachings of earlier thinkers. Abelard lists sayings of the
Fathers from Athanasius and Didymus, to Chrysostom,
Augustine, and Jerome.[32] Anselm of Havelberg considers the
different kinds of heretics whose teachings the black horse of the
Apocalypse represents: *Niger equus atra haereticorum doctrina est.*[33]
He lists Arians, Sabellians, Nestorians, followers of Eutyches,
Macedonius, Donatus, Plotinus, Manes, and points out that
there are many more.[34] St. Anselm could not have produced so
impressive a list either of patristic writers or of heretics, because
his reading had been so much narrower than that of either
Abelard or Anselm of Havelberg. He certainly knew of the
Arians and the Sabellians;[35] but it is doubtful whether he would
have felt such listing of authorities or of heretical viewpoints

[30] Abelard, *Theologia Christiana*, p. 325; Thierry on Boethius, p. 494.26–33.
[31] S, 1.177.15.   [32] *Theologia Christiana*, pp. 328ff.   [33] *Dialogus*, p. 76.
[34] Ibid., p. 78.   [35] S, 2.15–16.

helpful. This again distinguishes him, both personally, and as a scholar of his day, from Anselm of Havelberg and Abelard, to whom such exercises appeared valuable and interesting. A further aspect of the problem presented itself to Anselm of Havelberg and Peter Abelard. The Greeks had arrived at their view by arguing a case in their own language, while the Latin Christians had worked out their position in Latin. The extent to which discussions of Trinitarian doctrine were dependent upon technical precision in the use of language was clear to St. Anselm,[36] but he, unlike a small number of his twelfth-century successors, was unable to take account of the exact differences Greek usage made. Abelard points out that the difference of doctrine goes deeper than the mere surface appearance of the words: *hoc est contrario modo, non diverso verborum sono, quia et nos Latine dicimus quod illi Graece*[37] ('That is in a different way not merely by a difference in the sound of the words, for we say in Latin what they say in Greek'). In his debate, Anselm of Havelberg had to make practical provision for circumventing the difficulty posed by the language-barrier. We have seen how he assembled bilingual witnesses. He explains that at the very beginning of the discussion it was decided that he and his Greek opponent would argue not about words and usages, but about meanings: *non videbimur verborum observatores, sed sententiarum investigatores.*[38]

He and Nechites do not succeed entirely in their objective, but the technical discussions drawn from the *artes* which Anselm introduces merely add an additional dimension of discussion about language to what is being said about differences of meaning; the argument never turns entirely upon a point of linguistic analysis. Anselm, for instance, criticizes Nechites' argument (that to claim that the Holy Spirit proceeds from Father and Son is to imply that there are two *principia* in the Trinity) like this:

Hanc tuam argumentationem cum tam festinato enthymemate nequaquam suscipiendam judico. Ex hoc enim vero quod premissum est, non sequitur illud falsum quod illatum est:

verum est autem quod spiritus sanctus procedit a patre et a filio, sed falsum est quod duo sunt principia; ideoque nulla est ibi cohaerentia.[39]

[36] S, 2.178.4–5.   [37] *Theologia Christiana*, p. 326.1951.
[38] *PL* 188.1164.   [39] *PL* 188.1166.

(I do not think that your argument with its hurried enthymeme is to be accepted. For the false conclusion which is drawn does not follow from the true premiss. It is true that the Holy Spirit proceeds from the Father and the Son, but it is false that there are two sources; therefore there is no connection between them.)

Anselm's view is that since Father and Son are one God they cannot be said to be more than *unum principium*. He has employed his technical skills of dialectic to detect the fallacy in Nechites' argument, and although they are discussing meanings, it must be conceded that they are acting as *verborum observatores*, too, despite their first intention.

More items drawn from the study of the *artes* are to be found throughout the dialogue. Anselm refers to the *transpositio* of the names of the Persons in some Scriptural texts.[40] He argues that this in itself implies that the three Persons are one God because they are in a sense 'interchangeable' in position, just as the Holy Spirit is third in the Trinity not in dignity, but only in order (*numerandi ordine*).[41] We meet the idea that the names *Pater*, *Filius*, and *Spiritus Sanctus* may be regarded as *nomina defectiva*, if we say that in that the Father is not the Son nor the Holy Spirit, the name 'Father' is deficient (*in hoc sit deficiens*).[42] The Holy Spirit is said to proceed *secundum relationem*, according to his relation, not according to his substance (which is common to all the Persons of the Trinity) nor according to his Person (which is his own: *quae ad se dicitur*).[43] None of these devices or topics for discussion is peculiar to Anselm of Havelberg. These were common areas of interest of the day in which the technical principles of the *artes* were applied to the resolution of theological problems. There are traces of similar preoccupations in St. Anselm's treatise. Anselm of Havelberg has not found in practice that it is possible to set aside contemporary questions of usage and issues of linguistic philosophy and concentrate on the investigation of differences in meaning only. He is consistent only in his refusal to be drawn into argument over individual Greek words. He knows the word προβολεύς to be equivalent to the Latin *emissor*. But 'because the proper significance of this Greek name is uncertain, I do not

---

[40] *PL* 188.1175–6.   [41] *PL* 188.1172.
[42] *PL* 188.1177.   [43] *PL* 188.1178.

wish to base any certain conclusion on its definition for the moment'. (*Quia vero huius Graeci nominis propria significatio incerta est, nihil certum super interim diffinire volo.*)[44] The principal difference between him and St. Anselm in this respect is that Anselm of Canterbury saw in the first place no immediate difficulty in the fact that the Greeks had arrived at their conclusions in Greek, and in the second place, he was not so much hedged about as Anselm of Havelberg was by technical considerations. He discusses substance and relation, unity and plurality, modes of 'proceeding',[45] because they seem to him, as they did to Anselm of Havelberg, the obvious issues to be resolved, but he applies his mind to them with a freshness which it would have been much more difficult for the Bishop of Havelberg to achieve. By his time the study of the *artes* governed and directed contemporary thought in this area, but it also restricted it. Although Anselm of Havelberg has enjoyed the stimulus of talking to Nechites in person, he has directed the debate into the conventional channels of Latin scholarship.

St. Anselm employs a striking argument from symmetry in the closing stages of his *De Processione Spiritus Sancti*. He suggests in Chapter 16 that there are six *differentiae*: to have a father, not to have a father, to have a son, not to have a son, to have a spirit proceeding from oneself, and not to have a spirit proceeding from oneself. Each of these is peculiar to one of the Persons of the Trinity, or shared by one Person with one of the others, and the distribution gives each one peculiar and two shared qualities.[46] Symmetry is preserved. Anselm of Havelberg has a less developed but not dissimilar argument from symmetry: The Father begets, but not himself; the Son is begotten, but not by himself; the Holy Spirit proceeds, but not from himself.[47]

This can, however, scarcely be taken as an indication that Anselm of Havelberg was in general sympathy with St. Anselm's procedures. On the contrary, he expresses a strong distaste for the method of argument by analogy which Anselm

[44] *PL* 188.1180.

[45] S, 2.205.18–19 (*duo principia*), S, 2.190, 1 (*relativa*), S, 2.199–200 (modes of proceeding).

[46] On the argument from symmetry see my article, 'The use of technical terms of mathematics in the writings of St. Anselm', *Studia Monastica*, 18 (1976), 75.

[47] *PL* 188.1171.

defends in the *De Processione Spiritus Sancti*.[48] Anselm of Havelberg argues that the analogy must be an *inepta similitudo*, used
by those who stretch beyond their reach in theology, and yet
remain far below their goal (*se supra se in theologiam extendentes, et
tamen multum infra theologiam remanentes*).[49] The particular image
he has in mind is used by Anselm in the *De Processione* and in the
De Incarnatione Verbi, and it seems to have made a sufficiently
strong impression on the next generation of theologians for it to
be the object of a rare reference to Anselm's work by Peter
Abelard in his *Theologia Christiana*.[50] The image is not an original invention of Anselm's. It was borrowed by him from Augustine, but his development of it seems to have helped to give it a
new currency in twelfth-century schools.[51] The image involves
a comparison of a watercourse made up of spring, river, and
pool, with the Trinity. Anselm of Canterbury had used it
originally for a single purpose: to illustrate how the divine
substance was one (the water in the watercourse) in all three
Persons, and how the Holy Spirit proceeds from both Father
and Son.[52] He had not intended the analogy to be over-
extended, because it is clear that if it is pressed too far it seems
to imply that the Holy Spirit proceeds from the Father through
the Son. It seems unlikely that Anselm of Havelberg is drawing
directly on St. Anselm in giving his account of the image. He
does not refer to the river as the Nile, and he introduces
additional elements, such as the notion that the pool or *stagnum*
can be seen as the *stagnum huius saeculi*, the pool of this world.[53] It
is much more probable that the image was already known to
the Greeks, as Anselm of Canterbury implies that it was,[54] and
that the Bishop of Havelberg is trying to detach himself and his
cause from a body of contemporary discussion which he feels to
be unproductive, and even detrimental to the case the Latin
Christians have to put forward. It is evident that Anselm of
Havelberg is, again, writing in a climate of opinion more
developed and more complex than that with which St. Anselm
had had to contend a generation earlier, and in which the topics

---

[48] S, 2.203.7–205.16. I should like to thank the editors of the *Journal of Ecclesiastical History* for permission to reproduce material from my article, 'St. Anselm and Bruno of Segni: the Common Ground', 29 (1978), 129–44.

[49] *PL* 188.1207.   [50] *Theologia Christiana*, pp. 304, 333–5.

[51] See my article, 'St. Anselm's Images of Trinity', *JTS* xxvii (1976), 46–57.

[52] S, 2.31–2.   [53] *PL* 188.1207.   [54] S, 2.203.24. It is used by Greek Fathers.

for discussion have been much explored already. He has had to take into account detailed difficulties and objections which St. Anselm was free to omit.

The same contrast is apparent in the way in which the two authors handle the question of the use of leavened or unleavened bread in the Eucharist. Both cite Scriptural texts in support of the case for the Latin practice.[55] But St. Anselm has taken up the defence of his Church only because he has been specifically asked to do so,[56] and his general view is that the matter is not of great importance, although the Roman practice is preferable to the Greek.[57] Anselm of Havelberg is more combative. He accuses the Greeks of going against universal custom (*universalis consuetudo*),[58] and he points out that nowhere in Scripture is leavened bread said to be a good thing; Christ consecrated unleavened bread at the Last Supper, and unleavened bread was always offered as a sacrifice in the Old Testament.[59] Anselm of Canterbury would not have been able to see the matter as something of so little real importance a few decades later, because he would have had to take account of the more highly developed views and the more decided standpoints of contemporary scholars.

Towards the end of Book III of his *Dialogus* Anselm of Havelberg remarks that he thinks he has proved his case both by clear reason and by firm authority (*quam evidenti ratione, quamve firma auctoritate*).[60] At the beginning he had proposed a scheme of reasoning based on Nechites' assertion that three things are relevant to their discussions: reason (*ratio*), *canonicarum scripturarum auctoritas*, the authority of canonical Scripture, and the pronouncements of *generalia concilia*,[61] general councils. Abelard, too, seems to have felt that the pronouncements of Councils were important. He discusses the Councils at which the statements of the Creeds were worked out.[62] St. Anselm makes use scarcely at all of Scriptural authorities, and never of the pronouncements of Councils, but chiefly of reasoning, in the treatises against the Greeks. Here, too, he has a freedom to omit which Anselm of Havelberg neither wanted nor claimed. He takes a scholarly pleasure in

[55] S, 2.224–31.　　[56] S, 2.223.4–10.　　[57] S, 2.224.7–12.
[58] PL 188.1211.　　[59] PL 188.1234, 1238.　　[60] PL 188.1236.
[61] PL 188.1165.　　[62] Theologia Christiana, pp. 325–6.

citing Greek authorities: Athanasius, Didymus, Origen—even
Jerome, who, as he says, knew Greek, Latin, and Hebrew—
who say that the Holy Spirit proceeds from both Father and
Son.[63] He has, as he makes plain, deliberately cultivated an
open-mindedness which enables him to accept what any
authority says without prejudice, so long as it is in conformity
with Christian doctrine:

Ego nulli Christianorum, Graeco sive Latino, seu cuiuslibet gentis fideli
Christiano, donum sancti spiritus intercludo, nullum contemno, nullum
abjicio, nec abjiciendum judico; sed omnem hominem recta loquentem, et ea
quae contra apostolicam doctrinam non sunt, scribentem, libera mente sus-
cipio et amplector.[64]

(I do not rule out the possibility of the gift of the Holy Spirit to any Christian,
Greek or Latin, or the faithful of any race; I do not condemn anyone; I do not
cast out anyone or think that anyone should be cast out; but I receive and
embrace with an open mind every man who speaks the truth and writes what
is not against apostolic doctrine.')

Anselm of Havelberg has made a decision which he evidently
regards as a markedly tolerant one, and above all, a decision
which has had to be consciously made. St. Anselm never faced
such a decision because his acquaintance with authorities other
than Scripture itself, Augustine, Gregory, and some of the other
Latin Fathers was negligible. He left authority out of account
and concentrated on reasoning deliberately,[65] but not because
the range of authorities available to him was confusing, or
because he felt that some authorities ought not to be accepted at
all.

The substance of Anselm of Havelberg's argument again has
a good deal in common with that of St. Anselm at first sight, but
his order of treatment is quite different. Both begin with the
statement of common doctrine and of the specific point of
disagreement which we have already examined. Anselm of
Havelberg and Nechites then agree that they will first consider
how the difference may be settled by reasoning,[66] before they
begin to look at authority. Nechites accordingly points out that
philosophy teaches the impossibility of there being two first
principles (*duo principia*). Either one must be insufficient (if we
are to postulate that there are indeed two) or one must be

[63] *PL* 188.1202.   [64] *PL* 188.1204.   [65] S, 1.7.2–12.   [66] *PL* 188.1165.

superfluous (*vel utrumque insufficiens esset, aut alterum superfluum esset*).[67] An argument of a similar kind is used by Anselm of Canterbury in the *Monologion* to prove that the Highest Good must be one.[68] He was perfectly familiar with this fundamental *datum* of the Neoplatonic philosophy of the day. He knew, too, of the argument that if we say that the Holy Spirit proceeds from Father and Son we imply that he has two sources. His answer to this is very much the same as Anselm of Havelberg's:

Quod si dicunt non eum posse esse de duabus causis sive de duobus principiis, respondemus quoniam, sicut non credimus spiritum sanctum esse de hoc unde duo sunt pater et filius, sed de hoc in quo unum sunt.[69]

(But if they say that he cannot have two causes or two beginnings, we may reply that we do not believe the Holy Spirit to be of that in respect of which Father and Son are two, but of that in respect of which they are one.)

Anselm of Havelberg says that Father and Son are *unum principium* just as they are *unus deus*.[70] The argument and its rebuttal was evidently something of a commonplace of such discussions.

Anselm of Canterbury uses it as a starting-point for some consideration of the special ways in which the notions of 'cause' and 'effect' and 'beginning' may be said to apply to the Godhead; he develops the philosophical implications of the matter for the special case of God.[71] For Anselm of Havelberg the development of the point takes a different form, because he is aware of the existence of contemporary discussion, which he feels obliged to take into account: *apud nonnullos aliqua quaestio est*[72] ('for some this raises a question'), he concedes, as he goes on to consider the three ways in wmich we may say that there is a beginning in God, a *principium in deo*.[73] The three ways are these: *substantive in seipsum* (substantially, in relation to himself); *relative autem invicem in Trinitate* (relatively, as the Father is the *principium* of the Son); and again *relative*, but this time in the sense that God is the beginning or Creator of created things.[74] The idea that God may be regarded as *principium* in that he is Creator is in St. Anselm, too,[75] and he builds a good deal of his argument in the *De Processione Spiritus Sancti* on a discussion of substance and relation.[76] There is no major topic raised by

[67] *PL* 188.1165.   [68] S, 1.13–22.   [69] S, 2.205.18–20.   [70] *PL* 188.1166.
[71] Ch. X.   [72] *PL* 188.1167.   [73] *PL* 188.1168.   [74] *PL* 188.1168.
[75] S, 2.205.22–6.   [76] S, 2.185–90.

Anselm of Havelberg in connection with the discussion of *duo principia* which is not to be found in Anselm of Canterbury's work, too, but the order of treatment in the two works is entirely different. It is clear that we are dealing with a common tradition of discussion, and not with direct borrowing on the part of Anselm of Havelberg.

At this point Nechites concedes that the case for the *unum principium* has been argued to his satisfaction. He raises another difficulty. If the Holy Spirit himself is the *unum principium*, how is it that he does not proceed from himself? *Simili ratione probari potest quod idem Spiritus Sanctus procedat a semetipso.*[77] ('By a similar reason it can be proved that the same Holy Spirit proceeds from himself.') Here Anselm of Havelberg introduces the argument from symmetry which bears so tantalizing a resemblance to that of Anselm of Canterbury. He points out that for each of the Persons there is some attribute which he has, but not in virtue of himself: God the Father begets, but not himself; God the Son is begotten, but not by himself, and the Holy Spirit proceeds, but not from himself. Similarly, it is the proper attribute of the Father that he begets the Son (*proprium est generare filium*), the proper attribute of the Son that he is begotten of the Father (*proprium est generari a patre*), and it is the proper attribute of the Holy Spirit that he proceeds from both as from a single source (*proprium est procedere ab utroque tamquam ab uno principio*).[78] In the fifteenth and sixteenth chapters of the *De Processione Spiritus Sancti* Anselm of Canterbury explores a series of explanations of this kind, in an attempt to demonstrate how there may be differences in the 'sameness' of the Godhead; again, we can only conclude that such demonstrations were frequently resorted to in arguments on the Procession of the Holy Spirit during and after Anselm's lifetime, since the method comes so naturally to Anselm of Havelberg's mind.

When his Greek opponent declares himself satisfied on this point, he suggests that the discussion is beginning to move away from its main objective. He asks *quae et qualis*, what kind of thing this Procession is.[79] The Bishop of Havelberg refuses to be drawn into such a discussion. He says that to ask such a question is like asking *quae et qualis* of the generation of the Son or the ingeneration of the Father; if we look into that 'we shall both go mad as we peer into divine mysteries' (*et ambo insaniemus divina mysteria perscrutantes*).[80] Instead, the two disputants consider some of the implications of the view which Anselm wants Nechites to hold. This involves a good deal of discussion of Trinitarian theology, of the special meanings of unity and simplicity, the absurdity of speaking of time and place in God, substance and relation, the technical difficulties of 'naming' God, much of which has close parallels among the topics Anselm of Canterbury covers. Anselm of Havelberg has more material, as we should expect; he introduces patristic authorities which St. Anselm explicitly excludes, because he knows that the Greeks will not accept the word of the Latin Fathers.[81] (In fact, although he considers a number of points raised by Scriptural texts as he goes along, and although he includes a brief explanation of the reasons why the Latins added the *Filioque* clause to the Creed they share with the Greeks in all other respects,[82] he does not in general depart from the first of the Bishop of Havelberg's proposed exercises: that of demonstrating the Procession of the Holy Spirit from Father and Son by reason alone.) It would not be true, then, to say that the *De Processione Spiritus Sancti* has the breadth of treatment or the scope of the *Dialogus*, nor that St Anselm has anticipated all the difficulties and objections with which Anselm of Havelberg has had to contend. But he has, nevertheless, shown himself to be familiar with most of them. His treatise belongs, in its subject-matter and in the technical considerations it embraces, to the same tradition of formal discussion of the Procession of the Holy Spirit as Anselm of Havelberg's work.

The principal difference between the two works lies not so much in the greater accretion of scholarship on which the later writer is able to draw, as in the quality of St Anselm's thought. Anselm of Havelberg concludes from both Greek and Latin authorities that the Holy Spirit proceeds from the Father *proprie et principaliter*, properly and firstly.[83] Anselm of Canterbury has looked at the same point; he shows in Chapter 14 that there can be no objection to this view on the part of Latin Christians, but he does so by redefining *principaliter* when it is used of God: *Quod si dicitur quia spiritus sanctus principaliter est de patre, quasi magis sit de*

[80] *PL* 188.1171.   [81] S, 2.177.4.   [82] S, 2.211–12, Ch. 13.   [83] *PL* 188.1204–5.

*patre quam de filio, non ita dicendum est, ut intelligatur ulla praedic-
tarum varietatum inesse.*[84] ('If it is said that the Holy Spirit exists
principally of the Father'—as Augustine says in one of his
sermons[85]—'as if he existed more from the Father than from the
Son, it must not be said in such a way as to imply that there is
any of the variety we have discussed in this'.) The 'variety'
Anselm has been considering is the diversity which is present in
things which can be more or less, earlier or later, greater or
lesser than one another. Since the Son is everything that the
Father is, no inferiority is imputed to him when we say that the
Holy Spirit proceeds principally from the Father.[86] This is in no
way as it would be in created things (*in rebus creatis*)[87] where
what is not first is second, in rank as well as in order. St. Anselm
has, in other words, explored a philosophical and theological
issue as he refines his definition, where Anselm of Havelberg
has been content to marshal his authorities. Even where he
argues his reasoned case earlier in the second Book of the
Dialogus he has felt it adequate to put forward technically sound
but generally brief and conventional arguments. Anselm of
Havelberg, despite his enthusiasm for novel applications of
historical theology, has not been inspired to original thought by
the problem he has tried to resolve in his second Book.

He is evidently pleased with his treatise. He feels that he has
made his point and convinced Nechites; as a missionary exercise the debate has been a success. As a book to be read by Latin
Christians the work has the novelty of including material taken
directly from the Greeks, both living and dead protagonists for
the Eastern Church's view. It is also a thoroughly workmanlike
rendering of the main points of debate which were current in
the schools of the West, including as it does topical items and
various technical devices drawn from the *artes*. It is the complete handbook to the *Filioque* controversy, up to date and
conceived and executed on a grand scale, with additional
material on differences of usage in the sacraments and other
matters where Greeks disagreed with Latins. Anselm of Canterbury's work is narrower, but it has gone deeper. Although he
has looked at issues which were still topical in Anselm of
Havelberg's day he has not supplied what the next generation
demanded by way of brief, technically informed discussion.

[84] S, 2.213.3–5.   [85] *PL* 38.459.   [86] S, 2.213.12–13.   [87] S, 2.213.30.

The Bishop of Havelberg's work owes little or nothing to his, it appears, because he speaks on behalf of another generation of theologians.

Conversion

The object of the missionary theology which took so many forms in the first half of the twelfth century was to bring about conversions to the right and orthodox view of the Christians of the Latin West. But even within the body of Latin Christians there was room for conversion from an apathetically held faith to a deeper commitment, and such conversions were a subject of considerable interest from the end of the eleventh century if not before. Guibert of Nogent describes a number of instances of changes for the better (*bonae mutationis exempla*)[1] in the hearts and lives of his contemporaries, and in particular he describes the conversions he himself and his own mother underwent.

The most usual way for a conversion to show itself was for the man or woman who had undergone the experience to commit himself to the religious life. Indeed the most familiar sense of the term *conversio* is its use as an expression to describe someone's decision to enter a monastery. Guibert sees these conversions as being of value because of the example they set to others. When one man takes the lead, others will follow, and he describes the way in which the conversion of a well-known figure has often led to a revival of monastic life in a given area, and to the living of better and more dedicated lives within existing religious houses.

But other meanings of the term are present in Guibert's mind, too. He understands from first-hand experience the spiritual and intellectual changes which conversion brings about. He describes how he found himself heavily beset by temptation in the early days of his own monastic profession at Fly. Some of the battles he fought with himself and with the Devil were battles of intellectual adjustment. As he set about resolving his difficulties and overcoming the objections to the faith which suggested themselves to him, he thought long and hard (*crebra conjecturarum mearum ruminatione*) and he turned over the pages of many books (*et diversorum versatione voluminum*).[2] He

---

[1] Guibert of Nogent, *De Vita Sua*, ed. G. Bourgin (Paris, 1907), p. 22.
[2] Ibid., p. 60.

benefited from all this intellectual and spiritual labour in the
end, although it cost him much effort.[3]

A generation earlier, Otloh of St. Emmeram had undergone
a similar experience as he found himself meeting temptations at
the beginning of his monastic life. Many of his difficulties came
consciously to mind only when he began to study the Bible
seriously for the first time.[4] He has described them in his
account of his own temptations, he says, so that others who
'desire to read Holy Scripture when they are first converted'
may be warned that the Devil is full of cunning and that 'he
attacks all who read the Bible'.[5] He, too, implies that a serious
commitment to belief which was likely to lead to the converted
man entering the monastic life, would also involve him in
studying Scripture systematically, and discovering, perhaps for
the first time, the cunning *qua omnes eamdem Scripturam legentes
impugnare solet* ('with which [the Devil] is in the habit of attack-
ing all those who begin to read Scripture'). The converted man,
if he is anything of a scholar—and by no means all the examples
Guibert gives concern men who showed a scholarly bent after
their conversion[6]—must reason out his faith like a convert from
another religion, if he is to progress beyond the initial experience of recognizing his conversion.

Both Guibert and Otloh found that a nagging sense of sin
and a general spiritual turmoil succeeded what William James
once described as 'a passion of willingness and acquiescence,
which removes the feeling of anxiety, a sense of perceiving
truths not known before, a sense of clean and beautiful newness
within and without, and an ecstasy of happiness'.[7] In some of
his early letters Anselm seems to have been trying to help young
monks in his charge or in exile with Lanfranc at Canterbury, to
work their way through this period of adjustment. Guibert
himself describes how Anselm taught him to 'manage his inner
man' (*qualis interiorem meum hominem agerem*)[8] on his visits to the
monastery at Fly. He says that he emphasized in particular
how important it was to use the power of the reason to help him
control his body (*qualiter super regimine corpusculi rationis jura*

---

[3] Ibid.   [4] *PL* 146.29.   [5] *PL* 146.51.

[6] *De Vita Sua*, pp. 22–30. Guibert mentions in particular Evrard of Breteuil, Simon of
Valois, and St. Bruno.

[7] Quoted in A. D. Nock *Conversion* (Oxford, 1933), pp. 7–8, from W. James, *The
Varieties of Religious Experience* (London, 1907), pp. 189, 209.   [8] *De Vita Sua*, p. 66.

consulterem).[9] Profound—and often entirely private and inaccessible to reconstruction—as the process of spiritual change was in converted men, it seems to have been most characteristically looked upon as something which could be helped along by the right use of the reason, and by conscientious reflection upon reading of Scripture and the Fathers. Conversion was, in other words, regarded as a changing of intellectual attitudes as well as of spiritual and emotional direction. The convert was to learn to give as good an account of his faith to the Devil when he came to argue with him, as he was intellectually and educationally equipped to do. The spiritual dimension was of the first importance, but we hear a great deal about the intellectual dimension, too.

Guibert of Nogent and Otloh of St. Emmeram are the authors of unusually explicit accounts of this process of working out of conversion. Each of them gives an account of his conversion which he has designed to have a particular effect upon his readers: Guibert wants to further the work of influencing others by example and so he digresses to point to the examples great men have set in their own areas of influence. Otloh has a rather different edifying purpose; he wants his readers to recognize and learn from their own spiritual experiences by comparison with his, and so he gives an account of his spiritual pilgrimage, and the inner vicissitudes which have beset him. Both of them tell us a great deal about the working out of the conversion experience in men who have not changed their faith, but who have committed themselves to it more firmly. Even if their experiences were not typical they are so richly and variously described that it is possible to recognize in them the common elements of other men's experiences. Anselm had to make an intellectual adjustment when he became a monk and added to the knowledge of the liberal arts which he came to Bec to augment, that body of Scriptural and patristic reading which informs his treatises. Odo of Cambrai, too, had been famous as a master of the *artes* before he decided to restore the monastery of Tournai; he, too, had to assimilate a knowledge of the Bible and the Fathers into the scheme of his learning.[10] We are told

[9] Ibid.
[10] Hermann of Tournai, *Liber de Restauratione Monasterii Sancti Martini Tornacensis, MGH Scriptores*, xiv (1883), p. 276.

little of any spiritual difficulties this may have occasioned to either scholar, but Guibert and Otloh help us to guess at the nature of the adjustments which had to be made, and what they may have cost.

Only in a strictly limited sense can such accounts of conversion be said to have any connection with the polemical and missionary theology which began to develop so conspicuously at the end of the eleventh century. But that sense is a significant one. They show how conscious educated men were becoming of the importance of thinking about their beliefs and making them watertight against assault from within or without. They demonstrate the place of reasoning and systematic study in the process. They show, in other words, exactly the same increasing intellectual self-consciousness and the greatly increased powers of criticism and self-criticism which underlie the work of the polemicists against Jews and Greeks of the first half of the twelfth century. The posture is perhaps sometimes a defensive one. But it is also a sign of the presence of a new energy.

Anselm himself underwent a period of adjustment when he came to Bec. We hear nothing of it from Anselm himself—unless the Prayers and Meditations preserve something of the struggle—but Eadmer says enough in his *Vita* to indicate that Anselm had to contend with a number of uncertainties before he was able to decide upon a monastic life at Bec.[11] He debated with himself whether to mortify his intellectual pride by going to Cluny, where the strictness of the observance of the Rule would leave him no time for scholarly pursuits, or to remain at Bec, where Lanfranc would outshine him and he would seem insignificant by comparison. We have here an aspect of the experience of conversion in an educated man which was to become increasingly pressing for many scholars of the next generation. For Anselm there was no strong temptation to make a career in the schools as Abelard did. Roscelin and Abelard, younger than Anselm, had a different world before them. It was not perhaps yet an academic world, but it was a world in which intellectual commitment to the Christian faith was not necessarily a concomitant of conversion to monastic life. The devout theologian need no longer be a monk.

[11] *VA*, pp. 8–11.

Consistency

Anselm never expected to find the smallest inconsistency in the teaching of Scripture or in doctrine; any apparent anomaly would, he was confident, disappear upon careful examination of what was really being said. He believed this to be the case because no inconsistency at all is possible in God himself (*quamlibet parvum inconveniens in deo est impossibile*).[1] The Word of God must reflect the nature of God. So firm was Anselm's assurance on this point that he made that very consistency a ground of proof. The best test of any argument about the correctness of a theological principle in Anselm's eyes was the 'fittingness' it appeared to possess. When we discuss theology, he felt, *convenientia* and *decentia* constitute grounds for acceptance which are every bit as compelling as *necessitas*.

This expectation of Anselm's that all disputed points of doctrine or Scriptural interpretation will prove susceptible of resolution in accordance with a single scheme of orthodox views was not a thoughtless one. It is clear again and again in his treatises that he had subjected the notion to the strictest tests; using the relatively simple dialectical procedures known to him he set himself the task of devising explanations of apparent anomalies by technically impeccable means. It is possible now, with the aid of a technically more advanced logic, to fault him at times. Already in the fourteenth century exactly this kind of fault was being found with him. In MS Balliol College, Oxford 63, fos. 89–99ᵛ a remark ascribed to John of Beverley makes the point: *utendo logica sua possunt sustineri argumentationes eius quoad formam*. ('using his logic his arguments can be sustained with regard to their form'.) The author is less sure of their force when they are applied to reality. But Anselm envisaged many of the technical difficulties which his attempt might raise in the minds of others. He certainly never cheated his readers of any argument he was able to discover, by consigning a problem to the catalogue of insoluble divine mysteries before he had done his utmost to resolve it. He comes close to doing so in Chapters IX–XI of the *Proslogion*, where he pauses to admire the paradox of God's perfect justice and perfect mercy; but he quickly returns to his task of explanation. It

[1] S, 2.26.4.

cannot be said that Anselm was either naïve or careless in making his assertion that there can be no inconsistency in a theology which has as its object of study so wholly consistent a God.

Janet Nelson cites his statement about consistency with the suggestion that it may reflect a widespread contemporary attitude of mind. As a result of the Gregorian reform of the Church, and of certain other changes in later eleventh-century society, she argues: 'there is a renewed emphasis on institutional unity, and the common religious heritage of Christendom as a whole; the trend is centripetal, towards increased conformity.'[2] No doubt what Anselm said did in fact represent the views of many of his less articulate contemporaries accurately enough in a general way, although he is, philosophically speaking, making a statement of another order altogether. Anselm was a thinker whose habit it was to set his conclusions before him before he began to reason. It is at the level of his first assumptions that he adopts the view that everything we know about God shows him to be consistent. In this respect perhaps he may be said to speak for his age: his natural inclination and his training alike led him to look for consistency in doctrine. He spoke both philosophically, in that he was able to see no theoretical objection to the notion, and more broadly and generally on behalf of many of his immediate contemporaries, who were not theologians, but who looked for coherence in the view of the faith with which the Church presented them.

Janet Nelson goes on to point out that 'twelfth century heresy was in an important sense anti-structural: that is why the issue of obedience was crucial and why doctrine was not necessarily involved'.[3] Her argument is that not all lapses from conformity had a clearly-defined basis in theological difference. Some were revolts against the ecclesiastical hierarchy. The working out of that trend towards 'increased conformity' which she detects in the Church at large in the later eleventh century met opposition, from within and without, from declared heretics and from those (like Abelard and Gilbert of Poitiers) who considered themselves to stand within the Church still, but whose views the Church found itself unable to tolerate. Men who took the bold step of 'literally opting out'[4] and becoming heretics did

[2] J. L. Nelson, 'Society, theodicy and the origins of medieval heresy', *Studies in Church History*, 9 (Cambridge, 1972), p. 73.   [3] Ibid., p. 74.   [4] Ibid., p. 75.

not, as she shows, necessarily present a reasoned case. Theirs was frequently not the intellectual alienation of men who could not agree philosophically with an Anselmian view of things, but rather a severing of bonds of a more strictly social kind.

Heretics cut themselves off from the institution of the Church, with all that that implied in terms of separation from the ordinary affairs of life. Important though the underlying social changes which made this possible are, for the support they gave to those who did wish to argue a case and explain their disaffection philosophically, they will tell us little about the grounds of thought which produced that changed attitude of mind which Anselm himself was already beginning to encounter in his later years; this was a change which made it difficult for many young scholars to accept his view that no doctrinal difficulty was too great to be resolved in accordance with the orthodox teaching of the Church. Over and above the shift of social attitude which encouraged Churchmen and rebels alike to emphasize and distinguish differences of practice and belief between conformity and nonconformity, a purely philosophical debate was taking place. It divided thinkers at a most fundamental level. It separated those who are naturally conformists from born sceptics, those who habitually look for ways of reconciling anomalies, from those to whom the existence of anomalies is in itself an indication that no such coherence is there to be found; those who are not prepared to alter a jot of received teaching from those who are ready to consider the possibility that reason might dictate radical changes. It was, above all, a change which gave both a licence to speak. In the eleventh century Berengar and Roscelin had not been silent. But men of less pronounced combative instincts found their tongues in the new climate of more widespread debate.

This was to be no short-lived display of philosophical disquiet on the part of those who were beginning to question the very possibility of consistency. The controversy was so vigorous and so sustained that a whole scheme of polemical or apologetic theology was gradually devised; it ran parallel with the development of a system of speculative theology and exerted a noticeable influence upon its development. Aquinas found it possible—even necessary—to write a *Summa contra Gentiles*, as well as a *Summa Theologica*. In the first he made an attempt to present Christian doctrine systematically, but specifically addressing himself to unbelievers. The subtitle of the work, *A Book on the Truth of the Catholic Faith against the Errors of Unbelievers*,[5] emphasizes the largeness of its scope. It presents a complete system, designed to meet the errors of all the *errantes*: pagans, Muslims, Jews, Christian heretics. It had to be couched in rather different terms, and to deal with its topics from another angle of approach, from the *Summa Theologica*, because it was intended to meet specific objections to orthodox doctrine which had been raised by all these categories of 'unbelievers'. But it amounts to a *Summa* because sufficiently numerous and varied objections were by now in circulation to provide material for a major work.

What was under way at the end of Anselm's life, then, was a lasting change of direction. A substantial body of thinkers continued to find it impossible to see how Christian doctrine can be entirely consistent, and their number certainly did not grow less in the course of the twelfth and thirteenth centuries. In the schools an increasing number of articulate young men with minds trained in the arts of argument were bold enough to declare their intellectual dissatisfaction with the assumption Anselm expressed so succinctly; perhaps not all theological statements can be expected to have the consistency and ultimate simplicity of the statements he finds acceptable about the nature of God. The degree of boldness required was not by Abelard's day as great as it had been for his opponent Roscelin when he attacked Anselm, in one critical respect. It was becoming, in some circles, academically and intellectually respectable to be open about one's reservations.

Peter Abelard's *Sic et Non* set side by side a large body of conflicting authorities, without comment (except for his introductory remarks to the whole collection). Had such a work come into Anselm's hands his first impulse would have been to examine the views expressed in it in detail so as to see whether their discrepancies might be more apparent than real. In an early letter—the only instance in Anselm's works where patristic authorities are said to be in conflict—Anselm goes to some trouble to show that there is no contradiction.[6] In a few decades

---

[5] *Liber de Veritate Catholicae Fidei Contra Errores Infidelium.*
[6] *Letter* 65, S, 3.183.57–184.68.

the climate of thought had so changed as to make Abelard's exercise appear stimulating, challenging—dangerous, certainly, as his own experience proved—but intellectually valuable to a substantial number of readers. Their wider awareness of the existence of such contradictions of attitude among the Fathers and within Scripture itself, and their technical grounding in the arts, made it impossible for many young men to reconcile a straightforward acceptance of the Church's teaching with that intellectual integrity their training was designed to breed in them. A rather similar phenomenon is familiar enough in our own day. What was new at the beginning of the twelfth century was the willingness of many young men to ask their awkward questions openly and the seriousness with which they were listened to.

It was certainly not the case, however, that every writer of the day felt himself obliged to accept these new canons of intellectual respectability. Beryl Smalley has indicated something of that uncomfortable consciousness that there were novelties abroad which is detectable in the late eleventh and early twelfth centuries.[7] Bruno of Segni rejoiced at the thought of the coming of a new heavens and a new earth,[8] but he had in mind no novelty which might threaten the solid acceptability of the Church's teaching to the minds of all educated men. Most contemporary writers who comment on the change, acknowledge themselves to be frightened by the innovations they see around them. Innovations of thought in particular were fiercely opposed. The result was a hardening of attitudes on all sides, on the part of the protagonists of orthodoxy and on the part of their self-confessed enemies, but also, and perhaps this is the most significant factor, on the part of those who had begun by asking questions, by being simply unsure, and who were subsequently put under some pressure to clarify their own position.

If the whole of doctrine cannot be accepted with a clear head and a satisfied faculty of reason, then it must be conceded that it is inconsistent. And if it is inconsistent it is difficult to see how we are to decide which points of doctrine are acceptable and which are not. Anselm's overriding argument from *convenientia*

---

[7] B. Smalley, 'Ecclesiastical Attitudes to Novelty c. 1100–1250', *Studies in Church History* 12 (1975), pp. 113–33.　　　　[8] *PL* 169.943–74, *Sententiae*, Book III.

has the great advantage of bringing together a whole scheme of thought into a single system. Once the possibility of fragmentation is admitted, no stone can be regarded as necessarily standing firmly upon another and theology no longer constitutes a unified system. The impact of the peculiar set of circumstances which obtained at the end of the eleventh and the beginning of the twelfth centuries seems to have been this: the pressure to conform to the orthodox view made men think afresh about what they believed; at the same time, better training in the art of argument made them more easily able to identify the precise areas of their disquiet. Once the demands of the philosophical principle of complete theological consistency began to be recognized, the way was open for further explorations of the possibilities of revision of doctrine. Apologists for every viewpoint became more vocal. The mere investigation of Anselm's proposition that theology is always consistent if it is sound will not on its own account for the change, but it is in a very real sense a key to it. The work of twelfth-century scholars consisted largely in constructing a systematic theology. Anselm saw no need to do so because the coherence of his system of thought never seemed to him a matter for question.

In the writing of the *De Processione Spirious Sancti*, however, we have seen the possessor of the best mind of a generation unable to succeed entirely in the one task he believed most firmly that it was always possible to perform. He failed to convince the Greeks that there was nothing in the Latins' doctrine of the Procession of the Holy Spirit which they need find out of keeping with their own Creed. He did not demonstrate the consistency of all Christian doctrine so irrefutably that no one was able to disagree with him later. He put forward views which he himself found convincing and which, no doubt, his monks would have found helpful, too. But in a larger and more hostile world he could not hope to sustain the doctrine that total consistency speaks for itself. It spoke clearly enough to him to the end and to others for many generations afterwards. But it could no longer be claimed for it that it possessed universal acceptability to all right-minded men. Twelfth-century theology was always to be marked by an awareness that there were debating-points to be settled. It is always in some measure, a polemical theology.

II

HABITS OF THOUGHT

THE SEARCH FOR THE TRUTH

The Instruments of Argument

THE work of four of the most prominent teachers of theology of the mid-twelfth century—Gilbert of Poitiers, Peter Abelard, Peter the Lombard, and Peter of Poitiers—appeared so obscure and misleading to Walter of St. Victor that he called them 'the four labyrinths'. He displays only a limited technical understanding of what they had actually said,[1] but he put his finger on that element in the speculative theology of the early and mid-twelfth century which caused the greatest general disquiet to conservatively-minded contemporaries. Novel technical procedures were being applied to familiar theological questions, and as a direct result it was becoming plain that the holding of misguided views could not always be put down to misunderstanding on the part of ill-informed objectors. It was clear that not everyone could be converted to an orthodox position simply by having it explained to him where he had gone astray, as Anselm had hoped and expected. When heretical men with trained minds adopt a viewpoint they will be able to explain precisely why they have done so. They may be particularly persistent in their contrary views. 'It is not those who have the wisdom of God who differ on this point, but those men who are wordly-wise, such as the heretics and grammarians with their childish quibbling.'[2] This bracketing of heretics and grammarians recalls Anselm's description of the *dialectici haeretici* in the *De Incarnatione Verbi*.[3] The phenomenon was not by any means new. But the number of informed and technically expert 'quibblers' was now far greater, and the collective force of their arguments weighed more heavily. Walter asks whether we now have 'a dialecticians' Christ, or a Christ of the Christians'.[4]

In a sense, what had happened is easy enough to understand. Two disciplines—of theology and of the secular arts—had been

---

[1] *Contra Quatuor Labyrinthos Franciae*, ed. P. Glorieux, *Archives*, xix (1952), 187–335.
[2] Ibid., p. 246.20–4. [3] S, 2.9.21–2. [4] *Contra Labyrinthos*, p. 275.17–18.

brought together, not for the first time, but never before in so thoroughgoing and extensive a manner. New possibilities continually presented themselves in changing permutations. The impression is somewhat dazzling even at this distance of time. To contemporaries it must have seemed more brilliant still, and at the same time, more than a little frightening. It is never a comfortable experience to feel the grounds of one's deepest certainties shifting, and that is exactly what was happening to many of Abelard's contemporaries as they tried to assess the lasting validity of what they were being told. That sense that things are getting out of hand of which they often speak was a natural enough response. Several times within a century generally accepted explanations (of the workings of the universe or of the 'origin of species', for example) have been called into question in our own day. We have all seen new methods revolutionize an accepted interpretation of something thought to have been safely settled, then fall out of favour in their turn, leaving behind them no grounds of certainty at all. This amounts to something rather more than straightforward revision and reassessment, a bringing of things up to date once and for all in the light of new knowledge. There is no longer a fixed point of reference which is found to be universally acceptable. The old view will no longer do; the new one has turned out to be of ephemeral value and all that it has left behind it is a realization that the task of rethinking still remains to be done. That was the position in which men like Walter of St. Victor found themselves. They cannot tell us much about the long-term effects of these changes because they lived in the midst of them. But they do show us something of the intellectual distress which they felt.

This distress arose in large measure from a residual confusion over what was now acceptable, methodologically speaking. The immediate reassurance of knowing what practical steps are to be taken in a crisis was denied in such circumstances. It was not in practice possible to go back because the new technical terms and habits of thought had become so entrenched in the theological literature. But it was urgently necessary to decide what methods were still useful, among the vast range of new procedures with which the previous half-century had made scholars familiar. The task was, in part at least, one of methodological revision, and at a technically exacting level at that.

If the mid-twelfth century seems to have been a time of confusion and mental discomfort for a significant number of thinkers, it was evidently, for others, an exciting time. The work of reassessment went steadily forward, and there is no evidence that those whose response to the changes was a negative one succeeded in bringing about any check. There were many for whom there were no grounds for serious disquiet about the methods they were using. But we cannot discount the numerous expressions of anxiety on exactly this count—of propriety or impropriety of method—which are to be found everywhere in mid-twelfth-century writings, and which were still being raised later in the century.

The Origins of the Artes

The first question to be decided is whether the techniques of the *artes* which were becoming so influential were created by God or invented by man; if we take the view that they were God's creation, we may than ask whether he intended them to be used in the study of divine mysteries. If we wish to use dialectic in the discussion of the 'substance' of God or the 'relation' between the Persons of the Trinity, Aristotle's *Categories* may be a valuable aid or dangerously misleading, according to the view we take of the ultimate authority of the *artes*. Ralph of Longchamps raises a further difficulty. It seems that we cannot even be sure that the answer will be the same for all the *artes*. Looking back on the discussions of the twelfth century, he remarks that there have been certain thinkers who have said that the arts have not always existed: *quidam dicunt artes non esse ab aeterno*, but that they have conceded that arithmetic is the exception: *concedunt tamen arithmeticam esse ab aeterno quantum ad deum.*[5] ('But they concede that arithmetic exists from eternity with respect to God.') The laws of mathematics seemed to some twelfth-century thinkers to possess a universal validity and a self-evidency which distinguished them from the axioms of all the other arts. But underlying all such attempts to consider the authority of the *artes* individually is the great preliminary question: what is their origin?

[5] Ralph of Longchamps, *Commentary on the Anticlaudianus*, ed. J. Sulowski (Warsaw, 1972), p. 175.17–18.

Towards the end of the tenth century, the Italian Gunzo, who came to Germany and became a monk there, wrote a letter in which he goes, chronologically at least, to the root of the question. When Adam named the animals, he asks, are we to believe that he knew grammar? He questions whether we are to take the view 'that the first man was created with a knowledge of all the liberal arts, which he lost when he sinned. If that is so, we men would all have a natural knowledge of all the arts; although we read that the will was corrupt in the first man, we do not read that a knowledge of the arts was lost.' Gunzo is examining the historical evidence which the Bible provides. He is not satisfied that there is any clear indication that the arts were created at the beginning because he cannot see any strong evidence that Adam knew their rules.[6]

Rupert of Deutz, a younger contemporary of Anselm's, approaches the problem more fancifully, by means of an allegory. He describes the disciplining of the seven liberal arts in a lively image in the part of his book *On the Holy Trinity* which deals with the work of the Holy Spirit. At first these members of God's household were thoroughly undisciplined: *vagabantur enim prius per circuitum, lascivae, garrulae et verbosae puellelae*[7] ('for they ran about in circles, frolicsome, chattering and talkative young women'). They did not work, but were full of idle curiosity. Then they were set to work: (*missae sunt ergo in opus*) and now they speak in a trustworthy way about their creator (*serio fideliterque quod expediebat de creatore loquerentur*) saying good things which redound to his honour (*bonumque ad honorem eius sermonem*).[8] Rupert is not, of course, really saying anything about the origin of the *artes*. He is trying to provide a brilliant visual image which will illuminate his readers' understanding. His immediate purpose is to show how the arts may be made to work in the service of God if they are properly handled and kept in their place. He allows, however, that the *artes* are designed to tell us something about God, that God himself is in charge of them and enforces the rules or disciplines under which they operate. That is the most important thing, since without that

---

[6] Gunzo, *Epistola ad Augienses*, ed. K. Manitius *MGH, Quellen zur Geistesgeschichte des Mittelalters*, 2 (1958), pp. 38.21–39.2.

[7] *De Sancta Trinitate*, ed. H. Haacke, *CCCM* 24, XL.vii.10, p. 2 48.387.

[8] Ibid., p. 2049.390–4.

concession the commentator on Scripture and the speculative theologian cannot in conscience make use of the technical aids of the *artes* at all.

In the generation after Anselm, Hugh of St. Victor takes a thoroughly common-sense view. Men were measuring fields, he says, before geometry existed. They devised the rules of geometry to meet their practical needs. Similarly, men wrote and spoke before there was grammar; before there was dialectic, they used reason to discriminate between truth and falsehood; before there was rhetoric they handled legal matters; before there was arithmetic they used numbers, and before there was music they sang; before there was astronomy they told the time by the stars.[9] The *ortus* or origin of each of the *artes* was a practical need. 'It was necessary for logic to be discovered, for no one can discuss anything properly unless he first knows the rules of correct use of language.'[10] Hugh, like Rupert of Deutz and Gunzo, is confronting the problem directly, but somehow failing to come to grips with the central issue. He does not consider whether, when the laws of the *artes* were finally formulated, they gave a systematic account of principles which God had already implanted in the working of the created world, and whether they may therefore be reckoned to have been designed by God as an aid for theologians. He implies that this was how he saw the arts, because that is the spirit in which he himself makes use of them. But he takes care not to elevate them to the status of special channels of information about divine mysteries. All three writers have taken much the same precaution. In doing so, they have disappointed us of a direct answer to our first question (what is the origin of the *artes*?) and to the second question (can they tell us anything directly about God?). But they have made it plain that the question was in their minds, and that it was coming to be seen as an immensely important and potentially uncomfortable one, perhaps best answered a little obliquely.

Had any of them stated unequivocally that God made dialectic so that men might find him out by means of formal reasoning, he would have put himself in a further difficulty. If dialecti-

---

[9] Hugh of St. Victor, *Didascalicon*, 2, 9, ed. C. Buttimer (Washington, 1939), p. 31; cf. 1, 11, ibid., p. 22.
[10] Ibid., p. 18.

cal or grammatical principles lead to conclusions at variance with orthodox doctrine, we must look for falsehoods in the premisses, faults in the framing of the propositions or in the sequence of the arguments or for errors in the doctrine. And if the laws of dialectic are God-given and hold absolutely (and have been followed to the letter in a given instance) there seems to be no alternative to revising the doctrine in question. Thus it was that Gilbert of Poitiers and his followers were prepared to go some way towards modifying theological doctrines because they believed that the teachings of the secular arts made it necessary. We have seen that Anselm took another view. He preferred to assume that both doctrine and the laws of formal argument were right and that any apparent discrepancy was to be eliminated by examining the exact sense in which terms and methods were being employed. Secular studies did not threaten to alter theological principles for him; they merely confirmed their soundness. But this was not an attitude he could have held so comfortably in Gilbert's day.

Wherever we look among the doctrinal issues considered by Anselm and the theologians of the next generation, the impression is inescapable that Anselm had a freedom his successors had not, to set aside all but what he regards as the main issue in hand, and to build upon his assumptions without examining every one of them first with the aid of the technical procedures of the *artes*. His knowledge of the *artes* is a help to him, and it informs and directs much of his discussion, but it never becomes a stumbling-block because it never obtrudes uncomfortably upon his thinking. It is arguable that he would have attempted to approach problem-solving in this way even if he had been born a century later, because the temper of his mind would have made it difficult for him to do anything else. But there can be no doubt that he would have found the task which confronted him far more difficult because the field of theological study had been made a minefield by the proliferation of technical difficulties. The simplicity of Anselm's formulation of doctrinal problems and the lucidity of his solutions is the more notable because it could not have been matched by anyone writing a generation or so later. That is a matter not only of Anselm's stature as a thinker, but also of a changing climate of thought.

The Search for the Truth

Abelard says that without a study of certain dialectical principles it is impossible to carry out satisfactory demonstrations
of the truth or falsehood of statements. It is in that exercise, he
reminds his readers, that dialectic makes its greatest effort:
maxime desudat.[1] Even though many of Abelard's contemporaries, too, acknowledge that the primary purpose of dialectic is to help them tell truth from falsehood, it is clear that not
everyone found it fully adequate. The more clearly it was
understood what dialectic could do, the more clearly perhaps
was it understood what dialectic could not do. It could not
bring about the inner conviction which is the ultimate touchstone of proof in matters of faith. Abelard himself turns to what
he calls an *interior magister*[2] for that, as Augustine had done.

The first question of all to be asked about the existence of
God, as Aquinas sees it in his *Summa Theologica* (*Q.* 2, *Art.* 1) is
whether it is self-evident. That is not a question we should
expect to find taking such a form in the minds of eleventh-
century writers. But twelfth-century scholars who made a
study of Boethius' *De Hebdomadibus* when it became a fashionable textbook, found there a discussion of self-evidency which
captured their interest. Boethius put forward the idea that
certain truths may make themselves felt directly, that they may
be immediately and irresistibly convincing. He defines such a
truth as a *communis animi conceptio*, a common conception of the
mind.[3] Everyone accepts it, and it requires the support of no
extraneous proof—indeed it is not susceptible of proof. It is *per
se nota*, known through itself, and it can be known in no other
way. Gilbert of Poitiers, Thierry of Chartres, and his pupils,
Clarembald of Arras, Alan of Lille, and other twelfth-century
thinkers helped to make the idea familiar to their contemporaries and thus to introduce it among the habits of thought of
the day.

The essence of the self-evident axiom is its obviousness.
Scholars who attempted to discover a similar ground of built-in
certainty for matters of faith and doctrine did not, in practice,

---

[1] Abelard, *Dialectica*, p. 121.5–7.
[2] *Tractatus de Unitate et Trinitate Divina*, ed. R. Stolze (Freiburg, 1891), Book II.1; cf. n.
of H. Ostlender, *Beiträge*, 35 (1939), pp. 33–7.   [3] *Theol. Tractates*, p. 40.

find a similar ready consensus of opinion in all men's minds. It was manifestly not true that doctrinal statements commanded instant general agreement because they were obvious. Yet there is at least a superficial likeness between the moment of acceptance of the truth of an axiom and the moment of assent to an article of faith. Several thinkers of the mid-twelfth century tried to pinpoint the quality of the experience of 'thinking with assent'[4] or 'perceiving with assent.'[5] The perception of the truth: *quo interius in mente veritas manifestatur*,[6] the process 'by which the truth is made plain in the innermost mind' was of even more pressing interest to them than the mode of perception of a Boethian axiom, because it had to do with the nature of faith.

In his *Commentary on the Creed* Simon of Tournai cites Augustine's view that to believe is nothing else than to think with assent (*credere nihil est aliud quam assensione cogitare*).[7] In Simon's discussion of the definition of facth, and in the thinking of several other contemporary writers, matters of faith differ from philosophical or mathematical axioms principally in that a further step of assent is required on top of the act of understanding which makes the actual meaning of the doctrine clear. The question of the existence of God constitutes something of a special case here. The truth of an axiom, as Boethius conceives it, is not to be denied by anyone who has understood it (*nullus id intellegens neget*).[8] That is what Anselm argues to be true of the idea of God's existence. He suggests that when we have properly understood the idea of God it will be impossible for us not to believe in him: *Nullus quippe intelligens id quod deus est, potest cogitare quia deus non est*.[9] ('No one who understands what God is can think that God does not exist.') It might be argued that Anselm is speaking here in the context of a philosophical demonstration of the necessary existence of God in the first few chapters of the *Proslogion*. His subject, strictly, might be regarded not as a matter of faith but as a matter of the axioma-

[4] N. M. Häring, 'Simon of Tournai's commentary on the so-called Athanasian Creed', *Archives*, xliii (1976), 152–3; cf. Augustine, *De Praedestinatione* 2.5, *PL* 44.963.
[5] 'Die Zwettler Summe', ed. N. M. Häring, *Beiträge*, N.F., 15 (1977), Book I, p. 25.
[6] Hereford Cathedral Library MS O.I.vi, fo. 85ᵛ. This 12th-century MS is from the Augustinian house at Cirencester.
[7] *Archives*, xliii (1976), 152–3; cf. Gilbert of Poitiers, *Expositio in Quicumque*, ed. N. M. Häring, *Mediaeval Studies*, 27 (1965), 31.   [8] *Theol. Tractates*, p. 40.   [9] S, 1.103.20–1.

tic self-evidence of God, which no one can fail to recognize if he has understood what he is being asked to accept. Aquinas later discusses Anselm's argument in the course of his own treatment of the question: is the existence of God self-evident?[10] Although he takes a different stand on the matter from Anselm, he, too, clearly envisages the issue as a special case, a unique article of faith where, if nowhere else, assent may automatically follow understanding, and it is argued by some that we have what approaches a 'doctrinal axiom'.

Not all the statements of the Creeds can command the same instant acceptance by believers and unbelievers alike. The difference is, as Abelard points out, partly a question of subject-matter. Faith must deal with 'things unseen', the *invisibilia* of Hebrews 11:1.[11] He quotes Gregory's remark that, 'Those things which are apparent or obvious (*apparentia*) command recognition, not faith' (*fidem non habent sed agnitionem*).[12] Axioms are generalizations about the properties of the natural world or the universe at large. Even if they cannot be exhaustively tested experimentally, they gain their force from the impression they give to anyone who hears them that they express universal laws, by which it seems that the universe does indeed work. As Aquinas puts it, they are of such a kind that, as soon as anyone hears their subject and understands what it is, the whole statement is immediately clear and acceptable to him: *statim nominato subiecto et intellecto quid sit, statim manifestum est praedicatum ei inesse*.[13] The *res invisibiles*, the invisible things which constitute the subject-matter of faith, are not like this. They are not grand abstractions or general principles, but something whose truth is of another kind and which requires another kind of perception.

Matters of faith are not, for example, related to one another as axioms are. We cannot reason directly from the existence of God to the Fall of Adam or to the Incarnation, as we can reason from the axioms of geometry to a theorem. Given a set of certainties about God's nature it was possible, as Anselm showed in the *Cur Deus Homo*, to argue that he could have

---

[10] *Summa Theologica*, Q.2, Art. 1.
[11] *Theologia 'Scholarium'*, ed. E. M. Buytaert, *CCCM* 12, pp. 406–7, para. 18.
[12] Gregory, *Hom. in Evang.*, Book II, *Hom.*26.8, *PL* 76.1201–2.
[13] Aquinas, *Expositio in Boetii de Hebdomadibus, Lectio* 1.15.

chosen to redeem the world in no other way. Anselm perhaps came closer than any of his immediate successors to making the attempt to construct a second set of axioms of faith upon the first. But even he could not do so without admitting to the discussion a number of additional factors which are not 'necessary' and which are not inseparable from the idea of God. Adam fell, as Satan did, by a free act of his own will. The 'axiomatic' necessity for the Incarnation and Redemption sequence to take the course it did follows from the state of affairs after the Fall, not solely from the primary facts of the existence of God, and of the divine nature.

An important distinction was commonly made by twelfth-century thinkers between the two categories of truths of faith which are involved here. Augustine taught that only the existence of God and certain of his attributes can be reckoned self-evident to holders of every philosophical and theological or religious viewpoint. Even pagans can believe that there is one God, that he is just, omnipotent, beautiful, and so on.[14] But the doctrines of Trinity and Redemption are another matter. One twelfth-century writer explains that 'Master Alan [of Lille] says that the articles of faith are those particular "invisible things" which belong peculiarly to the Christian religion, such as the nativity and the Passion' (*res ille invisibiles, que ad Christianum pertinent religionem, ut nativitas, passio*).[15]

A concession was made by Thierry of Chartres which shows how much more alert twelfth-century thinkers were becoming to the presence of distinctions or a more or less technical kind between perceptions of the truth. 'Everything is not capable of being understood in the same way', he says (*Non enim omnia uno modo habilia sunt ut intelligantur*).[16] Things are to be understood not all 'in one way, but according to their nature' (*non uno modo sed secundum naturam suam*).[17] The nature of what is to be known determines the way in which it may be known. In addition, it is possible to identify a variety of modes of knowing or faculties of knowledge in the soul, the *motus mentis* or the *vis anime per-*

---

[14] Augustine illustrates the point extensively in *De Civitate Dei*, Book VII, and it is a notion taken up by various 12th-century commentators on Romans 1:19–20.

[15] R. de Lage, 'Deux questions sur la foi inspirées d'Alain de Lille', *Archives*, xiv (1943–5), 326.31–3.

[16] Thierry on Boethius, p. 268.3–5.

[17] Ibid., p. 269.8–10.

cipiendi.[18] We find sense-perception (*sensus*) distinguished from *imaginatio*, the power of conjuring up images of things which are not actually present to the senses, *ratio* (reason), and *intelligentia*. the faculty of assessment which works upon the arrangement-of-what-is-known which the reason carries out.[19] Within this increasingly complex system of modes of recognition of the truth, the kind of 'knowing' involved in an act of faith holds a special place.

Hugh of St. Victor places faith above opinion and below knowledge in the order of certainties (*supra opinionem et infra scientiam*).[20] Simon of Tournai elaborates a little on this: 'Faith is above opinion because it involves assent and below knowledge because it rests on no [objective] cause of certainty.'[21] Nicholas of Amiens also makes use of the scheme which places faith above *opinio* and below *scientia*.[22] In some 'questions about faith' based on Alan's work we find another list: *ignorantia* is the complete absence of knowledge, *dubitatio* a state of knowledge where reason and authority incline to neither side; *putatio* takes place where reason and authority combine to suggest that something is probably so, and then comes *opinio* itself, where reason and authority agree that something is certainly so.[23]

The twelfth-century work of subdivision and classification does not end there. Matters of faith are felt to be true only by the believer who contributes an act of agreement on his own account. Hugh of St. Victor emphasizes this element of will in faith: *Fides est voluntaria certitudo absentium*[24] ('Faith is a voluntary certainty about what is not present'); it is, in other words an act of willing assent to the truth of 'invisible things'. In Hugh's opinion, God's decision not to make himself known by an act of self-revelation which would be entirely self-evident to every rational creature involves a deliberate restraint. Those who are to have faith must make some contribution to their faith of their

---

[18] N. M. Häring, 'Two redactions of a commentary on a Gallican Creed by Simon of Tournai', *Archives*, xli (1974), paras 12–13, p. 46.

[19] Thierry on Boethius, p. 269.22–3; cf. M. T. d'Alverny, *Textes inédits d'Alain de Lille* (Varis, 1965), pp. 302–6.

[20] *PL* 176.43, *Summa Sententiarum* I.i; cf. *PL* 176.331, *De Sacramentis* I.x.2.

[21] Simon of Tournai on the Gallican Creed, *Archives*, xli (1974), para. 10, p. 46.

[22] Nicholas, *De Articulis Catholicae Fidei*, *PL* 210.601, see *Textes inédits*, pp. 68–9 on the question of the authenticity of this piece.

[23] De Lage, ed. cit., pp. 334.298–9, 335.307.

[24] Hugh of St. Victor, *Summa Sententiarum* I.i., *De Fide*, *PL* 176.43.

own free will and on their own account, by assenting fully to what God shows them in part.[25]

Within the act of faith there is also a perception. Gilbert of Poitiers asserts that there must be a *veritatis cuiuslibet rei cum assensione perceptio*[26] ('a perception of the truth of something with assent'). Perceptions of the truth cannot be mistaken in the case of the self-evident axioms of mathematics or philosophy, because they make their truth felt as soon as they are understood. But Simon of Tournai considers the possibility that in other kinds of perception there may be the possibility of error. Perception, he says, is to the mind as walking is to the body, since perceiving is one of the mind's natural functions.[27] But like feet in walking, mental perceptions may go astray. Only when the perception is a perception of the truth can it be said to be an act of faith. The *perceptio veritatis* alone can be called 'faith' (*et haec sola fides appellatur*).[28]

Sometimes the mind does not accept the truth even when it has perceived it, and that is why we must add 'with assent' to our definition: *Sed quoniam non semper veritati percepte consentit animus—quoniam scilicet se non nosse percepisse—ideo sequitur 'cum assensione'*.[29] He gives an example: 'I see a pale man. I think he has been studying (*studuisse*). But I do not accept this view (*nec tamen assentio*). His pallor could be caused by illness or by his being in love, as well as by studying.'[30] Even if perception (here, of the man's pallor) and assent to a given explanation are present, we do not have faith unless what is believed is true. An essential element in faith is the truth of the perception we have consented to accept.

Further, it is not enough for a man to go through this sequence of understanding, perception, willing assent, if he is merely thinking about the workings of the natural world. He must direct his faith to the 'invisible things which belong to religion' (*res invisibiles ad religionem pertinentes*).[31] What Hugh of St. Victor envisages as the 'proper proportion' of *cognitio* and *devotio*, of intellectual understanding and the assent of religious

---

[25] *PL* 176.45.   [26] Gilbert on Boethius, p. 71.11–12.

[27] Simon on the Gallican Creed, *Archives*, xli (1974), para. 11, p. 46; cf. Alan of Lille, *Summa Quoniam Homines*, ed. P. Glorieux, *Archives*, xxviii (1953), 137.

[28] Simon of Tournai, *Archives*, xliii (1976), p. 153.   [29] Ibid.

[30] Simon on the Gallican Creed, *Archives*, xli (1974), para. 10, p. 46.

[31] *Archives*, xliii (1976), p. 153.

emotion in faith, involves more than a balancing of intellectual assent and assent by an act of will. If faith is to be worth anything it must be exercised not merely upon what is true but upon the actual *invisibilia dei*,[32] the proper subject-matter of faith.

No special act of will or intellect is required of the man who accepts that an axiom is self-evident, because he cannot help but accept its truth. Nevertheless, all the states of understanding below 'certain knowledge' involve the knower in taking up an attitude towards the object of belief. He must decide whether to doubt, or to think probable, or to be of a certain opinion. Faith itself can grow or develop, but only towards a firmer emotional commitment. If it becomes knowledge it ceases to be faith. Hugh of St. Victor explains that faith grows in feeling (*secundum affectum crescit*), as it is inspired to greater devotion and strengthened in constancy[33]—that is, as its emotional component grows greater. Faith may grow in understanding too (*secundum cognitionem fides crescit*), but then it moves towards knowledge (*eruditur ad scientiam*).[34] The emotional or devotional component in faith is especially praiseworthy in Hugh's eyes.[35] The believer has merit, as the holder of an axiom has not.

In the search for theological truth, the twelfth-century scholar often found the aids dialectic provided helpful. But in the end they proved inadequate for the larger tasks with which he was faced when he tried to discuss the truths of faith. Factors had to be taken into account which lay outside the scope of the *ars disserendi*, the art of argument. The principal practical reason why the *artes* were of only limited usefulness to the student of theology was that the truths they were technically equipped to assess were not the truths of Christian belief. Dialectic could teach a man to think but not to believe.

Grammar, Dialectic, and the Special Case of God

Half-way through his career Abelard turned from the dialectical studies in which he had made his reputation, and took up theology. He had come to feel that theology offered him both a greater intellectual challenge and the opportunity to make himself a larger reputation. There is no equivalent clear-cut

[32] *PL* 176.45.   [33] *PL* 176.332, *De Sacramentis* I.x.4.   [34] Ibid.   [35] Ibid.

change of direction in Anselm's work, unless we count the alteration which must have been worked in him by his decision to become a monk, and the ten years he spent at Bec reading the Fathers before he began to write for publication. Similarly, there is no exact comparison to be made between the textbook resources which were available to Anselm and those Abelard had at his disposal. It is impossible to be sure exactly which textbooks of the *artes* Anselm had studied, and exactly which methods of formal argument he knew; although some details are clear, there is much that remains uncertain.[1] Abelard's textbook sources were probably more numerous—especially if we include the *Prior and Posterior Analytics* and the *Sophistici Elenchi* which it seems likely that he was able to read at some stage—although the bulk of his technical knowledge must have been substantially very similar to that of Anselm.[2] But for both thinkers the relation between dialectic and theology was of more than superficial interest. It touched deeply on their work at innumerable points of detail.

We need not look far to discover at least three factors in Abelard's situation which distinguish it from that of Anselm. No scholar who had travelled as much from school to school as he had done could remain confident for long that there was normally only one interpretation of even the simplest point in the *Categories* or the *De Interpretatione*. He was successively confronted with almost as many possiblities as there were masters. He refers in the *Dialectica* to the views of a number of contemporary masters: Roscelin, Ulgar of Angers, William of Champeaux, Garmundus of Tournai,[3] in much the way that we see theologians later in the century discussing the conflicting opinions of their contemporaries and immediate predecessors along with those of old-established authorities. The very technical procedures of dialectic were a debating-ground for Abelard and his contemporaries as they were not for Anselm. In the few works where Anselm deals explicitly with dialectical methods he gives the impression that the rules of formal reasoning are to him like skill in reading and writing, something to be used with

---

[1] For a convenient summary of the evidence as to the textbooks Anselm knew see J. Hopkins, *A Companion to the Study of St. Anselm* (Minneapolis, 1972), pp. 16–36.

[2] Abelard, *Dialectica*, pp. xiii, xvii.

[3] Ibid., pp. xix–xxi.

care and exactitude, but not to be disputed over. They are merely tools to be kept in good order.

Secondly, the introduction of new textbooks and the proliferation of commentaries was already beginning to have an effect in Abelard's day. He and his contemporaries were repeatedly forced to revise their opinions. Thirdly, and as a direct result of this, it is clear that an interest in the devising of new methods and in the refining of old methods was abroad. When Anselm framed a novel argument he never asked himself to what category of the logical art it might be said to belong. The ultimate touchstone of his confidence that his arguments are sound is the general reasonableness they possess.

Problems of propriety of application arose when theology was introduced into dialectical studies, just as they did when dialectic was applied to theology. Such experiments often show up most clearly as technical difficulties of reconciliation between the two major disciplines. Abelard deals with several theological problems in his *Dialectica*, where again and again dialectic is put in a somewhat defensive position as it confronts theological truths which appear to confound the laws of reasoning. Abelard's main purpose in the work is to give an account of the logic of his day, but since the *Dialectica* is an original treatise, not merely a commentary on the Boethian texts Abelard has used,[4] he is able to allow himself considerable scope for the development of some of these special problems. The theological matters which arise seem to have been quite commonly discussed in connection with certain grammatical and dialectical principles in Abelard's day. Anselm deals with many of the same matters. He, too, regards them as topics quite properly—even necessarily—considered in relation to theology. It is important not to lose sight of the fact that there runs beneath the surface of contemporary debates about the general applicability of the technicalities of the *artes* to the resolution of theological problems, a steady current of ordinary common practice. Specific topics are habitually discussed in technical terms in a quite uncontroversial way. It is possible to see the influence of dialectic quite quietly at work in twelfth-century speculative theology in a dozen areas.

[4] Ibid., p. 4.

The roots of the difficulties which presented themselves lay, as contemporary writers were well aware, in the fact that dialectically and grammatically speaking, God always presents a special case. Abelard believed that God is the source of all language.[5] But we have at our disposal only limited human language, a created thing which can speak of its Creator only in the restricted manner of created things. He remarks in his gloss on Porphyry that 'we accept that it is the custom of human language to presume to speak of the Creator as if he were a creature'. (*Nam licet consuetudo humani sermonis de creatore quasi de creaturis loqui praesumat.*)[6] Yet this limited and imperfect human language which can do no better than to speak of God in the terms it uses to refer to his creation must, in being language at all, reflect the Word which is God himself. Anselm makes the same assumption in the *Monologion* where he explains how all words and all language derive ultimately from the great universal words in the mind of God. These words are 'natural' and they are the same for every race of men.[7] The different languages men actually use are derived from these in some way, but they gain their meaningfulness from the universal *verba*. In practice, Anselm was content to accept that, although human language is too limited to allow us to discuss God adequately, yet the rules of language and logic we possess are our only means of doing so at all. He, like Abelard and his contemporaries, was obliged to try to reconcile the rules of language he knew with the special tests posed for those rules by what we know of God's nature.

It came as no surprise to them to discover that God was a special case. We use words like 'refuge' and 'consolation' of created things, but we also use them of God. It seems reasonable to ask whether their 'proper' usage is confined to things in the created world and their reference to God is in some sense an extraordinary usage, or whether they are used 'properly' only of God.[8] Such problems of signification were compounded as Latin-speaking theologians gained an increasing knowledge of the workings of other languages used by Christian writers. In

[5] J. Sikes, *Peter Abailard* (Cambridge, 1932), p. 50.
[6] *Peter Abaelards philosophischen Schriften*, ed. B. Geyer (Münster, 1919–33), p. 27.11.
[7] S, 1.25.12.
[8] Alan of Lille, *Summa Quoniam Homines*, ed. P. Glorieux, *Archives*, xxviii (1953), p. 149 (10b).

mid-twelfth-century theological writings there is a good deal of discussion of the implications of Greek and Hebrew terms. Anselm knew that the Greeks meant the same as the Latins when they spoke of God's single essence and three Persons, even though they appear from their choice of terms to mean the opposite.[9] But Robert of Melun sees the technical difficulties in another light: *mihi nondum apparet*, 'It is not yet clear to me', he says in the course of a long discussion of signification, why Greek words do not have the same proper signification as Latin ones.[10] The problems are more numerous for him because he has more variation of usage to take into account than Anselm. He knows more about the different languages in use among 'the races of men' than Anselm had any inkling of when he wrote the *Monologion*. Anselm saw the major philosophical problems involved clearly enough. But while both Anselm and those who came after him (and who chose to make use of their knowledge of the arts of language in theological discussions) were first and foremost linguistic theologians, the points where technical problems touched on theology were far more numerous for later scholars. Technically speaking, God seemed far more noticeably to constitute a special case.

This is particularly evident in that borderline area between grammar and dialectic which Anselm discusses in his *De Grammatico*. The problem with which this treatise is concerned is whether *grammaticus*, (a) literate (man), is to be regarded as a substance or a quality. If the word *grammaticus* is used (as we should now say) as an 'adjective', it seems to signify a quality. A literate man is a man who has the quality of literacy. If it is used as a noun it signifies 'a literate man' in its own right. It seems, therefore, to signify a substance, the man himself.

The difficulty is especially apparent in Latin because of the Latin language's convention of allowing the same word-form to act as a noun and as an adjective; but the general problem of paronymy of which this is a special case is a universal problem of linguistic philosophy.[11] Anselm has chosen his example from many stock examples of the day because it brings together, particularly well, grammatical questions to do with the parts of

---

[9] Cf. S, 4.95-7, *Letter* 204, S, 1.8.14-18.
[10] Robert of Melun, *Sententiae*, ed. R. Martin, SSL 21 (1947), pp. 38-40.
[11] On the *De Grammatico* see D. P. Henry's *Commentary* (Dordrecht, 1974).

speech and the agreement of nouns and adjectives, and dialectical issues (signification, the categories of substance and quality), and he hopes that it will help the beginner in dialectic[12] to see where his grammatical knowledge will be helpful to him in his new study and where it may prove a hindrance (unless he is clear-sighted about the different ways in which the two arts handle words). Anselm has, then, found for himself and his pupils a problem in the resolution of which grammar and dialectic will be forced to confront one another directly. The principles involved are fundamental ones, normally encountered early on in the study of either art. This is not a discussion about technical minutiae, but an exploration of the basic differences between the two chief arts of language.

For contrast we might take another discussion about *grammaticus* which occurs in Alan of Lille's *Summa Quoniam Homines*. Alan puts the case of two men, one of whom is called *Grammaticus* because that is his own proper name, his *proprium nomen*. The other is known as *Grammaticus* because he is good at grammar (*alteri vero per excellentiam sit adpropriatum*). Which of the two, Alan asks, is 'properly' (*proprie*) called *Grammaticus*? He who is called *Grammaticus* because he exercises himself in grammar (*quia grammatice particeps est*) is certainly quite properly called *Grammaticus*, but Alan suggests that he might even more properly be said to be called *Grammaticus* 'appropriately' (*appropriate*).[13] The twelfth-century scholar has fallen back on refinement of technical terminology. That is not to say that he has failed to take account of the underlying problems of signification. But he has avoided detailed discussion of such matters, in favour of a device which enables him to give a quick ready answer.

Technical advances sometimes set aside the deeper issues involved, as perhaps they have done here, but often they brought fresh aspects of old problems to the fore, and helped to define a familiar area of difficulty rather more precisely. This is particularly evident in the discussions of verbs and tenses. Abelard explains that when we predicate 'being' of God (*cum. . . esse de Deo praedicamus*), we do not use the term with reference to time.[14] Nothing which is said of God can apply to

---

[12] S, 1.173.6.   [13] *Summa Quoniam Homines*, p. 144 (9c).
[14] Geyer, ed. cit., p. 333.26.

him only sometimes. Because verbs have tenses, however, they cannot be used without implying that the action of the verb takes place in the past, the present or the future. *Verbum*, 'verb' is also the general term for 'word' and the expression we use for the Word of God himself. 'No word is said more properly of God than this Word', says Alan of Lille. 'For this word (verb) denotes substance (*notat substantiam*), and it is said by natural philosophers to have nothing to do with movement in time.[15] For it is not like other words (verbs) which signify successive actions; it does not signify as to motion, but rather it signifies essence.' (*Non enim, sicut alia verba, quae actiones successivas significant, in motu habet significationem, sed potius significat essentiam.*)[16] Alan is struggling to express a distinction between 'word' and 'verb' which the terminology of his day did not allow him to do easily. The verb, taken strictly as a part of speech in grammar has, as Isidore points out, a past, a present, and a future, and we use it to explain what we do. The same term, *verbum*, can mean words in general, he says, including all the parts of speech.[17] Alan has put his finger on an aspect of the difference between the two which makes it of central importance to theology. According to Boethius theology proper deals only with that which is without motion, for the divine substance is without motion (*motu caret*).[18] But a verb, strictly defined, has to do with motion (*in motu habet significationem*). Yet *Verbum* is the very word we use for Christ himself, in whom there is no motion or change. Such matters are not difficulties capriciously raised by a use of the *artes* in connection with theology. They are the inescapable concomitants of the attempt to use language precisely, and they call into question the soundness of the technical principles of the arts, as well as the acceptability of points of doctrine.

In the *Dialectica* Abelard looks at the relation of 'time' and 'place' to God. These two Aristotelian categories have, like all the others, a special quality in God.[19] This is because God contains all things and exceeds everything in his magnitude (*universa magnitudine suae maiestatis excedit*).[20] God presents a

---

[15] *PL* 210.640. [16] *PL* 210.640., Rule 39.
[17] Isidore, *Etymologiae*, ed. W. M. Lindsay (Oxford, 1911), 2 vols., I.ix.2–3.
[18] Boethius, *Theol. Tractates*, p. 8. [19] Abelard, *Dialectica*, p. 79.7.
[20] Ibid., p. 61–5.

special case which seems to break the rules of the dialectical categories of time and place. Anselm reminds his readers of the same paradox in the thirteenth chapter of the *Proslogion*: 'Whatever is restricted by the bounds of time and place is less great than that which no law of time or place binds. Nothing is greater than God and so he is restricted by neither time nor place, but he is everywhere at all times (*ubique et semper*). Anselm employs Abelard's vocabulary. God is, he says, *incircumscriptus*. He does not explicitly link what he says with the *Categories* tradition, but it clearly underlies his habit of associating the two as directly as it does Augustine's similar practice. Anselm has felt it both natural and necessary to make some reference to God's unique relation to these two categories, as he discusses a series of attributes of God in the later chapters of the *Proslogion*.[21]

Abelard notes that the rules of dialectic are submitted to severe tests by theological considerations at several more advanced points in the study of dialectic. Affirmations or negations may be true or false at different times. (*Fiunt enim affirmationes et negationes verae vel falsae circa alia tempora*.)[22] But this cannot be true of statements about God, which must be eternally true or false. It is necessary to bear this in mind, he says, when we make statements of an affirmative or negative character. We should also be aware that in some connections the past may be the same as the present or the future. The heavens, for example, are always revolving and will always revolve but they did not always do so; God always exists, and always did exist and always will exist.[23] The use of tenses in constructing affirmative or negative propositions will therefore require one set of considerations to be borne in mind if we are speaking of God and another if we are speaking of created things. Abelard is acutely anxious to warn the scholars he is helping to train that theological issues raise special problems in dialectic itself.

Whether we seek examples in the field of grammar or dialectic (or, to a lesser extent, any of the other arts) we shall find instances of special theological difficulties at every turn. So close were the technical problems of the *artes* and theology at certain points, that there is some difficulty in making dialectical

---

[21] S, 1.110–11.   [22] Abelard, *Dialectica*, p. 210.24–5.
[23] Ibid., p. 212.32–5.

principles work as effective tools of argument in these contexts where they are themselves brought into question. These were not matters where there was any possibility of leaving the teaching of the *artes* out of account because many of the theological problems involved were identifiable only in the terms of grammar and dialectic. The difficulty about the *Verbum* simply does not exist if we are not trying to think in terms of verbs and nouns. Such matters do not perhaps constitute a very large part of the dialectician's or grammarian's ground. It would be misleading to suggest that they substantially altered the direction of secular studies. Abelard introduces the special case of God into the *Dialectica* often only incidentally, or at the end of a long sequence of explanation of the straightforward dialectical rules. But theology can be seen to be putting grammar and dialectic to the test, just as they tested doctrinal principles in their turn.

By the middle of the century many scholars were beginning to find Anselm's position difficult to maintain, even if they wanted to do so. They found that it was not in practice always possible for them to resolve a discrepancy in such a way that both theology and the arts were proved to be sound. Some of them found it necessary to entertain the possibility that either doctrine or dialectic might be found to be in error. Others persevered in the attempt to force the two systems of thought to coincide. Still others tried to leave the *artes* out of theology altogether. It was becoming clear that here lay an area of choice, methodologically speaking. At the very least it was now an area of self-consciousness about methods and principles, as it had rarely been for Anselm.

2

FINDING ARGUMENTS

CICERO explains in the *Topics* (II,6) that there are two branches of the art of argument: the finding of arguments (*inventio*) and the judging of arguments (*iudicium*). *Inventio* is naturally prior to judging, he explains, because until arguments have been discovered, it is impossible to judge them. Cicero claims that the Stoic dialecticians of his own day tended to neglect the finding of arguments in favour of *iudicium*. He has tried to redress the balance in his treatise by discussing at length the ways in which an argument may be 'found'. Although Gilbert Crispin mentions both *inventio* and *iudicium*[1] as the constituent parts of logic, it was a balance which stood in need of redressing in the twelfth century, too. Perhaps it was simply that there was no shortage of old arguments to be reviewed and of new ones put forward by pupils and mature scholars alike; certainly the dialecticians of the twelfth-century schools gave a good proportion of their energies to the refinement of techniques for judging arguments.

But Anselm has something to say about the process of *inventio*. He says that after he had constructed the chain of arguments which make up the *Monologion* he began to ask himself whether it might be possible to find a single argument which would prove that God truly exists, that he is the highest Good, and so on. The expression he uses is: *si forte posset inveniri unum argumentum*[2] ('if perhaps one argument might be found'). When he thought he had discovered it, he wanted to communicate to others the pleasure it had given him to find it (*quod me gaudebam invenisse*).[3] Again, he uses the term *invenire*. The choice of term is not without significance. Cicero's *De Inventione* deals with the methods of 'finding arguments' which were in use among the rhetoricians of his day. He claims that 'every kind of argument can be found' under the headings he has listed (*atque inveniri*

---

[1] Gilbert Crispin, *Dispute of a Christian with a Heathen*, ed. C. C. J. Webb, *MARS* 3 (1954), 59.   [2] S, 1.93.6.   [3] S, 1.93.20.

quidem omnis ex his locis argumentatio poterit). [4] A number of scholars of Anselm's generation and the next were familiar with these works, and with Boethius' *Commentary* on Cicero's *Topics* [5] and his *De Differentiis Topicis*. It is doubtful whether any writer with any knowledge of the art of argument could have spoken of 'finding an argument' without some notion of its technical sense. The use of technical terms was not so far developed in Anselm's day that we can take it for granted that he has a precise technical meaning in mind. Indeed it is evident from what we know of the processes which led up to the finding of the *Proslogion* argument that Anselm had done something very much more than carry out a straightforward technical exercise. [6] But his use of the expression *invenire argumentum* suggests that the technical term was familiar to him.

In the *De Inventione* Cicero defines 'invention' as the process of 'thinking of true or apparently true things' (*excogitatio rerum verarum aut verisimilium*), [7] things, that is, which will make a case seem probable or credible when it is argued in a lawcourt or in the political arena. Cicero's definition, with its emphasis on *excogitatio*, the thinking-process, was still being quoted long after Anselm's death as a standard working definition. [8] This 'thinking up of arguments' does not, as a rule, involve the invention of entirely new arguments, an innovative process, but rather a process of discovering arguments which are already implicit in the issue in question. This is what Cicero taught his readers to do. Even in the most profoundly original of his arguments, the ontological argument of the *Proslogion*, Anselm tried to make explicit something which had always been implicit in the very nature of thought. He looked for an argument which was, in a sense, already there.

Cicero goes on to list the headings under which arguments may be marshalled. In arguments about persons, for example, we may discuss the name, the nature, the way of life, the good or bad fortune, the character, the emotions, the concerns or interest, the purposes, the deeds, the accidents, the sayings of the man in question. When we look at 'nature', we shall need to

---

[4] *De Inventione* and *Topics*, ed. M. Hubbell (Gondon, 1968), *De Inv.* I.xxx.50.
[5] *PL* 64.1044 ff.   [6] S, 1.93, cf. *VA*, pp. 29–31.   [7] *De Inv.* I.vii.9.
[8] Ralph of Longchamps, *Commentary* on Alan of Lille's *Anticlaudianus: In Anticlaudianus Alani Commentum*, ed. J. Sulowski (Warsaw, 1972), p. 142.12.

consider whether the person in question is human, whether he is male or female, what is his race, his place of birth, his family, his age.[9] The exploration of the problem is to follow a formal pattern, so that the orator may discover by observation and investigation those facts about his subject which will yield him arguments. This is certainly a process of 'discovery' rather than 'invention'. Cicero says that the arguments are *abscondita*, hidden away, and that 'when the places where those things are hidden is made plain and pointed out (*demonstrato et notato loco*) it is easy to find them (*facilis inventio est*).[10] 'Topics' are the areas of investigation or headings under which the orator may systematically look for the arguments he needs. Once he has memorized the list of topics, half the work of *excogitatio* has been done for him, and all that remains is for him to make his discovered arguments fit the case in hand. The process as Cicero envisages it is essentially one of reconstruction, of rediscovery of points which are already implicit in the situation, but which are temporarily hidden.

In one area of twelfth-century usage *inventio* is a technical term for something which has been newly invented. A novel use of a word may be said to have been arrived at *ex inventione*. Abelard speaks in his *Dialectica* of *naturales voces*, natural sounds, which have a meaning which has not been contrived by human invention (*quas non humana inventio imposuit*), but which nature alone has caused to have meaning. The example Abelard gives is that of a barking dog: *ut ea quam latrando canis emittat ex qua ipsius iram concipimus*[11] ('like that [sound] a dog makes, by which we know him to be angry'). The passage occurs in the course of a discussion in which Abelard distinguishes between senses which are in some way built into sounds, and which may therefore be 'discovered' in them, and sense which are imputed to sounds (*imposuit*)[12] by human *inventio*.[13] The vocabulary of imposition[14] and signification[15] and references to *vocabula*[16] and contrasts with propriety of usage[17] are all to be found in connection with *inventio* in the commentaries on Boethius of Thierry of

---

[9] *De Inv.* I.xxiv.34–xxx.50.   [10] *De Inv.* I.xxiv.35; *Topics* II.6.
[11] Abelard, *Dialectica*, p. 114.20–3.   [12] Ibid., p. 111–17.
[13] See *LM* II¹, p. 227 and K. M. Fredborg, 'The dependence of Petrus Helias' *Summa super Priscianum* on William of Conches' *Glose super Priscianum*', *Cahiers*, 11 (1973), p. 19.
[14] Thierry on Boethius, p. 446.48.   [15] Ibid., p. 444.70.
[16] Ibid., p. 196.46.   [17] Ibid., pp. 191.58, 149.62–70.

Chartres, whose mastery of the liberal arts was famous[18] and whose technical expertise is beyond question.

But in connection with the finding of arguments, the meaning of *inventio* continued to be confined, generally speaking, to 'discovery'. Thierry discusses the words with which Boethius opens his *De Trinitate*. Boethius addresses the work to his father-in-law Symmachus with a request for his opinion of the argument he has 'found'.[19] Thierry says that Boethius made this 'discovery' (*inventum*) 'by working out his solution to a question'. It is this solution which he calls his 'discovery'.[20] What Boethius has done, in other words, is to 'find an argument' in the best rhetorical tradition.

He has, moreover, had in mind some additional considerations which are in Anselm's mind, too, and which mark the finding of theological arguments as a process somewhat different in character from Cicero's finding of arguments. Boethius is aware that the subject-matter with which he has chosen to deal in the *De Trinitate* is peculiarly difficult, and that it is concerned with the *divinitatis celsa*, the heights of divinity. It is therefore susceptible of understanding by human reason only up to a point.[21] Where the matter in hand has to do with faith, a special kind of investigation is required if we want to discover arguments which bear on it.[22] The same elements are present in Anselm's thinking about the finding of theological arguments: the emphasis upon the unique difficulties involved, the recourse to reason within a context of faith, the notion of 'seeking'. The rational mind alone among created things is able to seek God (*ad eius investigationem assurgere valeat*).[23] The end and purpose of that seeking is the 'finding' of God (*eiusdem inventionem*).[24] This pattern of seeking-by-rational-inquiry and finding is to be found in the *De Veritate*, where the pupil declares himself to be willing to accept whatever his master finds by such means (*quidquid inveneris, ego servabo*).[25] Even if the process of seeking is effortful, as Anselm concedes in the *Cur Deus Homo* that it is (*in quaerendo valde videatur difficilis*),[26] the moment of finding brings its reward: *in solvendo tamen omnibus est intelligibilis*

---

[18] R. W. Southern, *Mediaeval Humanism* (Oxford, 1970), p. 81.
[19] *Theol. Tractates*, p. 2.4–5.   [20] Thierry on Boethius, p. 127.99–128.1.
[21] *Theol. Tractates*, p. 4.22–4.   [22] Ibid., p. 4.30–4.   [23] S, 1.77.17–20.
[24] Ibid.   [25] S, 1.177.8.   [26] S, 2.48.7.

et propter utilitatem et rationis pulchritudinem amabilis. [27] ('In its resolution it is understandable to everyone, and delightful because of its profitableness and the beauty of its reasonableness.') The rational inquiry comes full circle here, and the seeker's satisfaction in the arguments he has found consists at least in part in the appeal his discovery makes to his own reason.

Anselm's assumption is that the power of reason has been implanted in man by a rational God for no other purpose than to enable him to engage himself in the search which will end in such discoveries about God. The finding of arguments is a stage in this process. Such arguments must, of their very nature, be discoveries of what is already there, not fresh inventions. Anselm speaks in the *Cur Deus Homo* of the possibility that God will reveal to him more reasons than he has yet been able to think of. In the meantime, his arguments 'have only that certainty which attaches to things which seem true to me for the moment, until God will deign to reveal something better to me in some way'. [28] Anselm does not think that he has invented any of his *rationes*; he has merely been permitted to make some discoveries about things as they really are.

The place of faith in the proceedings is conspicuous in Anselm's thought. The *Monologion*, in which Anselm sets out his first chain of discovered arguments about the nature of God, [29] was conceived of first as a meditation *de ratione fidei*, [30] on the reason for faith. Anselm goes most deeply into the question of the relation between faith and reason in his search for arguments in the little homily at the beginning of the *De Incarnatione Verbi*. He begins by challenging those who think that they can make discoveries by reason alone, that it is open to them to find arguments (*capere*; *comprehendere*) without the aid of faith. [31] They will not, he points out, find sound arguments in that way, but only misleading ones. [32] Yet no difficulty or impossibility of understanding stands in the way of the man who approaches the task in faith. [33] The process of finding arguments of a theological kind is a guided investigation at every stage. The reason functions as God has designed it to do and faith ensures that it does not go astray.

---

[27] S, 2.48.7–9.   [28] S, 2.50.9–10.   [29] S, 1.93.4–5.   [30] S, 1.93.2–3.
[31] S, 2.6.7–10.   [32] S, 2.9.17–19.   [33] S, 2.10.15–16.

There are, however, respects in which Anselm's finding of arguments resembles Cicero's process quite closely. It is most unlikely that when Anselm wrote the *Cur Deus Homo* in his sixties he made detailed use of technical skills acquired in his youth when he heard Lanfranc lecture on the *De Inventione*, or even earlier.[34] But he could have found a number of the arguments he uses in the *Cur Deus Homo* by means which Cicero describes. Anselm's borrowings from the textbooks of the *artes* are always hard to detect because he has so thoroughly absorbed the technical terms and methods they taught him that he has made them his own. This is what seems to have happened here; the general principles Cicero outlines merely suggest ideas and help to direct his thinking from time to time.

There is a rhetorical air about the treatise which is shared by no other work of Anselm's because he is arguing a case, a *causa*, which has a distinct flavour of the courtroom. He faces opponents (the *infideles*) who are real, not hypothetical, objectors. He has to argue his case against articulate partisans of another view.

A crime has been committed. Man has stolen from God and owes him reparation: 'Nothing is less tolerable in the order of things than that a creature should steal from God the honour he owes him, and not pay for his theft.'[35] Some thinkers have argued that the Devil has a claim here, too, since mankind submitted to him of his own free will. If reparation is made to God, he will lose his control over mankind. This is not a claim which Anselm is prepared to endorse, however. He is more concerned with the repercussions of the case for God and man. A death has occurred as a result of this crime. Christ has chosen to give himself up to death for the honour of God. God's justice and mercy are discussed.[36] God is judge over the proceedings and paradoxically also the plaintiff, the victim, and the expiator of the crime. Man is the accused, but he is also, in Christ, the expiator and the victim. It is in the context of this forensic exercise that a rhetorically-inspired presentation of the case is peculiarly appropriate. It certainly seemed so to Hugh of St. Victor, who speaks in Book I,8 of the *De Sacramentis* of the

---

[34] Lanfranc's work as scholar and teacher is discussed at length in Margaret Gibson, *Lanfranc of Bec* (Oxford, 1978).   [35] S, 2.71.7–8.   [36] S, 2.111.2, S, 2.131.27.

'cause' of man against God and the Devil. 'These three', he says, 'come to court, man, God and the Devil.'[37]

The rhetorical flavour of Anselm's putting of his case is very noticeable in places. In Book I,6 he holds an imaginary exchange with the *infideles*, the hecklers to whom he is addressing himself. As he proceeds, Anselm falls increasingly into the use of rhetorical questions: 'But in whose power is hell or the Devil, or whose is the kingdom of heaven, but his who made everything?' 'Why is it that he should do what you say so as to show his love?' 'Does he not show the good angels how much he loves them, although he does not bear such things for them?' 'Surely the omnipotence of God reigns everywhere?' As he addresses himself to the unbelievers his tone becomes more and more that of the presenter of a case in a court of law. Anselm's habit of appealing to *decentia* and *convenientia*, appropriateness and fittingness, has often been noted.[38] It is a usage common to Anselm's contemporaries, too, and it seems to have had an acceptable rudimentary technical sense in the field of dialectic.[39] But it makes an appeal to the agreement of an audience or a readership which is essentially of the kind Cicero has in mind when he says that arguments must be found which will make a cause seem 'probable' or 'plausible'.[40] Many of Anselm's arguments in *Cur Deus Homo* have force for him (as he intends them to have for his readers) because they fit the case and seem appropriate. Their force is no less than that of syllogistic demonstration in Anselm's eyes, but they belong at root to the Classical rhetorical tradition rather than to dialectic.

The atmosphere of the lawcourt is heightened by Anselm's profound concern with *iustitia*. He is most anxious to make it clear exactly where justice lies, especially in relation to the Devil. If Satan has a just claim to compensation when man is wrested from his grasp, the issues at stake are rather different from those which arise if he has no such claim. Anselm refers to the 'cause', *causa*, the actual court-case involved: *quam causam debuit agere deus cum suo, de suo, in suo*.[41] ('What cause ought God to fight with his own, concerning his own, on the subject of his

---

[37] *PL* 176.307–9.
[38] See, for example, J. Hopkins, *A Companion to the Study of St. Anselm* (Minneapolis, 1972), p. 249.   [39] It is, for example, to be found in Abelard's *Dialectica*.
[40] *De Inv* I.vii.9.   [41] S, 2.56.6.

own?') His point is that since Man and Satan alike are God's creatures, his possessions, neither can engage in a lawsuit against him with any justice on his side. The vocabulary of vindication, retribution, payment of debt[42] which runs through the treatise is again the vocabulary of the court of law.

It is not, then, surprising to find Anselm looking under what are (loosely at least) the Ciceronian topic-headings, when he wants to find arguments. Cicero suggests that when a person is being discussed, the orator should consider his name, nature, and character (*nomen, natura, habitus*).[43] This is exactly what Anselm does when he looks for arguments from the nature of God to substantiate his claim that there was no other way in which man could properly have been redeemed. He considers how it was possible for God to humble himself by becoming man: *Non ergo in incarnatione dei ulla eius humilitas intelligitur facta, sed natura hominis creditur exaltata.*[44] ('No humbling of himself is therefore understood to have been brought about in the incarnation of God, but the nature of man is believed to have been exalted'), he answers. 'So it is that nothing is imputed to the divine nature when something is said of Christ concerning human weakness. (*Ita sit, nihil imputetur divinae naturae, quod secundum infirmitatem hominis de Christo dicitur.*)[45] Later, Anselm asks whether we can take it for granted that Christ was able to die *secundum humanam naturam*, according to his human nature, since according to his divine nature, *semper incorruptibilis erit*[46] ('he will always be incorruptible'). Man's nature differs from the divine nature at exactly those points which enable Anselm to show how Christ was able to do as God what we could not do as man, and how he owed a debt as man which he did not owe as God (*cum non deberet nisi homo, non posset nisi deus*).[47] Moreover, as God, Christ could not allow his honour to be violated, but as man, he could identify himself with a being capable of violating that honour.[48]

Anselm looks at *affectio*, too, as Cicero recommends,[49] and points out that it is his love for mankind which has moved God to redeem humanity.[50] He considers the *studia* and *consilia* of God,[51] his concerns and purposes, in the extended discussion

---

[42] S, 2.57.22. [43] *De Inv.* I.xxiv.34–5. [44] S, 2.59.27–8. [45] S, 2.60.1–2.
[46] S, 2.109.4–5. [47] S, 2.127.1–2. [48] S, 2.72.24. [49] *De Inv.* I.xxv.36.
[50] S, 2.51.2–3. [51] *De Inv.* I.xxv.36

on the number of angels and men God planned from the first to
be the inhabitants of the heavenly city,[52] and the divine plan
that God had for man (*quod deus de homo proposuerat*).[53]

Cicero also provides a series of suggested headings for discussing actions.[54] Anselm, too, looks at the actions of God in
carrying out the Redemption. He asks whether it could have
been done in any other manner, by an act of mercy alone, for
example, or by an angel acting on behalf of God.[55] He discusses
actio itself, whether the same action may be just and unjust in
different circumstances;[56] for whether a blow is struck because
it is deserved, or despite its being undeserved, the blow itself is
the same *actio* or deed.

In the *De Veritate* Anselm's pupil refers to the definition of the
truth which Anselm adumbrated in the *Monologion* but did not
work out there fully. Anselm concedes that he does not
remember himself to have 'found a definition of truth' there
(*non memini me invenisse definitionem veritatis*)[57] The 'finding of
definitions' is yet another of the branches of *inventio* which
Cicero discusses[58] which is to be found in Anselm; there could
scarcely be a more explicit acknowledgement of the notion that
formulating a definition is a process of *inventio*. Indeed, several
of the points which Anselm suggests must be borne in mind in
formulating a *perfecta definitio*,[59] are to be found in Cicero's
Topics, or in Boethius' commentary on the work, or in Marius
Victorinus' *On Definition*.[60] In the field of dialectic definitional
procedures were becoming increasingly clearly defined in
Anselm's day and immediately afterwards, and it is not necessary to postulate a specifically rhetorical influence here;
nevertheless, in such contexts as that in which Anselm asks in
the *Cur Deus Homo* I,11: *Quid sit peccare*[61] ('What does it mean to
sin?'), definition is being used for rhetorical purposes. Anselm
defines the topic in question so as to make it plain exactly what
he intends to prove about it. Here, he says that to sin is to act
against the will of God, and that only a rational creature in
possession of free will can therefore be said to sin; equally, as he

---

[52] S, 2.74–84.   [53] S, 2.52.9.   [54] *De Inv.* I.xxvi.37. ff.
[55] S, 2.52.14–24.   [56] S, 2.57.14–28.   [57] S, 1.176.21.
[58] *De Inv.* I.xii.17.; cf. *Topics* II.9, V.27–VII.32.   [59] S, 1.225.3.
[60] S, 1.225.24–8, and see Victorinus, *De Definitione*, which is printed in *PL* 64.891–910
among Boethius' works; Boethius' commentary and treatise on the *Topics* are also in *PL*
64.1040–1216.   [61] S, 2.68.2.

later demonstrates, Christ was unable to sin because he could not act against his own will, and therefore he could not act against the will of God. Upon his definition he is able to construct several arguments of crucial importance to his case.

Cicero also suggests the use of examples (*exempla*),[62] and analogies of various kinds. Anselm uses one striking *similitudo* in the *Cur Deus Homo*, in his analogy between fallen man and a precious pearl which belongs to a rich man. The owner, he argues, will surely pick it up after it has been struck out of his hand by his enemy (the Devil) and clean it, and put it away safely in his store?[63]

Thus it is that Anselm 'finds' his arguments in the *Cur Deus Homo* by recognizably Ciceronian methods and in something of the spirit of the Classical rhetorician.[64] By looking at the persons involved, the events and actions which take place, the issues at stake, the rights and obligations, he discovers the *rationes* he seeks.

This was not a possibility which was open to him, however, in the finding of the ontological argument. There is no atmosphere of the courtroom in the *Proslogion*; there are no opponents, no events or actions, no controversial issues at stake, no questions of right or obligation, none of the circumstantial details which provide so much material for exploration in the *Cur Deus Homo* and which help to make Anselm's arguments there so richly varied in form and content. In the *Proslogion* we are concerned with a single argument, which Anselm had to 'discover' independently of familiar aids. If we look at the process of searching and finding as it is described by Eadmer and by Anselm himself it is clear that no workmanlike procedures suggested themselves. Anselm struggled long and hard to find the argument because he could not readily find a means of approach; he did not know where to begin his search:

Ad quod cum saepe studioseque cogitationem converterem, atque aliquando mihi videretur iam posse capi quod quaerebam, aliquando mentis aciem omnino fugeret.[65]

('When I often and assiduously turned my thoughts to it, sometimes it seemed to me that I was about to grasp what I sought, and sometimes it entirely eluded my mind's grasp.')

[62] *Topics* X.41–5 and III.15.   [63] S, 2.85.6–24.
[64] On the question of whether or not Anselm knew Cicero's *Topics*, or Boethius' works on topics, see J. Hopkins, op. cit., p. 34.   [65] S, 1.93.10–12.

Eadmer, too, implies in his account that Anselm could not at first find any means of systematically searching for and finding what he sought.[66] Yet the notion that he wanted to 'find an argument' clearly underlay Anselm's efforts; it is simply that the rhetorical and dialectical methods with which he was familiar did not meet his needs. That is not to suggest that the 'finding of arguments' in the *Cur Deus Homo* is mechanical. But familiar technical procedures were potentially helpful there in a way that they were not in the search for the ontological argument. In this special sense, the ontological argument can be said to have been as much an invention as it was a discovery.

Analogies and other Arguments

Like the Stoics, whom Cicero accuses of neglecting *inventio* in favour of *iudicium*,[1] the dialecticians of Abelard's day were most actively interested in the problem of judging and assessing arguments. It is something of a commonplace for them to say, as Abelard does, that dialectic is the art of telling true arguments from false,[2] that judgement is its prime function. Yet, nominally at least, Abelard saw dialectic as an all-round study. He wrote upon 'topics' in his *Dialectica* as well as upon 'categories' and the use of the syllogism. And as well as explaining how to test different kinds of argument he lists the types of argument which may be discovered.

Among the types of formal argument he knew, he says that the syllogism holds pride of place: *Syllogismus et natura et firmae probationis privilegio principalis supereminet*.[3] ('The syllogism, both by nature and because of the uniquely firm proof it gives, stands supreme.') Less satisfactory than the syllogism, in Abelard's eyes, is the enthymeme, a form of rhetorical syllogism, in which either proposition or conclusion may be omitted,[4] and the whole argument makes its impact by implication rather than by plain statement. A second, and quite distinct, type of argument is the *inductio*, or argument by analogy, from which is derived the *exemplum*,[5] the single example or parallel. These two principal types and their subtypes were all, according to Cicero, first to be found and then judged.

---

[66] *VA*, pp. 29–30.

[1] *Topics* II.6–8.   [2] Abelard *Dialectica*, pp. 152.28, 278.17.   [3] Ibid., p. 466.20–1.

[4] Ibid., p. 463.22–3.   [5] Ibid., p. 463.6–8.

Arguments by analogy were a sometimes controversial feature of theological discussion. Their technical type was clearly recognized. Abelard remarks in his *Theologia Christiana* on 'an analogy introduced above' (*ex similitudine superius inducta*),[6] and makes use automatically both of the technical expression *inductio* and of the term *similitudo* which is to be found in Cicero's discussion of analogies in the *Topics*.[7] But as *argumenta inventa* they were often felt to be peculiarly unsatisfactory in theological contexts. Scripture itself is full of *exempla*, and Stephen Langton was not alone among the theologians of the later twelfth century in finding it perfectly natural to allow Scriptural analogies to suggest to him the helpfulness of using *exempla* of various kinds in his sermons.[8] Parables and illustrative stories are one thing, however, and analogies which are intended to throw light on divine mysteries are another. Recourse was had to analogies to attempt to explain the unity of the Trinity in particular, only because no other kind of argument was found to be adequate. There are many who found such analogies themselves inadequate, if not dangerously misleading.

The difficulty of applying any analogy to a divine mystery was clearly recognized. William of Champeaux despairs of finding anything in nature which will allow him to explain the Trinity by comparison: 'There is one God and three, one in substance and three in Persons. How I am to explain this I do not see, for nothing in the natural world can be found which is like it' (*cum in nulla rerum natura simile quid possit inveniri*).[9] It is difficult if not impossible to find what Abelard calls a *similitudinis ratio*,[10] a principle of likeness, between God and any created thing. Rupert of Deutz points out that the corporeal things on which we base our analogies (*de quibus similitudines ducuntur*),[11] are bound to be only shadowy and transitory images of the enduring truth.

Abelard goes further in his discussions of the principles which underlie the use of analogy in theological argument. He,

---

[6] *Theol. Chr.*, p. 315.1604.   [7] *Topics* X.41.
[8] B. Smalley, *Exempla in the Commentaries of Stephen Langton* (Aberdeen, 1933), pp. 1–2.
[9] Lottin, p. 192.85–7.   [10] *Theol. Chr.*, p. 306.1310.
[11] Rupert of Deutz, *De Sancta Trinitate*, ed. H. Haacke, *CCCM* 24, *De Operibus Spiritus Sancti* I.7, p.1829.249–54.

too, indicates that whenever we frame an analogy we transfer
the words (*vocabula transferimus*) from their proper application to
creatures in an attempt to apply them to the Creator.[12] In
certain circumstances he sees this as an act of presumption,
particularly on the part of the pagan philosophers who have
tried to talk about God in analogies as if to disguise their
presumption.[13] We cannot find adequate analogies (*minus
plenarias similitudines invenimus*), for that which is unique and for
which there is no comparison.[14] If that is firmly understood—for everything which is said of God is said obliquely and
in parables[15]—we may proceed to make some limited use of
whatever aids to understanding are available to us. Abelard
himself seems prepared to make some such concession. He
mentions a number of the analogies for the Trinity which were
in common use in his day despite the fact that, as he says, 'Some
modern thinkers complain that these things have nothing to do
with the force of the question.' (*nonnulli murmurent novi, dicentes
quidem haec nihil attinere ad vim quaestionis.*)[16] On this extreme
view, the use of analogies in theology is simply irrelevant.

Abelard's own interest in the possibilities of development of
the technical skills he had learnt from the study of the *artes* leads
him, not to dismiss the *similitudo* altogether, but to look a little
more closely at its possibilities and limitations. He considers
how similarity differs from identity. There is no 'likeness'
except between distinct entities (*discretis rebus*) because everything which is like is in some way also unlike or else it would be
identical. (*Omne quippe simile in aliquo dissimile est.*)[17] But this
unlikeness must not be too great. A good natural likeness makes
for a better comparison (*Facile quippe est ex similibus similia coniici*)
where one thing is by nature similar to another (*ipse per naturam
vicinior*).[18] He distinguishes between truly congruous examples,
which may be brought in to strengthen an analogy,[19] and the
slight parallel which may have its uses, even if it cannot be
pressed very far.[20] There are, in other words, pronounced
differences in the value of analogies in Abelard's eyes. He

---

[12] *Theol. Chr.*, p. 245.1628 (III.133).
[13] Ibid., p. 238.1388 (III.118).
[14] Ibid., p. 246.1640 (III.134).
[15] Ibid., p. 245.1635 (III.134).
[16] Ibid., p. 303.1196 (IV.82).
[17] Ibid., p. 231.1181 (III.95).
[18] Ibid., p. 347.38 (V.3).
[19] Ibid., p. 414.394.
[20] Ibid., p. 418.507.

speaks of bringing a stronger parallel to bear (*validiorem* . . . *similitudinem* . . . *induxisse*).[21] We have in Abelard an example of the ways in which a trained mind could make something of the natural inadequacies of the method of argument by analogy without losing sight of its particular shortcomings for use in theological discussion.

Even if there had been no support for the notion of argument by analogy in the rhetorical textbooks, the existence of *similitudines* in the Bible would have given rise to discussion of this method of argument. Bruno of Segni takes the statement that 'The light of the body is the eye', identifies it as a *similitudo* and proceeds to develop it point by point, so as to show that without that light the hand and foot and the other members of the body could not carry out their work. He does not consider the technical properties of the analogy, but he knows that it is a *similitudo*.[22] Supported by such precedents and fortified with a knowledge of analogical method, mid-century theologians make a restrained but frequent use of analogies in their theological arguments. Simon of Tournai often introduces such a comparison in the *Disputationes*. He shows a proper concern for technical soundness. *Ut ergo abusio sit in comparativo*[23] ('to force the comparison'), he says, contemplation is better than administration (because it is good in itself) just as honey is sweeter than gall. This comparison, he feels, is unsatisfactory because it is impossible to say that something is 'more good' than something else which is not good at all in itself and which seems so only in special circumstances. It is equally absurd to say that honey is 'sweeter than' gall, because gall is not sweet at all. The grammatical comparative is simply inappropriate here. In discussing the technical problem, however, Simon has used an analogy quite naturally; the method itself seems to him to be a helpful one.

He introduces further comparisons or analogies by *sicut*. (Christ loved John more if we are to judge by outward exhibitions of love, but he loved Peter more if we are to judge by the feeling he had for him; just as, a *paterfamilias* loves a member of his household more than his son if we are to judge by the outward signs of regard he shows him, but he loves his son more

---

[21] Ibid., p. 304.1208.   [22] *PL* 165.120, *Comm. in Matth.*

[23] Simon of Tournai, *Disputationes*, ed. J. Warichez, *SSL* (1932), p. 28, *Disp.* IV, Q.2.

in his heart.)²⁴ *Ut* introduces numerous analogies, among them a comparison between two men who fall into mortal sin although one is a better man than the other, and a single place to which two slopes run down, one higher than the other.²⁵ *Ut ita, quasi, velut,* in the *Disputationes* and elsewhere, introduce what Simon clearly saw as a form of argument technically identifiable as an argument from likeness, *a simili.*²⁶

He has given some thought, too, to the special considerations it may be helpful to bear in mind when making comparisons. As a rule, he acknowledges, if we were to compare gold with silver gold would seem better. 'But some silver, like the mark, would be chosen in preference to some gold, like the bezant, for a mark of silver can be worth more than a bezant of gold.'²⁷ Like Abelard, he has gone to some trouble to develop a theory of argument by analogy, although he has done so in a rather different spirit, and he does not stop to consider the major question of the usefulness of such arguments in theological discussion. He has given the analogy a humbler place. Although he is dealing with theological topics he does not in general attempt to illuminate the reader's understanding of divine mysteries by means of analogy, but merely to make sensible use of parallels from ordinary experience as a simple means of assistance to his reader's understanding.

The great images of Trinity²⁸ pose theological and philosophical problems of another order, and it is here, where the analogy is most severely tested, that it is most often felt to be inadequate for theological purposes. Anselm shows in the *De Processione Spiritus Sancti* how great a strain contemporary controversy was already putting on the method. The analogy between the Trinity and a river or watercourse made up of spring, stream, and pool had seemed to him an illuminating one when he was writing the *De Incarnatione Verbi.*²⁹ But he had intended it to be no more than an aid to understanding. There are, he concedes, great differences between the Trinity and such a river (*magna dissimilitudo*), yet there is also some likeness (*nonnulla similitudo*)³⁰ which makes the image helpful. Anselm

---

²⁴ Ibid., p. 26 (*Disp.* III, Q.2.).   ²⁵ Ibid., p. 30 (*Disp.* IV, Q.3).
²⁶ Ibid., p. 45 (*Disp.* XII, Q.1), p. 60 (*Disp.* XVII, Q.3).
²⁷ Ibid., p. 45 (*Disp.* XII, Q.1).
²⁸ See my article, 'St. Anselm's Images of Trinity', *JTS* xxvii (1976), 46–57.
²⁹ S, 2.31–33.   ³⁰ S, 2.33.2–3.

cannot be accused of having made over-large claims for his adaptation of this Augustinian image. In the new analogies he invented for use in preaching he was always careful to match the analogy with the subject in question precisely, point by point, and not to press it too far. A monk is compared with a good penny, God with a mighty king, the Devil with his enemy, and so on, as Anselm makes up little stories and brief descriptions of parallel cases for the edification of his hearers.[31] The force of his own analogies often lies in their capacity for being perceived as a whole. He took care to keep them simple and contained, so that they would not mislead. When he used an image of the Trinity he tried, as far as his subject-matter would allow him, to abide by the same rules. The Greeks against whom he wrote in the *De Processione Spiritus Sancti* would not, however, let the matter rest. They attacked the image of the river at all its weakest points, and they forced Anselm to defend his use of the image.

In the *De Incarnatione Verbi* Anselm had explained the precise points at which the analogy seemed to him helpful. It would be natural to call any part of the watercourse 'the Nile'. Any two parts of the watercourse might equally be called 'the Nile'. Or all three might be referred to collectively as 'the Nile'. In each case it is the same Nile which is referred to, not two or three different Niles. But no one would call the spring the river or the river the pool. The names of the parts of the watercourse are peculiar to each. It is impossible to say where the watercourse is divided into its parts, because it is a continuous quantity. In a limited sense, the three parts are one. Because of the arrangement of the parts of the watercourse, the stream runs from the spring only (as the Son is begotten by the Father only) while the pool proceeds from both stream and spring (as the Holy Spirit proceeds from both Father and Son).

It is clear enough that the same image was appropriate to the discussions of the *De Processione Spiritus Sancti*.[32] Yet Anselm does not introduce it at once, and when he does so, it comes towards the end of a prolonged attempt to discuss some of the

---

[31] *Memorials*, p. 370, and see my article, 'St. Anselm's Analogies', *Vivarium*, xiv (1976), 81–93.

[32] It is interesting to note that Anselm had recourse to the analogy of point on point in both treatises, too.

principles it illustrates without its aid. It begins to seem that he
is unwilling to employ it again if he can avoid doing so. He
remarks, almost wistfully, at one point, that he has made use of
it before, in the *De Incarnatione Verbi*, and that there are indeed
many respects in which it is applicable to the mystery of the
Trinity: *Multo enim in horum consideratione . . . inveniuntur, quae uni
deo et tribus personis per quandam similitudinem aptantur.*[33] There,
however, he had been able to limit the scope of its application.
But he had also exposed the image to the critical gaze of those
Greeks who had presumably not troubled to read of it in
Augustine.[34] These critics had found fresh applications which,
they claimed, supported their own view. The river, for
example, seems to proceed or be derived from a spring in a
more direct way than the lake proceeds from the river: *sicut rivus
magis illi videtur procedere de fonte quam lacus de rivo.*[35] This splitting
of hairs of meaning had never been Anselm's intention. Neither
had he pointed out that the river and the lake are not 'in' the
spring, but outside it, as the Greeks now reminded him,[36] nor
that the lake comes from the stream only after an interval.[37]
God cannot be 'outside' God, nor can there be any intervals in
God. Anselm is reluctant to abandon the image altogether
because he still feels that it may be helpful in a more limited
frame of reference. Besides, to do so would have involved his
making some modification to the *De Incarnatione Verbi*. Instead,
he defends it as far as he can, makes clear the points at which it
should not be extended further, and provides further parallels
to support it.[38] But the Greeks have brought him face to face
with the limitations of the analogical method in disputation.
What a willing pupil finds instructive, a critical opponent will
try to demolish.

   Anselm achieved little by exposing the river analogy further
to his reading public, except perhaps to put it into common
circulation for a few decades. He certainly failed to convince the
Greeks, either of their error of doctrine concerning the Procession of the Holy Spirit, or of their lesser mistake in questioning
the value of the Nile analogy by over-extending its implications. On the contrary, he seems to have made it only too plain

[33] S, 2.204.24–7.   [34] S, 2.177.4–5.   [35] S, 2.204.4–15.
[36] S, 2.204.3–6.   [37] S, 2.204.4.
[38] For example, S, 2.203 ff., a man begotten by his own father is also a son of Adam.

to scholars of the next generation that attempts to explain the doctrine of the Trinity by analogy were of strictly limited usefulness. Abelard makes few direct references to Anselm's works, but he gives some space in the *Theologia Christiana* to this particular image, and his view of its possibilities is highly critical.[39] Anselm is not perhaps to be blamed for this turn of events, since it had not been his original intention to return to the analogy in the fashion he found himself obliged to do.

What emerges most clearly from the episode is the change of attitude which distinguishes Abelard's view of the usefulness of such analogies from that of Anselm himself. Abelard, too, had reservations about their use in general, as we have seen, but his reservations were of a different kind from Anselm's. Anselm used the analogy as a simple means of bringing out by comparison some specific points in Trinitarian doctrine which could perhaps be understood by reference to the created world, even if the mystery of the Trinity as a whole was inaccessible to the understanding of created beings. Like Abelard, he was heir both to a tradition of biblical commentary in which Scriptural *similitudines* were discussed, and to the teaching of dialectical and rhetorical textbooks about argument by analogy. But unlike Abelard he was not anxious to develop the procedure further in any technical way. Abelard's reservations were, in part at least, based on disquiet about technically effective methods, while Anselm's anxiety appears to have come to the fore only when he saw that the analogy might lead his readers astray. To Anselm's concern for the establishing of the truth, Abelard has added a concern for technical propriety.

He has also felt it necessary to catalogue the standard analogies he knows. He mentions the image of the sun, whose light and heat are indistinguishable from their source, but which perform different functions and have different effects. The analogy is used by Anselm, too, and developed by him in his pastoral teaching to include a description of the way in which the Virgin conceived. Sunlight may shine through a lens and kindle a piece of wood without altering the lens in any way. The burning wood can then be extinguished. Thus Christ was able to die, although he was divine, and the Virgin remained a

[39] *Theol. Chr.*, pp. 304–5.

virgin after his birth.[40] Abelard knows that it is a commonly-
cited analogy—and indeed it is to be found widely in the
writings of his contemporaries. He mentions the comparison
between God and a craftsman or painter, which is also used by
Anselm, in the *Monologion* and the *Proslogion*.[41] To the Anselmian images, which are chiefly Augustinian in inspiration,
Abelard adds the Boethian example of the sword, which may be
referred to by various names even though only one sword is
meant.[42] He includes a discussion of the image of a musical
instrument: it is played by art, and it is also played by hand;
from the action of art and hand together comes the sound.[43] He
puts forward his own famous analogy of the mould and the
impression.[44] These are not set out in order in the form of a
catalogue of alternative possibilities. Some receive fuller treatment than others, and each is introduced individually where
Abelard finds it appropriate. But it is evident that the
thoroughness which makes him consider the technical problem
of using analogies at all also encourages him to assess each of
the standard analogies which appear to have been in use in his
day. The skilled technician's conscientiousness has led him to
'find' all the arguments he can of this type, so as to make his
discussion of the Trinity as well documented as possible.
Where Anselm would have been content to understate the
possibilities of the standard Trinitarian analogies had he been
allowed to do so, Abelard is anxious to defend himself against
attack by anticipating technical objections, objections of principle, and objections of omission alike.

It is in this spirit that Abelard has 'found' his arguments-
by-analogy.

[40] *Theol. Chr.*, p. 303.1194; S, 2.200.7–9.; *Memorials*, pp. 302–3.
[41] *Theol. Chr.*, p. 335.2195.
[42] Ibid., pp. 249, 254–5.; cf. *Theol. Tractates*, p. 16.
[43] Ibid., p. 303.
[44] Ibid., pp. 248, 318.

3

JUDGING ARGUMENTS

Distortions of the Truth: Sophistry and Paradox

'IT might be proved from that, if it were incorrectly understood, that an ass is a man.'[1] Garlandus Compotista's *Dialectica* contains numerous examples of the ways in which arguments may mislead. As he explains the principles of argumentation he shows how each type of argument may go wrong, and he systematically teaches his pupils to detect common errors. Adam of Balsham's *Ars Disserendi* places a similar emphasis on the importance of fortifying young dialecticians against the errors into which they are likely to fall in argument, and of helping them to detect errors in other people's arguments.[2] The art of judging arguments which was of such paramount interest to the masters of dialectic of the late eleventh and early twelfth centuries was never so urgently needed as it was when fallacious arguments were put forward about theological issues. An example is mentioned by Thierry of Chartres in his commentaries on Boethius: 'Socrates is a man; Plato is a man; they are more than one man, not one man. This implies that diversity of persons makes plurality of nature. Therefore . . . God the Father, God the Son and God the Holy Spirit are three Gods, not one God.'[3] Arguments of this kind have the surface appearance of valid arguments; they may indeed be perfectly valid when they are applied to created things. But when they are used in the discussion of matters of doctrine, they pose a far greater threat to the truth than the amusing nonsense with which we began, which seems to prove that an ass is a man.

A thorough understanding of the possibilities and dangers of sophistical arguments was brought to the West with the Latin

---

[1] Garlandus Compotista, *Dialectica*, ed. L. M. de Rijk (Assen, 1959), p. 144.1–2. and see ibid., p. 193 for a list of sophistries used by Garlandus.
[2] Adam of Balsham, *Ars Disserendi*, ed. L. Minio-Paluello, *Twelfth Century Logic*, I (Rome, 1956), esp. II.li.
[3] Thierry on Boethius, p. 65.7.

text of the *Sophistici Elenchi*,[4] but even in the later years of the
eleventh century and the first decades of the twelfth some
general knowledge of sophistry and its dangers was abroad.
Everyone knew that sophistries were not to be trusted. The
general warning which William of Conches gives in his *Glosa
super Platonem* is commonly to be found. William says that a
sophist is someone who uses deceitful arguments (*sophista est qui
callidis utitur argumentis*).[5] Peter Abelard puts into the mouth of
the Philosopher in his *Dialogus* an assurance that he will not
twist the argument as a sophist would do.[6] Accordingly, no
contemporary master encouraged his pupils to master the art of
sophistry because it would be of positive usefulness to them. It
was regarded as something to be learned for two rather negative reasons: firstly, it was important that the honest dialectician should be able to identify a fallacious argument so as to
eliminate or avoid it; secondly, it was essential that fallacious
arguments should not be allowed to mislead students of theology.

A sophistry is dangerous only in so far as it succeeds in
passing itself off as a sound argument. On the face of it, the
sophisticus syllogismus seems to be a valid syllogism.[7] Such an
argument, like the argument about Socrates, Plato, and the
plurality of natures, may seem to resolve one of the paradoxes of
the Christian faith contrary to the teaching of orthodox doctrine. Or it may appear to present a genuine paradox in itself,
to be set beside the real paradoxes of the Christian faith.
Theologians were continually being presented with such
genuine paradoxes: the doctrine of the Trinity; the paradox of
the two natures in the single Person of Christ; the fact that God
cannot suffer or die and yet Christ suffered and died. It is
possible—and some writers believed that this was the most

---

[4] *LM* I.1–112 on the early history of the study of fallacy and on the earliest glosses of
the twelfth century on the *Sophistici Elenchi*. On James of Venice's work in introducing
the *Sophistici Elenchi* into the West see L. Minio-Paluello, 'Iacobus Venetius Graecus,
canonist and translator of Aristotle', *Traditio*, 8 (1952), 265–304. On the evidence that
Thierry wrote on sophisms, see K. Fredborg, 'The *Logica* of Thierry of Chartres',
Cahiers, 7 (1971), 35–6.

[5] William of Conches, *Glosa super Platonem*, ed. E. Jeauneau (Paris, 1965), p. 82.

[6] Abelard, *Dialogus inter Philosophum, Judaeum et Christianum*, ed. R. Thomas (Stuttgart, 1966), p. 47.161–6.

[7] *Anonymous Aureliensis II*, ed. S. Ebbesen, *Cahiers*, 16 (1976), 48.

reverent response—to accommodate the difficulty the paradox presents to the understanding by worshipping what cannot be rationally explained.[8] But the response of those theologians of Anselm's day and after who were most deeply interested in the technical possibilities of the arts of argument was to try to apply the techniques of formal reasoning to the problem, and to resolve the paradox.[9] When we examine a sophism closely, it should be possible to discover a technical fault in the argument; any paradox it appears to present will then vanish. A genuine paradox, on the other hand, will not yield to any of the simple technical procedures by which a sophism may be detected. It presents philosophical problems of another order.

Two tasks, then, faced the would-be resolver of paradoxes. He had first to decide whether he was dealing with a sophistry or with a genuine paradox; and then he had to attempt to find a means of understanding the paradox. For both purposes, the technical skills of dialectic were especially well fitted, but for neither purpose were they entirely adequate. The skill of judging arguments was stretched to its limits by theological sophistries as well as by theological paradoxes.

Perhaps the most obvious difference between *sophisma* and paradox for Anselm's generation and the next was the fact that a fallacy normally deals with something trivial; Garlandus' sophistries deal with proofs that a man is a stone, every man is an apple, a dead man is an animal, a stone lives, an Ethiopian is not black when he is black, every ass is Jupiter, and so on. Anselm says that it is typical of irresponsible dialecticians who play with sophistries that they rush to their conclusions with a careless lightheartedness (*incauta levitate*).[10] It is quibblers (*cavillatores*)[11] who put fallacies forward. A Christian paradox, however, is a serious matter, and new difficulties of a technical kind begin to arise when sophistries masquerade not merely as sound arguments, but as serious theological arguments.

No student of dialectic could be taught even the elements of

[8] At one point in his discussion of the paradox of God's mercy and his justice, Anselm responds in exactly this way (*Proslogion* IX–XI).

[9] See my article, 'The "secure technician": varieties of paradox in the writings of St. Anselm', *Vivarium*, xiii (1975), 1–21.

[10] S, 1.285.1.

[11] *PL* 64.1045, cf. Garlandus, op. cit., p. 2.1.

his subject without encountering the existence of sophistries. Sophistry was the stuff of elementary school exercises. Hugh of St. Victor—whose early education is tantalizingly shrouded in obscurity—describes how he memorized his sophistical exercises as a young boy.[12] Garlandus, too, says that they are put into his treatise to exercise his readers (*gratia exercendi lectores*),[13] and to help them practise what they have learned. As soon as a student reached the stage where he was beginning to construct syllogisms, he had to be taught to avoid inadvertently falling into fallacy when he put his premisses together. In the case of the testing of theological arguments it was even more important that these matters should be understood early on. Anselm acknowledges that fallacies presented problems to beginners in the study of theology as they did in the study of dialectic. He says that it is those who begin to discuss Christian doctrine before they have fully mastered either dialectic or the principles of orthodox theology who are likely to run into trouble and to be diverted from the truth by a multitude of sophistries (*per multiplicia sophismatum diverticula*).[14] For his own part, he asserts in the *De Incarnatione Verbi* that he will allow no sophistry of the dialecticians to persuade him that God is like three angels, or that the Father was incarnate with the Son.[15] During these decades when dialectic was first being systematically applied to the study of theology it must have been especially tempting for beginners in either study to attempt to apply dialectical procedures for dealing with sophistries to the resolution of Christian paradoxes.

For those who wished to develop their knowledge of fallacies, either for dialectical or for theological use, beyond the elementary stage at which the sophism was apparently normally introduced, there was a little help to be found in the standard textbooks even before the text of the *Sophistici Elenchi* was available. Boethius provides some material in two of the textbooks of the *logica vetus*, the second commentary on the *De Interpretatione*,[16] and the *Introduction to Categorical Syllogisms*.[17] Her-

[12] Hugh of St. Victor, *Didascalicon*, ed. C. Buttimer (Washington, 1939), p. 114.18–24., Book VI.3.

[13] Garlandus, op. cit., p. 2.   [14] S, 1.284.31–285.1.   [15] S, 1.282.25.

[16] Boethius, *In Librum de Interpretatione, secunda editio*, ed. C. Meiser (Leipzig, 1877–80), pp. 129.10–134.7.

[17] *PL* 64.778–81, 803.

mann of Tournai says that Odo of Cambrai wrote a textbook on sophistries, but it has not survived.[18] Adam of Balsham developed the principles he knew as far as he could in his *Ars Disserendi*. He has a good deal to say about the six types of fallacy distinguished by Boethius and he examines their subdivisions and gives a list of tests for detecting sophistries.[19] Garlandus does not give an account of the theory of sophistry, but he points out the possible fallacies which may arise in each type of argument as he describes it. In his *Dialectica* Abelard discusses Boethius' teaching at a more theoretical level.

Two areas received particular attention from these writers. Abelard, like Adam of Balsham, pays special attention to sophistries which arise because of ambiguity in the use of terms.[20] Adam suggests various devices: dubious terms should be looked at in isolation, in juxtaposition to other words (which can be varied to see whether another sense emerges); literal and metaphorical meaning can be compared—and so on. He also has something to say about opposing statements. Hugh of St. Victor's sophistical exercises certainly included 'oppositions'. He made it a daily duty to rehearse set examples and their resolutions: *ut etiam sententiarum, questionum et oppositionum omnium fere quas didiceram et solutiones memoriter tenerem*[21] ('so that I might hold the solutions of almost all the sentences, questions and oppositions which I had learnt firmly in my memory'). In both branches of the subject, it seems that the usual practice was to learn to detect sophistry at least as much by studying examples as by learning the theory of the subject. Abelard gives a list of standard examples, to which he has added a few instances which he has apparently devised for himself.[22] Hugh of St. Victor says that he wrote out his sophisms on a page or two, for the sake of brevity and convenience, before learning them by heart.[23] Again, these were stock examples with which every schoolboy might be expected to be familiar, and which were probably of the kind Garlandus uses as examples.

[18] *Herimanni Liber de Restauratione Monasterii Sancti Martini Tornacensis, MGH Scriptores*, xiv (1883), p. 274.

[19] Adam of Balsham, op. cit. On the evidence that Adam, writing in 1132, used the *Sophistici Elenchi*, see L. Minio-Paluello, 'Adam of Balsham "Parvipontanus"', *MARS* 3 (1954), 136 ff.

[21] Buttimer, p. 114.18–24.　　　[22] For lists of examples see *LM* I.49–50.

[23] Buttimer, p. 114.18–24.

The development of the art of fallacy in these decades, then, did not make of it a finer instrument so much as a more generally useful defensive weapon. It is as a useful defensive weapon that Anselm clearly regards it in the *De Grammatico*. This—Anselm's only treatise on dialectic—was written during the years when Anselm was working on the three treatises in which he says that he was trying to introduce his pupils to the study of Holy Scripture.[24] There is no theology in the *De Grammatico*, but Anselm was clearly anxious to prepare his young students of Scripture to recognize sophistries by introducing them into this dialectical discussion.

Even if you prove fallaciously that no 'literate' is a man because what it is to be literate is not what it is to be a man, yet that will be helpful to you, since you may see laid bear in its fallaciousness that very sophism which deceives you in the guise of the truth:

Nam etsi sophistice probes nullum grammaticum hominem per hoc quod esse grammatici non est esse hominis: utile tamen tibi erit, cum ipsum sophisma quod te sub pallio verae rationis fallit, in sua fallacia nudum conspicies.[25]

The lack of higher technical development of the art made it of only limited practical usefulness in detecting the difference between sophistry and paradox; yet because the rules for detecting fallacies were still relatively simple, they allowed a thinker like Anselm some scope when he tried to adapt them to the honourable service of theology.

His freedom was not available to mid-twelfth-century theologians to the same degree because their knowledge of the technical pitfalls was greater, and also because they were acutely aware of specific instances where sophistry masqueraded as paradox in the study of theology in the schools of their own day. Anselm saw that in practice, a knowledge of the rules governing ambiguity and equivocation can be used either to detect a fallacy, or as a means of supporting a paradox by helping the reader to see how both elements of the paradox may be true. Such devices have, in other words, both a positive and a negative use. Accordingly, in some of the arguments of the later chapters of the *Proslogion*, he carries out a procedure which, had it been applied to a sophistical argument, might have been said to show that its conclusion was no paradox at all. But Anselm

[24] S, 1.173.2.   [25] S, 1.152.22–5.

tried to demonstrate the genuineness of the paradox by examining the precise meaning and application of the terms involved. In *Proslogion* Chapter VI he shows how it is possible for God to be perceptive although he is not a body, when it seems that the senses are all bodily senses, and can perceive only through the body. Anselm argues that the word *sensibilis* can mean not only 'able to perceive', but also 'able to know', and that in its second sense it is not improperly used of God: *non inconvenienter dicitur*.[26] In Chapter VII he considers how God is not able to do many things: to lie, for example, or to make what is true false.[27] He puts it that to do what one ought not to do is to act by a negation of power: it is a work, not of power, but of impotence.[28] There are things which God ought not to do and if he were to lie he would display a lack of power. He looks, as he did in the preceding chapter, at the usage of the words involved. We often say, he points out, that something is so, when we mean that it is not so. When someone denies that something exists, we commonly say, 'It is as you say', when it would be more accurate to say, 'It is not as you say it is not.'[29] Thus we ought to say, not that someone has power to do what he ought not to do, but that he has 'impotence', or 'no-power' to do it. Again, Anselm is marshalling arguments from exactness and propriety of usage to support an interpretation of the statement that God is omnipotent even though he cannot do certain things. This searching of the resources of language for devices which will enable him to make sense of nonsense and to reconcile apparent contradictions, has something about it of the sophist's art; but because it is being used to establish the truth and not to deceive, Anselm cannot have regarded the technique as sophistical in inspiration.

Chapter X contains a variant of an argument put forward in Chapter VIII. In Chapter VIII Anselm asks how God can be both merciful and incapable of suffering. He suggests that he is merciful in relation to us, because we feel the effects of his mercy, but not in relation to himself, because he feels none of the suffering of compassion, the fellow-suffering of mercy.[30]

---

[26] S, 1.105.3–4.
[27] Cf. S, 1.189.6–7, *De Veritate* 9, on the difference between truth and lying.
[28] S, 1.105.12.   [29] S, 1.105.18–23.   [30] S, 1.106.9–12.

Similarly, in Chapter X, he suggests that God is able justly to pardon the wicked because he is just in relation to himself, and not in relation to the deserts of those whom he pardons.[31] Again, terms are being defined in such a way as to generate a novel equivocal sense, and a special sense is then applied to God. God is both limitless and eternal in a way that is true of no other spirit, although other spirits are both limitless and eternal. That is the case because God's eternity knows no beginning, while other spirits have a beginning; and God's boundlessness differs from that of created spirits in that he is able to be everywhere at all times, and they cannot.[32] Devices remarkably similar to those suggested by Adam of Balsham for the detection of sophistries are being employed here in order, not to show up weaknesses in theological paradoxes, but to consolidate them.

Anselm was still practising a not dissimilar technique in the *Cur Deus Homo* when he tried to show how Christ could lie and yet could not lie,[33] how he had to save mankind in the way that he did, and yet was compelled by no necessity,[34] how he ought to suffer and yet ought not to suffer (*Quomodo debuit Christus et non debuit pati*).[35] He has not considered the possibility in framing any of these arguments that the paradox might be a fallacy; he is certain that all these theological and doctrinal paradoxes are true paradoxes, and therefore the application of verbal analysis can only confirm the truth of both their elements.

Had he been writing in the middle years of the twelfth century he would perhaps have been forced to approach the matter in a rather different spirit. There was no reason why Anselm should have considered the possibility that the arguments he uses to illuminate theological paradoxes might be fallacious, since their purpose is to support the truth by making it plain and comprehensible, not to mislead. Some of his arguments seemed fallacious to certain scholars of later centuries, however. Robert Holkot accuses him of using sophistry even in the formulation of the ontological argument:

potest dici quod ratio Anselmi est sophistica et errat in rei veritate. Unde,

---

[31] S, 1.108.26–8.
[32] S, 1.110.12–111.5.   [33] Ch. 10, Book II, S, 2.107.6.
[34] Ch. 9, Book I, Ch. 17, Book II.   [35] Ch. 18, Book II.

sicut nos decipimur licet hoc non percipiamus, ita enim fuit de isto doctore qui in multis etiam pertinetibus ad logicam deceptus fuit valde.[36]

(It may be said that Anselm's reasoning is sophistical and mistaken as to the truth of the matter. Thus, just as we are misled if we do not see this, so it was for that scholar himself, for he was much deceived in many things which have to do with logic.)

Views as strong as this on the shortcomings of Anselm's technical skills of argument were not to be put forward until the fourteenth and fifteenth centuries, but, within half a century of Anselm's death, the habit of looking for fallacies in the handling of doctrinal paradoxes was becoming widespread.

Simon of Tournai shows in his *Disputationes* exactly that alertness to the presence of fallacy in such contexts which appears to have constituted no real source of anxiety for Anselm in the *Proslogion* and the *Cur Deus Homo*. When he considers whether the body of Christ is always where it is at one time (*An corpus Christi semper est ubi semel est*),[37] he points out that one of the arguments which is normally advanced is a *fallacia*, and he explains why it is fallacious (not by pointing out the technical error, but by giving a parallel example which shows up the absurdity of the argument). Elsewhere, he offers a *solutio* to what he acknowledges to be a *fallacia*, by making a distinction between what may be the case in the natural world, and what may be true in a theological connection (*In naturalibus hoc possibile . . . Sed in theologicis, in hoc casu . . .*)[38] His awareness of the presence of what may be technically described as fallacies in the context of arguments designed to explain theological paradoxes is clear enough, although he rarely uses the term *fallacia* itself.

More commonly he simply recognizes an argument to be misleading or false, without calling it a fallacy. When he discusses the ancient but currently newly controversial issue: *Utrum Christus assumpserit aliquem hominem*,[39] whether Christ assumed a particular man, he gives a series of arguments which lead to an illusory paradox: 'Therefore he who assumes is he who was

---

[36] The remark is cited in R. W. Southern 'St. Anselm and his English Pupils', *MARS* I (1941–3), p. 3 n.3, from Robert Holkot's *Quaestiones super quatuor libros sententiarum*, Lyons, 1497, I, q.4, fo. d.vii[r].

[37] Simon of Tournai, *Disputationes*, ed. J. Warichez, *SSL* 12 (1932), p. 69, XX, 3.

[38] Ibid., p. 297, CII, 1.   [39] Ibid., p. 58, XVII, 1.

assumed, which is absurd'; 'Therefore the Son of God is one person and the Son of Man another, which is the Nestorian heresy.'[40] We meet *quod falsum est*[41] ('which is false'). The explanations, or *solutiones*, which follow provide alternative arguments which Simon considers to be sound.

In pursuing what seems to be a deliberate policy of keeping technical terminology and methods to a minimum, Simon is nevertheless unable to avoid making some use of the formal arts of argument. He clearly does so reluctantly. When he tries to explain how *motus* and *quies*, movement and stillness, may be simultaneously in the body of Christ, although they are contraries (*contraria sunt*), he points out that in the special case of Christ who emerged from the womb without opening it, and who went to his disciples through closed doors, such contraries are possible. But this, he admits, is not the place to apply the rules of dialectic (*Hic enim non est locus regule dialectice*).[42] Elsewhere, technical terms of dialectic have a place: *subiectum propositionis*; *univocatio*;[43] *nomen appellativum*,[44] but on the whole only the simplest terms, which would be familiar to a reader whose knowledge of the art was relatively elementary. A point of grammatical practice has the same ring about it. Words denoting will or desire or emotion (*verba voluntaria et desiderativa sive affectiva*), may be construed 'according the to the grammarians' rules' with infinitives of the present or the past or the future tense, according to the feeling involved (*pro varietate affectuum*).[45] Thus when we ask whether God always willed what he once wills we are creating an unnecessary difficulty for ourselves by taking the tenses of the verb too literally. To a certain extent, no doubt, some compromise with the technicalities of the *artes* was forced upon Simon by the way in which paradoxes were put to him by his students, who had fashioned them—or learned them from others who had fashioned them—out of the anomalies the technicalities of the *artes* tended to generate. 'Was Peter Christ, if Christ assumed [a particular man] Peter?'

Iste homo . . . fuit substantia, fuit animal; ergo rationale vel irrationale. Si animal rationale, ergo homo, ergo Christus vel alius homo. Sed non alius, Ergo Christus.[46]

[40] Ibid.   [41] Ibid., p. 69, XX, 3.   [42] Ibid., p. 69, XX, 4.
[43] Ibid., p. 92, XXX, 2.   [44] Ibid., p. 126, XLIV, 1.
[45] Ibid., p. 103, XXXV, 1.   [46] Ibid., p. 60, XVII, 3.

(That man was a substance; he was an animal; therefore he was rational or irrational. If he was a rational animal, then he was a man; therefore he was Christ or some other man. But he was not another man. Therefore he was Christ.)

This argument, which Simon proceeds to refute, plays on the traditional definition of a man as a rational animal which was a commonplace of elementary dialectic. In this way, whether he chooses or not, Simon is obliged to take some account of the elementary technicalities of the *artes* in examining real or apparent paradoxes, even if he avoids any thorough use of the theory of fallacy itself.

His procedures for showing up fallacies are straightforward enough. They involve, typically, a search for equivocation hidden within the framing of an argument. *Scientia dicitur multipliciter*[47] ('Knowledge has many meanings'), he says. *Nomen geniti et nascibilis duo insinuant.*[48] ('The word "born" and the words "able to be born" have two senses.') They belong to the level of skill in the handling of fallacies at which Anselm's generation worked, rather than to the more advanced level of the specialists of Simon's own day. It is not that Simon himself has made use of a greater technical skill than Anselm possessed, but rather that he has been presented with a far larger number of paradoxes, some large, some small, some genuine, some spurious, and he has therefore been forced to look at paradoxes not, as Anselm prefers to do, with religious awe, but with a clinical and suspicious eye.

A new attitude to the relation between sophistry and paradox, in speculative theology at least, seems, then, not to have been dependent upon the development of a higher degree of sophistication in handling sophistries which came about in the schools as a result of the introduction of the *Sophistici Elenchi*. It is impossible to tell from the *Disputationes* whether Simon of Tournai knew the work. But it is evident throughout his treatise that he and masters like him had to make a distinction between genuine paradox and spurious paradoxes generated by fallacious arguments, in every branch of theology. It was no longer possible to adopt the Anselmian approach, to set a few great paradoxes up as objects of reverence, and to seek to show how

---

[47] Ibid., p. 126, XLIV, 1.   [48] Ibid., p. 40, IX, 2.

they might be understood by any means which appeared illuminating. Even if the new air of scepticism was not a direct result of the more highly developed knowledge of sophistry mid-twelfth-century scholars possessed, it was almost certainly obliquely influenced by it. Without necessarily advancing beyond the few simple principles available to elementary students of dialectic in Anselm's day, theologians became more conscious of the possibility that fallacies might be present in theological argument; they learnt to look for them everywhere. A twelfth-century compendium of the *Sophistici Elenchi* describes several systems for the classification of *equivoca*.[49] Its author goes beyond Adam of Balsham in rather the way that Simon goes beyond Anselm in his search for fallacies in theological speculation. It is not so much that Adam of Balsham has been superseded, as that a new dimension of technical complexity has been added to what he has to say. Perhaps rather similarly, Anselm's bold delineation of means of understanding the great Christian paradoxes has been replaced, in Simon's work, by a cautious analysis of all doctrinal paradoxes to see whether they are genuine, a concern for the settling of a multiplicity of sometimes rather smaller issues.

Contradictions

At the beginning of the *De Libertate Arbitrii* Anselm's pupil asks his master what he has to say about the apparent contradiction between the freedom of choice of human free will and the operation of God's foreknowledge, predestination, and grace. They seem, he says, to be in opposition to one another (*videtur repugnare*).[1] When, many years later, Anselm wrote the *De Concordia*, he completed the task he had begun in the earlier treatise by defining freedom of will, and examined the interaction of that freedom with foreknowledge, predestination, and grace. Again, the keynote of the discussion is the apparent *repugnantia* involved.[2] An increasing emphasis was placed on the importance of identifying and resolving apparent contradictions within Christian doctrine in the late eleventh and early twelfth centuries, and there are few areas where the habits of

[49] S. Ebbesen, 'A Twelfth Century Compendium of Aristotle's *Sophistici Elenchi*', *Cahiers* 10 (1973), 12.
[1] S, 1.207.4.   [2] S, 2.246.1.

thought bred by the study of dialectic were more helpful to theologians.

A major contributing factor to this new interest seems to have been the readiness of pupils and mature scholars alike to question what they read when it seemed to them to go against common sense. Honorius Augustodunensis says that 'some people ... murmur' (*quidam etiam* ... *mussitant*)[3] over the explanations of the workings of providence and predestination with which they have traditionally been provided. Objections were raised on the specific grounds that contradictions appeared to remain unresolved. In the *Cur Deus Homo* Anselm mentions unbelievers who say that the Incarnation seems to them a contradiction of all that reason argues (*quia ratione putant illam repugnare*).[4] He later accuses those same unbelievers of contradicting themselves (*repugnatis vobismetipsis*).[5] *Repugnantia* had become a fashionable topic[6] among theologians.

In the *Inevitabile* Honorius' pupil asks him to make plain 'briefly, in a way which can be grasped, what [the Fathers] in their long treatises did not make it possible even to glimpse'.[7] A vast body of patristic opinion on these matters has had to be taken into account. It is not that these contradictions or apparent contradictions had only recently become apparent. But they had only comparatively recently become the subject of widespread discussion in the schools, and thus of pressing contemporary interest.

The influence of the schools had almost certainly heightened the awareness of scholars who dealt with such problems that they were discussing a phenomenon well known to dialecticians. Such terms as *repugnantia, contradictio, oppositio*, the technical terms of dialectic, are also used to describe apparent contradictions in doctrine. The terms are not as precisely defined in these decades as they were to become in the course of the twelfth century; they are used to indicate degrees of opposition from complete mutual exclusiveness to mere difference, but nevertheless they are technical terms in common use, whose dialectical connotations were familiar to many thinkers.

Abbo of Fleury had long ago emphasized the technical point which presented the greatest difficulty to those who thought

---

[3] *PL* 172.1199, in the *Inevitabile*.   [4] S, 2.42.10–11.
[5] S, 2.54.2–3.   [6] S, 1.207.7.   [7] *PL* 172.1197.

they had found contradictions in doctrine: *In contradictoriis . . . semper altera vera est, altera falsa*.[8] ('In contradictories one is always true, the other false.') The same point is made more than once by Garlandus in his *Dialectica*.[9] Anselm confronts the problem of the truth of two seeming contradictories directly in the *De Concordia*, where he suggests that if we postulate that both the foreknowledge of God and freedom of choice for man exist, we shall be able to see clearly whether it is impossible for both to exist at once (*videamus utrum impossibile sit haec duo simul esse*).[10] Here he is doing exactly what Garlandus recommends. Garlandus says that it is possible to draw inappropriate conclusions from contradictories (*potest concludi de contradictoriis inconveniens*) unless a penetrating understanding is brought to bear on them (*nisi acutus intuitus adhibeatur*).[11] Anselm has examined the contradictories closely in order to see whether they are really contradictories at all, so as to decide what sort of conclusion is to be drawn about them.

He often finds on closer examination that there is no contradiction at all. He speaks in the *Monologion* of a contrariety which merely seems to be present: *Patet itaque quantum sat est ad dissolvendam quae insonabat contrarietatem*.[12] ('And so it is clear that this is enough to dissolve the contrariety which sounded as if it were there.') A generation later, Gilbert of Poitiers is more technically explicit about the way in which this is to be done. 'Not every contradiction raises a question', he says. If either part or both can be shown to be false, there is no problem to be solved. Only if both parts seem to be true is there a question to be resolved (*si utraque pars argumenta veritatis habere videtur, quaestio est*).[13] He, too, emphasizes the fundamental principle that 'contraries abhor one another and flee from one another',[14] but he can go very much further in identifying and resolving them than Abbo of Fleury was able to do at the end of the tenth century. As technical precision developed in the first half of the twelfth century still further considerations began to enter in, especially in the realm of theology. Clarembald of Arras discus-

---

[8] Abbo of Fleury, *Opera Inedita*, ed. A. van de Vyver (Bruges, 1966), p. 34.17.
[9] Garlandus, *Dialectica*, pp. 53.33, 54.8–9.
[10] S, 2.246.4–5.   [11] Garlandus, *Dialectica*, p. 53.25.
[12] S, 1.41.15–16.
[13] Gilbert of Poitiers on Boethius, p. 63.18.   [14] Ibid., p. 204.50.

ses the apparent contradiction which arises in Trinitarian theology because what can be demonstrated by analogy with the natural world leads to one conclusion and the 'theological truth' of doctrine dictates another.[15] Anselm's *famosissima quaestio* of the relation between freedom of will, divine foreknowledge, predestination, and grace, belongs to this category of theological problems of real or apparent contradiction. His approach to the problem is quite clearly technical. He begins by defining his terms.

Anselm tries to meet the *repugnantia* which seem to arise, by constructing definitions which will serve in every forseeable context. In addition, they must enable him to show that any conflict which seems to bring orthodox doctrine into question is more apparent than real. In the *De Libertate Arbitrii* he defines freedom of choice as the power to preserve rightness of will for the sake of that very rightness. He makes his pupil question whether this is the *perfecta definitio* in order to show his readers that it will stand up to rigorous testing. 'Ought we not to add', asks his disciple, 'that that power is so free that no force can overcome it?'[16] Anselm answers by taking him point by point through the proper procedure which dialectic lays down for constructing a definition. Cicero states in the *Topics* that it is sensible to begin by saying what the thing to be defined has in common with other things (what genus it belongs to) and then to narrow the definition systematically until it cannot be applied to anything else (*quod nullam in aliam rem transferri possit*).[17] This is what Anselm does: first he looks at the general category in which the thing may be placed, and then at the subordinate categories, first at *genus* and then at *differentia*, as Cicero recommends.[18] 'Power', says Anselm, is the genus to which freedom belongs. We say that it is 'the power to preserve' in order to distinguish it from other powers, such as the power to laugh or to walk. We add 'rightness' to show that it is not the power to preserve gold, or anything else which is not rightness. We add 'of will' to demonstrate that it is not the power to preserve the rightness of opinion or of a rod (here *rectitudo* means 'straightness'). We add 'for its own sake' to show that

---

[15] Clarembald of Arras, *Life and Works*, ed. N. M. Häring (Toronto, 1965), p. 90, para. 1.
[16] S, 1.225.6–9.   [17] Cicero, *Topics* VI.29.   [18] Ibid., VII.31; cf. S, 1.225.13.

this is not done for the sake of money or by the light of nature, as a dog takes care of its pups. To add a note, as the pupil has suggested, to the effect that this freedom of choice cannot be overcome by any power would be to enter into another area of discourse altogether. Anselm points out that what he has intended is solely to define the freedom of choice every man possesses, regardless of what he does with it.[19] (He goes further, and distinguishes the freedom of will of God from that of men and angels in the next chapter, but his concern there is merely to show that men and angels have been given their freedom of will and have accepted it, while God has his of himself.)[20] The procedure he has followed is conventional enough. Anselm has arrived at his definition by means which his educated contemporaries would have recognized as perfectly proper. But he has borne in mind throughout the need to build into it elements which will enable him to use it for the specific purpose of avoiding *repugnantia*.

Other definitions of free will or freedom of choice were current among Anselm's contemporaries and in the next generation. Hugh of St. Victor says that free will or free choice can be defined like this (*sic potest diffiniri*):[21]

Free choice is the possession of a rational will which chooses good when grace works with it, and evil when it does not. It consists in two things, in will and in reason. It is said to be free in that it is a will, and a choice in that it is reason. It is the task of reason to see what is to be chosen or not, and it is the task of the will to desire it:

Sic potest diffiniri: Liberum arbitrium est habilitas rationalis voluntatis qua bonum eligitur gratia cooperante, vel mala ea deserente. Et consistit in duobus: in voluntate et ratione. Liberum namque dicitur quantum ad voluntatem; arbitrium quantum ad rationem. Rationis est videre quid sit eligendum vel non; voluntatis est appetere.[22]

The most noticeable difference in Hugh's definition is that he is defining free will itself, not as Anselm has done, 'freedom of choice'. Augustine did the same in his *De Libero Arbitrio*, and free will (or free choice, to render more precisely Hugh's sense

---

[19] S, 1.225.31–2.   [20] S, 1.226.3–21.

[21] *PL* 176.101., *Summa Sententiarum* III.8; on the authenticity of this work as a composition of Hugh's see M. Chossat, *Summa Sententiarum*, Introduction, *SSL* 5 (1923).

[22] Ibid., and see *De Sacramentis* I.v.21, *PL* 176.225.

of the expression) is the subject under discussion in the Laon Sentences. There we find *sensualitas* added to *ratio* and *voluntas*, and we learn that reason discerns (*discernit*), will chooses (*eligit*), and sense carries out or agrees to what is chosen (*implet vel consentit*).[23] But the topic under discussion is not *libertas arbitrii*, freedom of choice or freedom of will, but *liberum arbitrium*. The difference this makes is clear enough. Hugh and his contemporaries at Laon were asking what were the component parts of the faculty of free choice, Anselm has attempted a definition of the nature of the 'freedom' which appears to conflict with the force of predestination.

This emphasis upon the faculty of free will rather than upon the freedom of choice of the will is brought out very clearly in another of the Laon Sentences, where three definitions are set side by side. Boethius, we are told, calls *liberum arbitrium*, *liberum de voluntate iudicium*, free judgement of the will; Augustine calls it *potentia bene vel male operandi*, the power of doing good or evil, and Anselm of Canterbury defines it like this: *ita definit: facultas servandi rectitudinem propter seipsam quia non concedebat potentiam male operandi esse in Christo*.[24] Anselm's definition has been adapted, so that 'the faculty' has replaced 'the power' in Anselm's original wording, and his definition of freedom of will or choice has been turned into a definition of free will or free choice itself.

The same shift has taken place in a treatise of the second half of the twelfth century, by Frowin von Engelberg: the *De Laude Liberi Arbitrii*. Frowin has borrowed heavily from Anselm, as well as from Bernard of Clairvaux, Augustine, Gregory, Hugh of St. Victor. He has used Anselm more extensively than any of his other sources and he has drawn on several of the treatises. Nevertheless he has sought not for a definition of freedom of will or choice, but for a definition of free will: *quid sit liberum arbitrium?*, he asks.[25] *Liberum igitur arbitrium est rationalis voluntas*[26] ('free choice is rational will'), he answers, and then he goes on to consider (along Anselmian lines) the various meanings of will, as the instrument of willing, the *affectus*, the desire, and the use of the will.[27] Anselm framed his definition with the inten-

---

[23] Lottin, p. 124, No. 172.   [24] Ibid., p. 253, No. 322.
[25] D. O. Bauer, 'Frowin von Engelberg (1147–78) *De Laude Liberi Arbitrii*, *RTAM* 15 (1948), 39.
[21] Ibid.   [27] Ibid.; cf. *De Concordia* II.12, S, 2.284–5.

tion of using it to help him demonstrate that there is no *repugnantia*. Many of his contemporaries and those who came after failed to see the problem as consisting largely in definition. Hugh of St. Victor suggests that the wisdom of God is to be called by various names: *scientia, providentia, praescientia, praedestinatio, dispositio*. By knowledge he knows what is; by foreknowledge he knows what is to be; by providence he governs things; by disposition he brings things about; by predestination he saves.[28] Hugh distinguishes between foreknowledge, which God has of both those who are to be saved and those who are to be damned, and predestination, which applies only to those who are to be saved.[29] There is nothing like this in Anselm, and indeed it is difficult to see how definitions and distinctions of this kind can have been designed in any way to help remove the apparent contradiction between freedom of choice, or free will, and predestination or foreknowledge.

He is able to suggest only that we speak improperly (*improprie dicitur*)[30] when we say that there is foreknowledge in God, since to God nothing is future and nothing is past, and what we see as foreknowledge is present knowledge to God.[31] Honorius speaks of the knotty problem of predestination, the *nodum praedestinationis*,[32] and he draws up a list of difficulties which has clearly been inspired by Anselm's setting out of the problem in the *De Concordia*. What is free choice? How is it that it does not contradict predestination and foreknowledge? How does the operation of grace fit into this scheme of things?[33] Less systematically brought to our notice, but persistently reappearing throughout the Laon Sentences, are references to coercion, freedom, will, judgement, reason, the *depressio*, or suppression of free will, in Adam and the fallen angels—a series of attempts to deal piecemeal with the *repugnantia* for whose resolution Anselm has tried to equip himself in the framing of definitions.

Anselm first tests the powers of his definition of freedom of choice to help him avoid contradictions, in the *De Casu Diaboli*. We know, he says, that men and angels do not have freedom of choice from themselves, but only because God gives it to

[28] *PL* 176.61, *Summa Sententiarum* I.12.
[29] *PL* 176.62. This is a notion to be found in Honorius, too, *PL* 172.1199.
[30] *PL* 176.62.   [31] Ibid.
[32] *PL* 172.1198.   [33] *PL* 172.1199; cf. S, 2.245.3–5.

them.[34] Several elements in the definition of freedom of choice: the notion of 'preserving rightness of will' and the question of the 'power' which enables a creature to do so are introduced, along with the idea of freedom. Those angels who did not sin were able to persevere in the truth. Satan was free to accept or not to accept the perseverance which was offered him. He had the power of choice (arbitrium) freely available to him. He received, as Anselm explains, both the will and the power to receive perseverance (accepit velle et posse accipere perseverantiam), but he did not persevere because he did not thoroughly will to do so (non pervoluit), as the good angels did.[35] We cannot, then, conclude that the evil angels were discriminated against, that God assisted the free will of some to do right and impeded others,[36] and there is no contradiction here between God's treatment of good and evil angels and the freedom of choice the angels had. God did not influence the will of Satan.

A further definitional procedure which makes possible the circumvention of contradiction occurs in the De Concordia. Anselm does not work out a definition of foreknowledge or predestination at length to match his earlier definition of freedom of choice, but he singles out two elements in their meaning which seem to create repugnantia when they are set beside the freedom of choice of human free will—that is, futurity and necessity. In De Concordia I.2 he invites his readers to examine the exact meaning of the words involved in the discussion of foreknowing: 'If anyone considers the exact meaning of the word (si quis intellectum verbi proprie considerat) he will see that when something is said to be foreknown it is stated to be future (hoc ipso praesciri aliquid dicitur, futurum esse pronuntiatur).'[37] We can, however, make a statement in the future tense which carries no binding force of necessity at all; or we can make a statement about the future in the future tense as to whose truth-for-the-future we are confident.[38] He gives examples: 'Tomorrow there will be a revolt among the people', and 'Tomorrow the sun will rise.' The first, he feels, is not necessarily true, while the second is. What God foreknows must be both future and true,[39] but not everything he knows is necessarily to

---

[34] S, 1.233–5, Ch. I.   [35] S, 1.238.32–3.   [36] S, 1.235–6, Ch. II.
[37] S, 2.248.5–6,   [38] S, 2.250.13–14.   [39] S, 2.246.8–9.

occur; some things occur by freedom of choice, and in such cases that is the way in which God 'knows' that they are to be.[40] Anselm is following contemporary convention in pointing to these two elements of divine foreknowledge. Hugh of St. Victor notes more than once that *liberum arbitrium* applies to the future only: our free choice cannot change the present or the past.[41] But Anselm has pinpointed the precise areas where God's foreknowledge touches on human free will, by a definitional method. Because God can know that something is going to happen without that something being itself subject to necessity,[42] a man may sin or not sin according to his free choice. God knows what he will do and he knows that he will certainly do it, but he does not exert any force of necessity or compulsion upon him.[43] So it is not impossible for God's foreknowledge and human free will to coexist.

The authors of the Laon Sentences maintain that God's foreknowledge extends to both good and wicked men, but that his predestination covers only the good.[44] The first question to be answered, according to Anselm, is why predestination can be said to apply not only to the good, but also to the wicked. (*In primis igitur ante quaestionis responsionem videndum est quia praedestinatio non solum bonorum est, sed et malorum potest dici.*)[45] The difficulty lies in the fact that that would seem to make God the author of evil. Anselm suggests that the difference is that God positively causes what is good, but that he is said to 'harden a man's heart', for example, only because he does not soften it, or to 'lead into temptation' only when he does not free from temptation. It is only in this negative sense that divine predestination can be said to apply to the wicked, too.[46] The working of the divine will raises further seeming *repugnantia*, to which we must return in a moment. Here, however, Anselm lines up his definition of foreknowledge with that of predestination by saying that whatever happens under one must happen under the other.[47] Both cover what is to be in the future, either by necessity or by the exercise of human free choice (*aut necessarium aut spontaneum*),[48] and therefore everything which is argued for one will work for the other, and there can be no more contradiction

---

[40] *De Concordia* I.4., S, 2.252-3.   [41] *PL* 176.102.   [42] S, 2.246.12-13.
[43] S, 2.246.19-21.   [44] Lottin, pp. 85-6, No. 103, p. 94, No. 115.
[45] S, 2.261.2-4.   [46] S, 2.261.2-7.   [47] S, 2.262.9-10.   [48] S, 2.262.8-9.

between freedom of choice or free will, and predestination, than between freedom of choice or free will, and foreknowledge.[49] Again, Anselm has fashioned his definition so that it will stand up to the test he wants to put it to, and again, that test is one of circumventing contradiction.

In the third part of the *De Concordia* Anselm's purpose is to show how grace accords with free will, just as predestination and foreknowledge do. The term he uses is the opposite of *repugnare*; he says that we shall find them to be in accord (*concordare*).[50] As before, a definitional procedure forms the preliminary to further discussion. Anselm insists that he wants to consider only the grace which is necessary for salvation (*illa, sine qua nullus salvatur homo*).[51] He will leave out of account all the good things God gives through grace in this life, without which man can be saved.[52] He has thus avoided the immense difficulty of defining grace in general, and restricted his discussion to the point in which grace resembles foreknowledge and predestination, that is in its apparent irreconcilability with human free will.

In answering this third *quaestio* Anselm develops further some thoughts on the nature and operation of the will which he had adumbrated earlier. God's foreknowledge and predestination do not, he feels, interact with the free choice of human free will in the same subtle and complex way as grace does. He brings out some of the possibilities of interaction, and some of the questions of balance which they raise, in the first chapter of this section.[53] The role of the will is therefore more obviously in evidence here. Anselm draws out of his original definition of the freedom of choice various new elements which will be of help to him here. He points out that the power to believe rightly and to understand rightly (*recte credere et intelligere*)[54] is given to rational creatures in order that they may will rightly (*ad recte volendum*). In these two powers therefore lies the power to preserve *rectitudo voluntatis*, rightness of will, which is said to be the essence of *libertas arbitrii* in the *De Libertate Arbitrii*. These are gifts of grace. Grace helps the free will in a multitude of ways—too many to be enumerated, says Anselm—to 'preserve' what it has received by way of 'rightness' (*Quibus autem modis post rectitudinem eandem*

---

[49] S, 2.262.13–17.   [50] S, 2.264.12–13.   [51] S, 2.264.17–18.
[52] S, 2.264.18–20.   [53] S, 2.263–4.   [54] S, 2.265.7–8.

acceptam gratia liberum arbitrium adiuvet ut servet quod accepit).[55]
Again, the notions of 'preserving' and 'rightness' in association
with the will are taken out of the definition of freedom of choice
and developed. Anselm is certainly still thinking about the
nature of that freedom itself; he has not slipped unnoticingly
into the contemporary habit of discussing *liberum arbitrium*, free
choice, in preference to *libertas arbitrii*, freedom of choice. He
refers back to the *De Libertate Arbitrii* by name, in order to point
out that 'the freedom of will of someone who holds the rightness
he has accepted cannot be forced to abandon that rightness
under any necessity' (*libertas voluntatis tenentis acceptam
rectitudinem nulla necessitate ut illam deserat expugnetur*).[51] This is
exactly the point established in Chapter V of the *De Libertate
Arbitrii* and raised again by the pupil at the end of the dialogue,
where Anselm explains to him that there is no need to include
this proviso that the freedom of the will cannot be overcome by
force in order to complete the definition.[57]

As he introduces grace into each aspect of freedom of choice
which comes under consideration Anselm shows how, far from
coming into conflict with that freedom, grace supports and
enables it. In Chapter X, for example, he suggests that the
uprightness of will (*rectitudo voluntatis*) which is received through
grace cannot be abandoned except by an act of free choice on
the part of the rational creature. Such a sin does not come about
because the *potestas*, the power to preserve rightness of will,
fails, for that is itself the freedom of the will (*quae potestas est ipsa
libertas arbitrii*). It happens because the will to preserve it
(*voluntas servandi*) fails; even that will is not deficient in itself, but
it is driven out by another will, the will to do something
incompatible with rightness.[58] At no stage is Anselm forced
either to abandon one of the elements in his definition of free
will or freedom of choice, or to allow for the possibility that the
operation of grace has interfered with the action of free will.
The two interact; they may work together, but grace never
compels the will of man against his inclination. Far from modifying his definition to accommodate the operation of grace,
Anselm has been able to enlarge it as he considers the interaction of grace and freedom of choice. His definitional method has

[55] S, 2.267.10–11.   [56] S, 2.267.7–10.   [57] S, 1.214–17 and S, 1.225.8–9.
[58] S, 2.278.19–25.

served him admirably as a means of showing that no contradiction is present.

In the *Philosophical Fragments* Anselm considers at length a fourfold division of the will which he seems to have thought of introducing into the *De Concordia*, and then left out because he felt perhaps that it would detract from the clarity of his exposition. In some manuscripts of the *De Concordia* there are references to the *voluntas efficiens*, *voluntas approbans*, *voluntas concedens*, and *voluntas permittens* of the *Philosophical Fragments*,[59] and both works make use of the analogy of the naked man who is clothed. In the *De Concordia* he has the power of keeping and using the clothing; in the *Philosophical Fragments* Anselm asks whether, if we see a naked man and wish him to be clothed but do nothing about it, we can be said to approve of his being clothed, and only in that limited sense, to will that he be clothed.[60] The efficient will, the approving will, the conceding will, and the permissive will, in man or in God, allow for a vast additional range of possibilities of avoiding *repugnantia*. In the *Philosophical Fragments* Anselm gives a few Scriptural examples. When God is said to have done everything that he willed,[61] it is his efficient will which is referred to. When we read: 'Those whom he wishes, he hardens',[62] we understand his permissive will to be intended. When we hear: 'God wishes every man to be saved',[63] we understand his approving will. Here, too, a method of *divisio* is being used which is a part of the technique of definition of terms which Cicero outlines when he says that definitions are sometimes carried out by *partitio* and sometimes by *divisio*.[64] Freedom of will or freedom of choice is one thing; the modes of operation of the will are another, and by subdividing these Anselm is able to show, even in these *pauca exempla*,[65] that no passages of Scripture need be seen as conflicting with one another. This is very much his train of thought at the beginning of the third section of the *De Concordia* where he lists various Scriptural quotations which seem to teach conflicting things about grace and free will; at the end of the chapter he says that they merely seem (*videntur*) to favour the view that grace alone is

[59] *Memorials*, p. 335; cf. S, 2.281.16–282.1, apparatus criticus.
[60] *Memorials*, p. 335, S, 1.269.20–1.   [61] *Memorials*, p. 335, Psalm 113:3.
[62] *Memorials*, p. 335, Romans 9:18.   [63] *Memorials*, p. 335, I Tim 2:4.
[64] Cicero, *Topics* V.28.   [65] *Memorials*, p. 335.

effective, or are thought (*putantur*) to support the notion that
free will alone wins a man salvation.[66] By close definition
of terms and rigorous examination of meanings, Anselm is
confident that he will be able to show that no *repugnantia*
exists.

The originality of Anselm's achievement in handling these
questions lies in his bringing together simple but technically
precise procedures of dialectic and apparent *repugnantia* of doctrine, and using one to throw light upon the other. His explanations had some influence among his contemporaries perhaps,
but if so, they were curiously diminished in the borrowing. The
fourfold division of 'will' occurs in the Laon Sentences, too,
where it is described as *alia divisio*, an alternative method of
division to set beside those to be found in the teaching of
learned masters (*doctores magistri*). It is not specifically attributed to Anselm of Canterbury, but some of the instances from
Scripture which are given are in the *Philosophical Fragments*,
too,[67] and it seems likely that the explanation was traditionally
associated with the interpretation of certain biblical passages.
What is significant, however, here and elsewhere,[68] is that the
philosophical possibilities the division suggested to Anselm do
not appear to have made themselves apparent to those who
borrowed from him or used the same authorities as he. The
author of the Laon Sentence has not seen here a means of
avoiding *repugnantia*, but merely an addition to his list of standard opinions about will. He is making a collection, rather than
looking for material for use in argument.[69]

Judging the Truth

Perhaps the most striking development of the twelfth century is
the notion that one kind of demonstration of the truth may
carry more force than another. An anonymous writer of the end
of the twelfth or early in the thirteenth century separates
'philosophical' from 'theological' definitions: *Quod postea dicitur,
quia tempus est pars eternitatis, dicimus, quod haec descriptio est*

[66] S, 2.264.6–8.   [67] Lottin, pp. 234–6, No. 290.
[68] Ibid., pp. 116–17, No. 153, deals with a Scriptural passage which Anselm uses as
an example in the *Philosophical Fragments*.
[69] Abelard, *Dialectica*, pp. 535–98 and see *indices verborum* on *repugnantia, contradictio,
oppositio*, etc.

philosophica non theologica. Quare non cogit nos.[1] ('As to what is said next, that time is part of eternity, we say that this description is philosophical not theological, and that it has no binding force for us.') The writer thus gives precedence to what he calls a 'theological' reason over a 'philosophical' one, and he implies that a theological truth is in some way a greater truth than a philosophical one. 'For the philosopher judges according to what appears to be the course of nature, and only that does he consider to be possible. The theologian passes beyond the bounds of nature and says that things are possible which are possible only to God.'[2] 'Philosophy' is here put firmly in its place as the study of the workings of the created universe. Theology deals with truths of another order.

The theme of Anselm's *De Veritate* is the unity of truth; in his final chapter he seeks to demonstrate how the truth in all things is one truth. He emphasizes that we speak improperly when we say that something is true 'of this or that thing' (*huius vel illius rei*). Truth does not derive from things and it cannot be said to be 'of' anything. Nothing is true unless is is as it 'ought to be', in accordance with the supreme Truth, the *summa veritas*.[3] Anselm does not expect to find one kind of truth in conflict with another or carrying any less force of truth than another. He has not arrived at this position all at once in the *De Veritate*. He works his way towards it from a consideration of different usages of the word 'truth' in ordinary speech. He begins by considering the truth of a proposition.[4] We more often say that a statement is true or false than that anything else is true or false.[5] He looks at truth of thought, will, action, the senses. But the direction of his thought is towards an uncontroversial demonstration of the way in which these and other varieties of truth can be subsumed under a single definition. When, here or in his other treatises, he tries to test the truth of a conclusion or a doctrine, he expects to find it in accordance with the other truths he knows. The ultimate test of the truth for Anselm is its harmony with every other truth.

Twelfth-century thinkers found it increasingly difficult to

[1] A. Landgraf, *Dogmengeschichte der Frühscholastik* (Regensburg, 1953), p. 62, from Cod. Vat. Lat. 10754, fo. 10ᵛ.
[2] Ibid., from Cod. Vat. Lat. 10754 fo. 12.
[3] *De Veritate* X.   [4] *De Veritate* II.   [5] S, 1.177.6–7.

share Anselm's view. They moved towards a greater diversity of conceptions of the truth, as it proved technically impossible to reconcile anomalies and contradictions—which were generated in many cases by technical means. The developments which made it appropriate to speak of theological and philosophical truth by the end of the century also made it necessary to accommodate a variety of truths, to be judged according to their kind. There is evidence that Abelard and his contemporaries took pleasure in the making of distinctions for what the exercise would show them of fresh aspects of the problem in hand. When Anselm makes distinctions, as he frequently does, he intends to show more clearly the underlying unity of what is being subdivided. The search for the truth has taken on a new character, and the habits of mind with which it was approached have altered so significantly that the very direction of the search has changed.

III

NEW THOUGHTS OF GOD

THE COMMUNITY OF THOUGHT

A NSELM gave more years to the attempt to show for what single compelling reason God became man than he did to any other theological issue. His contemporaries and the theologians of the next generation, too, found this a matter of especial interest and importance. It was the circumstances which led him to write the *De Incarnatione Verbi* which helped to turn Anselm's mind to the problem in the early 1090s. For more than a decade afterwards he was working on the *Cur Deus Homo*, the *De Conceptu Virginali*, the *Meditation on Human Redemption*; he went on until he felt that he had given an account of the matter which satisfied him. It was not because of any uncertainty of his own about what he believed that the task took him so long, but because the demands of his contemporaries for explanations of all sorts of matters both central and peripheral to the question were increasingly multifarious, and Anselm wanted to provide them with an argument which would possess the additional force of offering a unified and coherent resolution of all their difficulties.

Sometimes the explanations he provided were taken up directly and used in the composition of fresh works, as they were by Hermann of Tournai. Hermann acknowledges his debt to Anselm and to Odo of Cambrai, the scholar who had become Abbot of Tournai when the monastery was restored at the end of the eleventh century. In his *Treatise on the Incarnation of Christ* Hermann claims that he has introduced no argument of his own; he has depended on his reading and on what he heard from Odo's own lips when he gave his annual homily on the Incarnation, which he says he delivered every year for the feast of the Nativity.[1] Anselm's influence makes itself felt in Hermann's emphasis on the necessity for the Incarnation,[2] his idea that man stole something from God when Adam sinned, which he subsequently owed him,[3] his notion of the propriety and

---

[1] *PL* 180.11.   [2] *PL* 180.11–12.   [3] *PL* 180.16–19.

fittingness (*decentia*) of the method of redemption through the Incarnation.[4]

In Hermann's case, the reason for the thorough knowledge of Anselm's writings—and his profound respect for them—is not hard to find. In the generation after Anselm's death the monks of St. Martin's Tournai showed a special admiration for his work. They went to some trouble to acquire copies of his treatises, and of Eadmer's *Life*. A manuscript of the *Vita* was apparently copied soon after the completion of the work by Eadmer.[5] One circumstance in particular helps to explain this interest. Baldwin, who accompanied Anselm on his journeys in the later years of his life,[6] was a native of Tournai, and he and his brother Ralph retained an interest in the monastery.[7] According to the twelfth-century catalogue of the monastery library, four manuscripts containing Anselm's works were held there[8]—perhaps as a direct result of this connection.

Such evidences of direct influence are few, however. Anselm certainly had friends and pupils who later wrote books of their own on theological topics. Gilbert Crispin is the author of treatises on the Procession of the Holy Spirit and the origin of the soul, and of another on the Fall of Satan. Each of these survives in only one copy. Gilbert's work was not, on the whole, to the taste of the next generation, and, considerable though Anselm's influence upon him was, he had little success in carrying the Anselmian method on into the twelfth century. His only widely popular work, the *Dispute between a Christian and a Jew*, he addressed to Anselm, perhaps as a double token, of their friendship at Bec, and of the help Anselm had given him while he was writing the piece.[9] At a further remove, Honorius Augustodunensis borrowed from Anselm and others in composing his *Elucidarium* and *Inevitabile*, but it is unlikely that he

[4] *PL* 180.19–20.

[5] P. Schmitz, 'Un manuscrit retrouvé de la *Vita Anselmi* par Eadmer', *Revue Bénédictine*, xi (1928), 230.

[6] Ibid.; cf. *VA*, p. xvii, and *Herimanni Liber de Restauratione Monasterii Sancti Martini Tornacensis*, *MGH* xiv (1883), pp. 280, 292.

[7] Schmitz, loc. cit.

[8] Ibid., and cf. L. Delisle, *Le Cabinet des manuscrits de la Bibliothèque Nationale*, II (Varis, 1874), pp. 487–92.

[9] See A. Robinson, *Gilbert Crispin Abbot of Westminster* (Cambridge, 1911), on Gilbert's works, and B. Blumenkrantz's edn. of the *Dispktatio Judei et Christiani* (Antwerp, 1956), p. 6. On Gilbert's conversations with Anselm, see *AB*, pp. 90–1.

was in any real sense either a friend or a pupil of Anselm's; rather, he was an admirer.[10] Most often in the instances where Anselm and one of his contemporaries, or a scholar of the next generation, touch on the same ground in something of the same way, the indications are that the similarities reflect what we may call the community of thought. Anselm's originality in the handling and presentation of the topics he and others discuss takes its character from his independent use of what is often quite conventional material.

Hermann learned about Anselm as a boy (*adolescens*)[11] and his admiration is that of a scholar of the next generation for a great theologian who is still remembered for his personal influence as well as through his writings. What Hermann drew from Anselm he took in the spirit of a humble admirer. Odo of Cambrai had been a teacher of some renown at the cathedral school of Tournai, before he decided to give up secular studies for the life of a religious, in 1092.[12] He was more nearly Anselm's contemporary, and a scholar of some standing in his own right. He and Anselm worked in much the same climate of thought as theologians, and it is clear that Odo had access to a range of sources and a knowledge of what was topical which was very like that of Anselm.

Hermann's description of Odo's capacities as a master suggests that he had an exceptional enthusiasm for teaching. He attracted pupils from all over France and Flanders, and from farther afield, from Italy, Saxony, and Burgundy.[13] This is a feat which recalls that with which Lanfranc is credited: it was said that pupils from the best families (*ducum filii*), *clerici*, and *magistri* flocked to hear him.[14] Even if we make allowance for the possibility that Hermann is employing a convention here, something of the quality of Odo's teaching makes itself felt in his description. He says that Odo sometimes taught like the Peripatetics (*Peripateticorum more*), walking about in discussion

---

[10] On Honorius see *AB*, pp. 209–17.

[11] See J. Warichez, in his edn. of Simon of Tournai, *Disputationes*, SSL 12 (1932), pp. xi–xii.

[12] A. Herbomez, *Chartes de S. Martin Tournai*, I (Brussels, 1898), 1–3, No. I. See, too, J. Warichez, *Les Origines de l'église de Tournai* (Louvain, 1902), p. 188, and Simon of Tournai, *Disputationes*, p. x.

[13] *Herimanni Liber*, p. 274.

[14] J. A. Robinson, *Gilbert Crispin Abbot of Westminster* (Cambridge, 1911), p. 97.

with his pupils, and sometimes as the Stoics did, seated and answering questions (*et diversas quaestiones solventem*).[15] In the evening, and even late into the night, Hermann tells us, he was still to be found in discussion before the church door, pointing out the courses of the stars to his pupils with his finger (*et astrorum cursus digiti protensione discipulis ostendentem*).[16] How much of this is to be taken at face value it is hard to say, but Hermann has gone to some trouble over his account. He devotes a good deal of space to praising Odo's prowess as a master in the days before he undertook the restoration of the abbey of St. Martin.

It is not easy, nor perhaps very satisfactory, to make comparisons between Anselm's work as a teaching master in the early days at Bec and this account of Odo's powers as a teacher. We know little about Anselm's teaching of the *artes* except that he had apparently early achieved sufficient fame for Avesgotus to be anxious to send him his nephew as a pupil.[17] But Anselm told him that he had always found the teaching of grammar a wearisome business, and that he no longer took pupils; he had certainly ceased to be a working master of Odo's kind even in the early years after he had become Prior of Bec, although he continued to take an interest in the progress of the young monk Maurice who had gone to Canterbury.[18] Nevertheless, it is evident from the eagerness with which his conversation and his addresses to the community were preserved in later years, and from the skill in teaching which his treatises display,[19] that he had powers at least as outstanding as those which Hermann claims for Odo. Like Anselm, Odo turned his attention to the writing of works which may loosely be called theological rather than textbooks of the secular arts, although in his case the renunciation of his earlier studies appears to have been more a clear-cut issue of principle than a matter of giving up elementary teaching of the arts in favour of something more congenial. The difference has perhaps something to do with the fact that Anselm made the change twenty years before Odo did. In the meantime, the work of cathedral schools in particular had developed markedly, and at Tournai, as at Laon and at Paris, the teaching of the *artes* was becoming an increasingly special-

[15] *Herimanni Liber*, pp. 274–5.   [16] Ibid.
[17] S, III, *Letters* 19, 20.   [18] Ibid., *Letter* 64.
[19] See my article, 'St. Anselm and Teaching', *History of Education*, v (1976), 89–101.

ized business. It was becoming less easy for a scholar to slip naturally from secular studies to the study of the Bible and what we may already call speculative theology, as Anselm had done. It already required, as it did for Peter Abelard, the taking of a conscious decision to move from one subject-area to another.

Hermann bewails the modern tendency to teach the *artes* not from the reliable commentaries of Boethius, but from new textbooks designed to supersede or to supplement what he had said.[20] Odo wrote, according to Hermann (who does not appear to disapprove of his efforts) a two-part book on logic, dealing firstly with the recognition and avoidance of sophistries (*ad cognoscenda devitandaque sophismata*), and secondly with complexional arguments.[21] These probably resembled far more closely the *Ars Disserendi* of Adam of Balsham[22] than the *De Grammatico* of Anselm, the only completed work of Anselm's with any claim to be a textbook of dialectic. Again, the influence of the changes of the twenty years (or perhaps rather less) which separates the composition of the two seems apparent. When Odo began to write on theological topics, he again did so in ways which reflect the customs of his day. He composed formal expositions of Scripture[23]—a genre Anselm appears to have neglected altogether—a *Dialogue* between a Christian and a Jew[24] (a form employed by Anselm's friend Gilbert Crispin, but not by Anselm himself), as well as works of speculative theology in the form of treatises. He responded to the demands of his contemporaries for certain types of treatise which were currently popular, both upon the *artes* and upon theological matters.

Nevertheless, despite these significant differences, there is a striking element of common thought and concern in the work of Odo and Anselm, which shows that the preoccupations of those who were actively engaged in teaching in any of the areas where progress was most notably being made at the end of the eleventh century and the beginning of the twelfth, were gener-

---

[20] *Herimanni Liber*, p. 275.
[21] Ibid. On complexional arguments see Abelard, *Dialectica*, ed. L. M. de Rijk (Assen, 1956), p. xxiv.
[22] Adam of Balsham, *Ars Disserendi*, ed. L. Minio-Paluello (Rome, 1956).
[23] *PL* 160.1053–69.   [24] *PL* 16.1103–8.

ally very similar. There is, recognizably, a community of thought here. At a mechanical level, Odo shared Anselm's concern with exact copying of texts,[25] and especially of his own works.[26] He begs the copyist of his *Expositio in Canonem Missae*, to be meticulous in his rendering of the divisions in the text, to pick out the chapters with headings in larger letters, to illuminate the most important headings so that they will stand out.[27] His concern for propriety extends to the provision of an explanation of his reasons for making use of *philosophica ratio* in his book on original sin.[28] Anselm, too, felt the need to explain why he had based his arguments on reason and not on authority.[29]

Much more telling, however, is the common ground the two writers share in the subject-matter of their works on speculative theology, and in their handling of that subject-matter. It seems likely that, whether or not Odo had access to all the treatises of Anselm he would have needed, the ideas he and Anselm have in common were relatively commonplace topics for discussion in contemporary schools. A number of them have a place in the Sentences of the school of Laon.[30] But in any case, Odo does not quote or cite Anselm directly; he has made his own use of the ideas concerned.

Odo is familiar with the Augustinian view that evil is nothing,[31] which Anselm puts forward first in the *De Casu Diaboli*.[32] Like Anselm, he knows that a particular difficulty arises when we ask whether the word evil means 'something', since it is a commonplace of the grammarians that every noun signifies (*nomen omne significativum est*).[33] Like Anselm, he concedes that in so far as it behaves, grammatically speaking, like a significant noun, *malum* is a something, an *essentia*.[34] Odo does not, however, borrow Anselm's device of calling evil or nothing a *quasi-aliquid*, a 'sort-of-something'. Moreover, he has found a place for material which is not present in Anselm, for a discus-

---

[25] See, for example, S, 3, *Letters* 43 and 60.
[26] S, 1.94.8–13, S, 2.43.417.   [27] *PL* 160.1070.
[28] *PL* 160.1102.   [29] S, 1.7.2–12.
[30] The surviving Sentences are edited by O. Lottin, *Psychologie et morale aux xiie et xiiie siècles*, V (Gembloux, 1959).
[31] *PL* 160.1071.   [32] S, 1.246–51.
[33] *PL* 160.1073, and cf. S, 1.249.2, and Fredegisus, *Epistola de Nihilo et Tenebris*, *PL* 105.751 ff.
[34] *PL* 160.1073, cf. S, 2.146.20, *De Conceptu Virginali*.

sion of the view of the Manichees that *malum* is something, for instance.[35] He adds some remarks on the four kinds of opposition (*oppositionum modi*) which dialectic recognizes.[36] Here, and in his use of a technical terminology which Anselm makes use of, too, Odo's work strongly suggests that he and Anselm were drawing on a common context of contemporary studies, in which the influence of Augustine was of considerable importance.

Odo goes about the definition of sin in a recognizably Anselmian spirit. If sin is an evil, it cannot reside in anything which God has made, because God did not create evil. In the case of a murder, therefore, we cannot accuse the sword (for God made the steel) the hand which wielded the sword (for God made the hand) the movement of the hand which wielded the sword (for God is responsible for that, too). The murderer's soul cannot itself be the evil, for God made that. We must conclude that sin is in the rational spirit only, and that it lies, not in the soul, nor in the will, but in the *iniustitia voluntatis*, the unrighteousness of the will.[37] This is exactly the conclusion to which Anselm comes by not dissimilar means.[38] Odo has Anselm's notion of 'due justice', too. He speaks of the *debitum iustitiae* of the rational nature, as Anselm describes the soul in which there ought to be righteousness (*ubi debet esse iustitia*).[39]

But against this evidence of a possible direct influence, we must set the fact that Odo does not borrow from Anselm his explanations of the way in which the soul of Christ was able to be without sin, although he was human and therefore apparently subject to original sin like the rest of mankind,[40] nor does he place the same emphasis on the achievement of Christ as Anselm does. Odo argues that Christ suffered partly at least so as to set us an example: *dedit exemplum patientiae, ne nos in infirmitate deficiamus*.[41] As we shall see, this is most characteristically Abelard's view,[42] not Anselm's, and it seems again that Odo is drawing upon a wide range of contemporary discussion and putting forward a considered view of his own.

The existence of a common contemporary climate of debate

---

[35] *PL* 160.1072.
[36] *PL* 160.1073.   [37] *PL* 160.1071–2.   [38] S, 2.146–7 and S, 2.142–3.
[39] *PL* 160.1075, S, 2.147.12.   [40] *PL* 160.1084.   [41] Ibid.
[42] Peter Abelard, *Commentary on Romans*, ed. E. Buytaert, *CCCM* 11 (1969), pp. 113–18. It is also a view Augustine puts forward in the *De Trinitate*.

about certain topics is abundantly clear. It is a little ironic that
Anselm should have said that he was anxious to live until he
had solved the problem of the origin of the soul, since he did not
know of anyone who could do so after he was dead,[43] in view of
the fact that Odo evidently thought he could attempt the
solution. He gives a great deal of space to the question of the
relative merits of the argument that God creates new souls for
human beings daily, and the argument that the soul is passed
on by direct inheritance from the soul of Adam.[44] Anselm had
in fact said something about the matter in the *De Conceptu
Virginali*, and it was under discussion at Laon at the end of the
eleventh and the beginning of the twelfth centuries. It is the
subject of Gilbert Crispin's *De Anima*, too.[45]

In the *Disputatio contra Judaeum* Odo considers exactly the
problem about the number of men and the number of angels in
the City of Heaven which Anselm discusses in a digression in
the *Cur Deus Homo*. It is pointed out by both that if men were
created only to make up the number of fallen angels, then those
men who were accepted into heaven would be in a position
where they must rejoice at the fall of the angels which had made
room for them, and no blessed and perfected being can rejoice
at the misfortune of another. Therefore there must always have
been intended to be a certain number of men in heaven. Those
who find themselves there will never know whether they were to
have been of that number in any case, or whether they are of the
number of the additional elect who fill the places left by the
fallen angels. They will therefore not have any reason for
unbecoming rejoicing at the Fall of Satan.[46] In the same treatise, Odo comes to exactly Anselm's conclusion in the *Cur Deus
Homo* as to why only God could make satisfaction for Adam's
sin: *satisfacere vero Deus potest, sed non debet, homo vero debet; sed non
potest*.[47] In all these instances it might be argued that Odo is
perhaps indebted to Anselm; equally, in view of the additional
and alternative viewpoints he puts forward, it seems perfectly
possible that he is merely showing us something of the climate
of thought and discussion in which Anselm himself was working.

Odo got his learning in a larger arena, as Anselm did, and he

[43] *VA*, p. 142.   [44] *PL* 160.1077–8.   [45] BL, MS. Add. 8166, fos 37–39ᵛ.
[46] *PL* 160.1107, S, 2. 78.18–26.   [47] *PL* 160.1107, S, 2.101.16–19.

brought to the teaching of his monks something of Anselm's large-mindedness and wealth of learning. In his day, as in Anselm's time at Bec, St. Martin's must have been something of a powerhouse of holy learning, where the monks derived from an outstanding master a quality of instruction which was quite exceptional. Perhaps it was partly because of the kind of house it became under Odo's leadership that it was so well equipped to take an informed interest in Anselm's work when his treatises came into the library there. In the absence of Anselm himself and after the death of Odo, the love and respect Hermann felt for Anselm survived. But the use he was able to make of Anselm's work is disappointing. It is already clear that without the stimulus an Odo or an Anselm could provide in person, the peculiar qualities of their thought were bound to have a diminishing influence—the more so, perhaps, in the case of Anselm's writings, than in that of Odo's more pedestrian teaching. Despite Tournai's initial advantages, it did not remain for long a distinguished centre of Anselmian studies. It would be pleasing if the line could be continued to include Simon of Tournai. There are a few pieces of evidence to link Simon with the monastery, but there is nothing to suggest that he had been much influenced by Anselm's theology in his own theological speculation.

In any case, Simon's place is in the schools, and not in the context of monastic scholarship where Anselm worked, and to which Odo and Hermann properly belong. The community of thought in which we must set Anselm's theology of the Redemption was common to the monastic world and the burgeoning schools of northern France and Italy only for a brief period. The great masters of the late eleventh and early twelfth century were able to move from one context to the other, and they had something to say to the scholars of both worlds, but after a few short years the two contexts of study began to diverge more and more markedly in their development.

This widespread, if short-lived, community of thought was not confined to northern France and England. There are sufficient likenesses between the ideas of Anselm and those of the Italian scholar Bruno of Segni to have prompted speculation as to the reason for such *rapports*, as de Ghellinck calls them.[48] It is

<hr>

[48] J. de Ghellinck, *Le Mouvement théologique du xiie siècle* (Bruges, 1948), p. 83, n.5.

perfectly possible that Bruno and Anselm met and talked. There were several occasions on which they could have done so.[49] They would have discovered that they shared a good deal of common ground of a personal kind. Bruno was born not far from Aosta. Like Anselm, he left his home as a young man, but he went south while Anselm travelled north. Like Anselm, he found that he had a vocation to the religious life, but while Anselm entered Bec in his youth, Bruno went to Monte Cassino first as monk and then as Abbot, only after the turn of the century, and he was recalled to his episcopal duties in 1111. For most of his life—and perhaps as unwillingly as Anselm—Bruno was involved in ecclesiastical politics as Bishop of Segni; he was much in demand by several popes as apologist and ecclesiastical politician.[50] It may be that he had as little appetite for the work as Anselm.

Bruno had a gift for writing and teaching which stands comparison with Anselm's rarer gifts remarkably well. He is the author of Scriptural commentaries, sermons, and treatises which display a sympathetic understanding of the needs of audience and reader. Like Anselm, Bruno talks openly about the purpose he has in mind in writing. He tries to make his treatises brief and orderly and to make use of examples and analogies. In a sermon on the Trinity he points to the parts of the body one by one to drive home the point he is making: *hic homo, hic oculus, hic pes, haec manus, hoc caput*.[51] He indicates a member of the audience: 'For if this man, to whom I point with my finger, is both Simon and Peter. . .'[52] In his *Book of Sentences* Bruno asks at the end of each book what can be learned from the matters he has been discussing—how, for example, may the virtues be said to adorn the Church?[53] In Book III, he considers point by point how a new world will come into existence: a new man, a new heaven, a new earth, new clouds, new mountains, new trees, new animals, new powers, new sea, new birds, new rivers; the sequence cannot have failed to capture and hold his audience's interest because he makes sure that they will be

---

[49] R. Grégoire, *Bruno de Segni* (Spoleto, 1965), pp. 16–58, and esp. p. 41 on the possible encounter at the Council of Bari in 1098.

[50] On Bruno's life, in addition to Grégoire, pp. 16–58, see B. Gigalski, *Bruno, Bischof von Segni, Abt Monte Cassino, 1049–1123, Kirchengeschichtliche Studien*, Bd. 3, Hft.4 (1898), pp. 42–53.

[51] *PL* 165.978.   [52] Ibid.   [53] *PL* 165.901 and 940.

eager to know what comes next. Bruno must have been, like Anselm, an outstanding teacher with the power not only to make himself clear but also to make what he has to say memorable and interesting.

Rupert of Deutz emphasizes that the Bible is intended to be understandable to simple men; that is why it is called 'the people's Scriptures' (*Scripturae populorum*).[54] Both Bruno and Anselm took care that their expositions should be understandable to the simpler men in the community.[55] But Bruno gave his energies to conventional Scriptural commentary more extensively than Anselm did. In his *Introduction to Genesis* he sets out the plan he has adopted. He says that he has given a detailed treatment of the part of Genesis which runs from the Creation of the world to Noah's Ark because that is full of difficulties. Then he has gone through the chapters more quickly. In the first part every section has been expounded in order (*continue cuncta exposita sunt*); then he has taken a chapter at a time (*per singula quaeque capitula*). When we come to Jacob's blessings, we are again in an area which is difficult to understand, so the reader will find them handled by continuous exposition (*continua expositione digestas invenies*).[56] In rather the same spirit, Anselm explains what he has tried to do at the beginning of the *Cur Deus Homo* and gives instructions for the chapter-headings to be copied in front of the work, so that the reader will know how the argument is to develop.[57] Bruno compares two commentaries on the Psalms he has written, so as to warn his readers not to be confused if they find that there are differences in what he has said in the later one.[58] Anselm explains at the beginning of his finished version of the *De Incarnatione Verbi* that an earlier draft was put into circulation unknown to him and without his permission. He wants his readers to be clear that this is his finished version and that it represents his considered view. Both scholars have tried hard not only to write clearly and simply and to keep their readers' interest, but also to make sure that their purpose and intention in writing is properly understood by all.

Like Anselm, Bruno makes some use of his knowledge of grammar and dialectic, but his emphasis is on the difficulties

[54] *PL* 169.15.   [55] S, 1.7.10, S, 2.48.12.   [56] *PL* 164.147–8.
[57] S, 2.43.4–5.   [58] *PL* 164.695.

they raise for simple men and his tendency is to use technical terms—sparingly—as signposts. Anselm introduces technical considerations at another level altogether, and here Bruno cannot match him. Bruno asserts in the *Sententiae* that faith cannot rest upon arguments or syllogisms or human reasons, but only on the authority of Holy Scripture. (*Haec autem fides nostra non argumentis, non syllogismis, non humanis rationibus edita est, sed solis sanctarum Scripturarum auctoritatibus*.) 'Those who try to dispute about the supreme and almighty Trinity with Platonic syllogisms and Aristotelian arguments (*Platonicis syllogismis et argumentis Aristotelicis*) are fools and altogether insane.'[59] But having made a conventional protestation, Bruno shows himself willing to allow some space to arguments of this kind in his demonstrations. He says that where dialectic says one thing about the nature of substances and theology says another about the divine substance, we must recognize that the dialectical rule will not apply in the special case of God. (*in divina autem et aeterna substantia aliter fit*.)[60] He speaks of the 'person who speaks, the person to whom someone speaks, and the person of whom something is spoken' in an analogy with the first, second, and third persons of the verb.[61] He discusses the relation of the syllable to the word.[62] These are not advanced grammatical topics, but their presence shows how close to the surface of every educated man's mind was the habit of thinking about language in the technical terms of grammar and how aptly grammatical parallels came to mind, even where a deliberate effort was being made to eliminate them from the discussion.

In such general ways, it is clear that Bruno and Anselm were thinkers trained in a common tradition of elementary study of the *artes*, and that they shared a particular set of attitudes to the business of teaching which identifies them as monastic scholars of their day. But it seems that the common ground of their thought can be rather better defined than that, and that there is a much more significant area in which we may speak of a 'community of thought' on which both draw. Bruno could have read Anselm's *De Incarnatione Verbi*, or the *Cur Deus Homo* itself, both of which were sent to the Pope when they were finished. But the range and variety of the ideas he shares with Anselm cannot be entirely accounted for by a reading of either or both

[59] *PL* 165.977.   [60] *PL* 165.977.   [61] *PL* 165.976.   [62] *PL* 165.976.

of these works—or even indeed by a reading of all Anselm's writings. If Bruno knew them,[63] or if he had talked to Anselm, he had evidently talked to other scholars, too, and their discussions had enlarged his perception of the possibilities involved. In Bruno's *De Incarnatione Domini* there is common ground with Anselm both in subject-matter and in method, but this is no abbreviation of Anselm's arguments in the *Cur Deus Homo* and Bruno has added elements of his own. The main argument rests on the assumption that the redemption of mankind could be carried out only by means of a sacrifice, which would make good the evil done by Adam.[64] Anselm prefers the term *satisfactio* to *immolatio*, and his concept of reparation is more developed, but substantially, that is his view, too. As Augustine does, the author of the *De Incarnatione Domini* points out that four things are proper in a sacrifice. We must ask to whom it is offered, by whom, what the sacrifice is, and on whose behalf it is offered.[65] Anselm gives no such detailed four-part scheme; Bruno has outlined it for himself.

Anselm emphasizes that the sacrifice had to be made to God, that it is God who has been offended, and that there is no reason to placate the Devil.[66] This is an important point, because contemporary debate on this matter of the Devil's rights over man was vigorous and some contemporary thinkers argued that Christ's death paid a ransom to the Devil rather than a debt to God himself.[67] Bruno argues like this: 'Let us see whether it was proper for the sacrifice to be made to the Creator or to a creature. It seems just and reasonable, and so everyone agrees, that an oblation should be made, not to a creature, but to the Creator.'[68] Bruno has not made use of Anselm's fully-developed arguments on this matter, but his assertion has an Anselmian character. The force of his proof lies in the 'fitting-ness' of what he suggests. His method of demonstration is to look at two (or more) possibilities and to decide which seems the more appropriate. This is exactly what Anselm does, but again, rather differently. Bruno has added something of his own, and left out some elements in Anselm's account. The similiarity cannot be explained by direct borrowing.

[63] Grégoire, p. 155, Gigalski, p. 283.   [64] *PL* 165.1079.
[65] *PL* 165.1079; cf. Augustine, *De Trinitate* IV.xiv.19.
[66] S, 2.68–9.   [67] *AB*, pp. 93–7.   [68] *PG* 165.1079.

Bruno asks by whom the sacrifice had to be made, and what it had to be. Anselm's answer is that only a God-man was able to make satisfaction and at the same time be responsible for making satisfaction.[69] As alternative possible redeemers Anselm considers only angels, or man-alone, or God-alone.[70] Bruno systematically eliminates every other possibility, beginning with inanimate objects. He argues, stage by stage, that it would be unfitting for the sacrifice to be an inanimate thing, or an irrational being.[71] We are left with the rational beings. An angel would not be suitable because a sacrifice must be visible, and angels are invisible to man.[72] A mere man would be a sinner, so he would be an *indecens hostia*, an inappropriate sacrifice, for the redemption of the whole human race.[73] Only the Creator himself could make such a sacrifice, and he could do so properly and effectively only as a man.[74] These are Anselm's conclusions, and the process of the argument is not unlike his own in places, although Bruno has left in many stages which are omitted by Anselm and he has left out a number of Anselmian refinements. The technique of argument by elimination and the appeal to fittingness are in evidence, however. It is in a similar manner that Anselm demonstrates that it was necessary and appropriate for Christ to be born of woman alone, and not of both a man and a woman or of a man alone.[75] These were both modes of reasoning common in their day, and there is no reason to suppose that they were not being very generally applied to the resolution of the difficulty of explaining why God became man.

In the *De Incarnatione Verbi* Anselm considers why it was the Son and only the Son who was incarnate. He argues that if any other Person of the Trinity had become man, various anomalies would have arisen. If the Holy Spirit had done so, there would be two sons in the Trinity, one the Son of the Father, the other the Son of a human parent or parents. There would therefore be an inequality between two Persons of the Trinity, which is impossible. If the Father had become man, he would have been the grandson of the Virgin's parents. The Son would be the

---

[69] S, 2.52.13–24 and S, 2.101.3–21.   [70] *PL* 165.1081.
[71] Ibid.   [72] Ibid.   [73] Ibid.
[74] S, 2.69.6,9, S, 2.105.21, *et al.*
[75] *Cur Deus Homo*, Book II.viii, S, 2.102–4.

grandson of the Virgin and again there would be an inequality, two conditions of being grandson which were not the same, since the Son would have nothing of his grandmother in him. We know how cardinal a principle of Anselm's thought it was that there cannot be the slightest inappropriateness in God.[76] Only the Incarnation of the Son, therefore, raises no *inconvenientia* at all.

From whatever source he draws it, Bruno makes use of a version of this argument. The Father, he says, could not be the Virgin's son, because he would be a father *secundum divinitatem* and a son *secundum humanitatem*. This would be anomalous (*non conveniebat*).[77] If the Holy Spirit had been incarnate there would have been two sons in the Trinity, the Son by divine Sonhood and the Spirit as a human son. Again the possibility simply is not fitting (*non congruebat*) and Bruno dismisses it.[78]

Even if we allow for the possibility that Bruno had made himself familiar with Anselm's arguments here and elsewhere by reading his treatises, or for the possibility that they had talked together at length and that the additional or different elements in Bruno's explanations represent the fruits of their conversations rather than direct borrowing from the treatises, his possible contacts with Anselm alone will not entirely account for the similarities or for the differences between their two treatments of the subject-matter they have in common. It seems far more likely that each has been prompted to include these arguments by their topicality in the schools of the day, and among monastic theologians, that we have here an indication of the community of thought on which both were able to draw. Anselm's treatment differs from Bruno because his intellectual resources were greater,[79] and he was able to make a more developed use of the ideas which were in relatively common circulation. Bruno's account may bring us rather closer to the ground level of debate upon which Anselm constructed the great edifice of the *Cur Deus Homo*.

[76] S, 2.26.3–4. There are, as Grégoire points out (pp. 264–5) precedents in patristic writings for the theme of this argument, but he is unable to show that Bruno draws directly on any one of them, although he thinks that the likeness to Anselm's argument is 'fortuite'.

[77] *PL* 165.1082.   [78] Ibid.

[79] But Grégoire, op. cit., p. 254, compares Bruno's Christology favourably with that of Anselm.

2

CHRISTUS HOMO

THIS was, then, a period of considerable active interest in questions concerned with the Redemption. When many people are engaged in pioneering work in an important area of thought, we should not be surprised to find that a change of emphasis is taking place. A substantial change of direction marks the work of the early decades of the twelfth century, not least because in Anselm's day the subject was newly controversial.

He was obliged to spend time and effort on the mapping out of the ground if he wanted to give a comprehensive answer. In the late 1130s Abelard deals quite summarily with the matter in a few pages of his *Commentary on Romans*. He may or may not have borrowed directly from Anselm, but in any case he inherited the results of a period of considerable theological labour in the schools[1] on exactly this question—especially perhaps the work of the school of Laon under Anselm and Ralph with which he had early made himself familiar.[2] He was therefore in a position to put forward his viewpoint succinctly. He cuts rapidly through a number of arguments which Anselm of Canterbury was forced to consider in a more extended manner. Abelard appears to have solved the problem briskly and Anselm far more discursively. Yet Abelard's account has a unity which is more apparent than real. Anselm believed that a single solution was there to be found. It is difficult to believe that Abelard or any of his immediate contemporaries had any such quiet confidence.[3]

There were, broadly, three areas in which Anselm and his successors were actively at work. They wanted to know how it was possible, in purely practical terms, for one person to be

[1] J. G. Sikes, *Peter Abailard* (Cambridge, 1932), p. 206.
[2] See, in addition to the items discussed in the preceding chapter, the surviving fragments of the School of Laon, ed. Lottin.
[3] On the *Cur Deus Homo* see J. McIntyre, *St. Anselm and his Critics* (Edinburgh, 1954); on Abelard's soteriology see R. E. Weingart, *The Logic of Divine Love* (Oxford, 1970) and R. Pepermuller on the *Commentary on Romans*, in *Beiträge*, N.F. 10 (1972).

both fully God and fully man; this presented itself to many of them as a problem which required a solution of a technical dialectical kind. Secondly, they asked why God went to the trouble of becoming man in order to redeem the world, when it might be argued that he could have found some other way of doing so. Thirdly, they were becoming curious about the human life of Christ. Even if it was possible to understand why God became man, what had been the purpose of his spending so long on earth living among men? This last was not a question on which Anselm has much to say, in the *Cur Deus Homo* at least. There, he subordinates every other consideration to what he sees as the first necessity: the rescuing and restoration of mankind. Abelard gives a far larger place to the example Christ set mankind by living a perfect human life.

In being prepared to take account of a variety of viewpoints Abelard is typical of his time. There is no echo in his work of Anselm's intense concentration on the resolution of what seemed to him the single most important matter. When Anselm digresses to talk about the angels and the heavenly city, he does so with an apology, and an acknowledgement that what he is about to say does in fact constitute a digression.[4] We must, then, look for two kinds of change during these decades of the early twelfth century: alterations of opinion on certain specific topics, and a more general change of attitude to the theologian's task. We shall not find certainties to match or replace those of Anselm, and we shall not discover in his successors so supreme a confidence about the purposes of theological speculation as he enjoyed. David Luscombe points out that 'the most that can be read in [Abelard's] own writings or in those of his closest disciples, in this matter as often in others, are miscellaneous and limited analytical observations.'[5] That does not mean that Abelard's ideas are unformed or ill expressed. But his exposition lacks that grand scale and that large sense of order which characterizes Anselm's writing in the *Cur Deus Homo.*

The Two Natures

Problems of choosing terminology and of applying terminology

[4] S, 2.84.3, for example.
[5] D. Luscombe, *The School of Peter Abelard* (Cambridge, 1969), p. 271.

to theological discussions where its exact technical sense could
be brought into question, were felt especially keenly when
contemporary scholars talked about the two natures of Christ.
A commentator of the school of Thierry of Chartres remarks
that: 'We Latins who are short of words call the spirit and the
individual substance of a rational nature by the common name
of "person".'[6] In the middle of the century, Odo of Soissons
asks what is to be understood by the saying 'God assumed
man[hood]' (*quid est Deum assumpsisse hominem*),[7] since it seems
that the word 'God' and the word 'man' are both being used to
refer both to person and to nature (*communiter ponitur*). He
concludes that when we use the terms 'God' and 'man' in this
expression, 'God' is the name of the Person, 'man' the name of
the nature.[8] The difficulty as he sees it has to do with the correct
use of technical terminology. The same is true of a writer of the
'school' of Peter Abelard, the author of the *Sententiae Parisienses*,
who claims that we simply cannot make the statement 'God is
man' (*homo est Deus*), because a man is a *res composita habens
partes*, a composite thing made up of parts, and God is *simplex
indissolubile*, indivisibly simple.[9] The language we have at our
disposal will not allow us to discuss the dual nature of Christ
with technical precision, and it was the feeling of many mid-
twelfth-century scholars that if we cannot do that, we cannot
say anything helpful about the Incarnation at all.

The problems of naming and designating and defining were
much in Anselm's mind, too. In the *De Incarnatione Verbi* he
explains that we cannot speak of the Son of God as a person, or
name him, without referring to the Son of Man; nor can we
speak of the Son of Man without referring to the Son of God:
*Neque enim personaliter filiius dei designari potest vel nominari sine filio
hominis, nec filius hominis sine filio dei.*[10] But his instinct is to see
this fact as an aid, not a stumbling-block to his thinking.
Instead of looking for reasons why we cannot discuss the matter
at all adequately in the language available to us, he considers
the straightforward implications of what we can say. If when

---

[6] Thierry on Boethius, p. 236.17.

[7] Ŏdo of Soissons, *Quaestiones*, ed. J. B. Pitra, *Analecta Novissima Spicilegii Solemensis*, 2
(Paris, 1888), p. 33, No. 32.

[8] Ibid.

[9] A. Landgraf, *Écrits théologiques d l'école d'Abelard*, *SSL* 14 (1934), pp. 31.1 ff.

[10] S, 2.29.12–13.

we talk of the Son of God we also speak of the Son of Man, here, surely, is evidence from language itself that there is one Person in the Son and not two? His view would have seemed unsatisfactory to those of his successors for whom the existence of such an anomaly suggested quite different conclusions.

Anselm's technical language was in certain respects rather less developed than that of his immediate successors It is partly for this reason that although he perceives much the same philosophical difficulties as they do in the doctrine of the Incarnation he is less troubled by the detailed implications of those problems than they. When Anselm points out that in becoming man God assumed manhood; man did not assume deity, the expression he uses is *assumpsit hominem*.[11] This was to be a focal point for analysis in later decades as scholars tried to determine the exact sense of *assumere*. But Anselm did not have at his disposal language which would enable him to say, with a commentator of the school of Thierry: *Deus enim assumpsit hominem non homo assumpsit deum, quia deus est humanatus, non homo deificatus*.[12] ('God assumed manhood; man did not assume deity, for God became human, not man divine.') Such forms as *deificatus*, *humanatus*, are to be found nowhere in Anselm, nor anything like them. When we have said that Anselm perceived in the discussion of 'assumption' matters of technical linguistic difficulty just as his successors did we have said very little. What is important is not his recognition of the existence of such difficulties at the very heart of the discussion, but the fact that he found them superable, as his successors often did not, because their awareness of the technical problems was becoming more developed than his, and also because they wanted to give a place to the technical problems in their own right, while Anselm sought to show that such problems were illusory.

Simon of Tournai looks at a series of such questions, which seem to him to be raised by the notion of a God-man. Is the name 'man' to be as properly applied to Christ as the name 'God'?[13] What are we to make of the fact that all the special rules of 'category' or 'predication' which make God a being with no accidents break down when we speak of the manhood of Christ (who must, if he was perfect man, have possessed sub-

---

[11] S, 2.29.15–22; cf. S, 2.59.27–8.   [12] Thierry on Boethius, p. 251.88–9.
[13] Simon of Tournai, *Disputationes*, ed. cit., p. 186.20.

stance and accidents like any other man?).[14] Anselm restricts
himself to providing a clear and relatively simple explanation of
the main issue as he sees it. He does not attempt to develop
what he has said so as to encompass further paradoxes, such
as those Simon discovers. The tendency of twelfth-century
theologians was to give a slighter treatment of what Anselm
views as the central issues, and to add numberless accretions by
way of detailed objections and responses. Philosophically
speaking, this was less elegant, but it was unavoidable if theology was to meet the demands of later twelfth-century schools
for an explanation of every apparent anomaly between the
teaching of dialectic and grammar and that of orthodox doctrine.

Odo of Soissons shows us something of the energy which was
given to arguments about the sheer mechanics of the Incarnation in the mid-twelfth century. He says that if we ask how God
became man, we shall have to discard certain possibilities. For
example, if we say that God assumed *aliquem hominem*, a particular man, we should be conceding that he assumed a person, not
just a nature: *cum omnis homo sit persona*, since every man is a
person.[15] But he knows that that account will not satisfy the
sophistici. They will press the matter (*instabunt*). They will argue
thus:

There was no man who was not either Christ or another man.
Therefore God united with himself either [the man] Christ or
another man.
He did not unite himself with another man, so he united
himself with [the man] Christ.

Thus it seems that God became a particular man. There was
energy in the debate in Anselm's day, too, as his explanations in
the *De Incarnatione Verbi* show plainly enough. But Anselm
himself not only categorized such arguments as this as sophistries; he also omitted them from his discussion except in contexts where he was forced by circumstances to take account of
them. Odo and his fellows took a much more positive pleasure
in the intellectual exercise of confuting one another's viewpoints.

[14] Ibid., p. 187.21–2.   [15] Odo, ed. cit., p. 49, No. 50.

There is certainly nothing in Anselm which corresponds with
the three ancient versions of the doctrine of assumption which
seem to have been newly current in mid-twelfth-century
schools.[16] Some argued that the Word clothed himself in a
human body and soul so that he could appear to mankind
'dressed as a man' (*habitus*). Some argued that Christ was in
some way composite, made up of God and Man; this is an
opinion canvassed by Boethius in the *Contra Eutychen*, where he
has a good deal to say about the ways in which two things may
cohere in one. Others believed that 'a certain man', composed
like all men of a body and a rational soul became God and that
God assumed that man. This is the view Odo is considering in
the passage above. We find no notion of *habitudo* in Anselm and
no arguments for the view that God may be composite, even
when he is incarnate. Indeed, Anselm asserts unequivocally
that God has no parts.[17] When he uses the expression *assumpsit
hominem* he does not envisage that it will raise the difficulties
it did for John of Cornwall, for Odo of Soissons, for Peter
Lombard.

He certainly saw that it raised some difficulties. *Dicunt enim
quidam*, 'For some say', he notes: 'How can we say that there
were not two persons in Christ, just as there were two natures?
For God was a Person before he became man, and he did not
cease to be a person after he became man; and the man who was
assumed was a person, for it is accepted that every individual
man is a person.'[18] Anselm explains that Christ did not assume,
with the nature of man, the distinct set of properties which
belongs to a separate person; he retained the set of properties
(*proprietatum collectio*) which were his own, and which became
the properties of the man Jesus.[19] What is at issue here is a
familiar principle of dialectic. Aristotle explains the relation
between the individual substance and its accidents in the
Categories. Boethius considers how personhood belongs to sub-

16 See, for example, John of Cornwall, 'The *Eulogium ad Alexandrum Papam Tertium*',
ed. N. M. Häring, *Mediaeval Studies*, 13 (1951), 253–300., esp. pp. 259–60, and Peter
Lombard, *Sentences* (Florence, 1916), Book III, *Dist.* VI.1–6, and Luscombe, op. cit.,
pp. 268–71.
17 S, 1.45.18–19, S, 2.17.18–19.
18 S, 2.28.15. This passage indicates that Anselm knew at least the substance of
Boethius' treatment in the *Contra Eutychen*.
19 S, 2.28.22–29.22.

stance alone in *Contra Eutychen* III. Anselm has certainly fallen naturally into a habit of thought which is dialectical in inspiration, and which owes something to his reading of Boethius on the *Categories*, and possibly, even if indirectly, to the *Contra Eutychen itself*. Yet he has not seen a stumbling-block here, but an aid in his own arguments.

A commentator of the Thierry of Chartres 'school' reminds his readers that it is generally accepted that a man consists of body and soul (*anima et corpus*).[20] If we are to believe that God became man it seems that we must account for the 'human soul' of the man he assumed, or else concede that he was not fully man. This is a point which seems not to have carried any weight with Anselm; at any rate he does not raise it. In John of Cornwall's account of the three views current in his day the dual nature of man himself is mentioned several times and John seems to see that there are in fact three *substantiae* to be united in one in Christ: the divinity, the flesh, and the soul (*divinitas, carnis et anima*).[21] When Anselm discusses why it was not necessary for Christ to sin, he points out that in man the soul is weighed down by a corrupted body (*et anima aggravatur corpore quod corrumpitur*),[22] and that it is therefore drawn into sin. That is not the case, he says, with Christ, because of the unity of the assuming Person and the assumed nature (*facile monstrari valet per unitatem personalem assumentis et assumptae naturae*).[23] It does not seem to Anselm necessary to look for the 'soul' of the man who was assumed, or to try to explain why such a hypothetical 'soul' was not dragged into sin by the body in Christ. Because the manhood Christ assumed was a nature not a person, Anselm sees no need to account for a separate human *anima* (who would, certainly, have been another person or *substantia* to be taken into account). Anselm, then, sees no difficulty at all in an aspect of the Incarnation question which gives rise to so much twelfth-century debate, and that is at least partly because his conception of the issues involved is simpler. He is not looking for stumbling-blocks. 'Those who say' what he refutes in the *De Incarnatione Verbi* do not engage his philosophical interest with their arguments; he wants only to correct their error and pro-

---

[20] Thierry, ed. cit., p. 544.14–15.   [21] John of Cornwall, ed. cit., pp. 259–60.
[22] S, 2.149.26.   [23] S, 2.150.4–6.

ceed with his exposition of what he believes to be certain about the Incarnation.

Cur Deus Homo

Anselm's scheme for the *Cur Deus Homo* took shape slowly. He seems to have recast his book many times before he was sufficiently satisfied with it to allow it to be copied.[24] Abelard, by contrast, moves with boldness through other men's opinions, retaining and discarding, until he is able to reduce that part of his treatment which deals with alternative hypotheses to a remarkably brief compass. He marches over the ground, where Anselm feels his way cautiously. The selection of his material in this way from the subject-matter of public debate was quite new to him. There is about the fashioning of the *Cur Deus Homo* an air of controversy circumvented which is unprecedented in Anselm's writings. Before he wrote the *De Incarnatione Verbi* he had preferred to avoid controversy altogether, although there he was forced to deal with it. But in the *Cur Deus Homo* we see Anselm aware that a change is abroad, and that he must write, not merely a sound account—for he intended his work to be of permanent value—but also an up-to-date one, if he is to satisfy his contemporaries.

At no stage in his revisions does Anselm appear to have permitted himself to move far from his central question: why did God become man? His instinct is to settle the main point once and for all, rather than to allow himself to be drawn into more general speculation. The question *Cur Deus Homo*? posed a variety of difficulties for contemporary scholars. Why did God not find some other means of redeeming the world? Could he have done so? Could he have chosen not to redeem the world at all? Anselm recognized the existence of these difficulties and he meets them systematically, but he conceived of the problem with a directness and simplicity which later scholars could not match because their thinking was unavoidably cluttered with additional detailed considerations. Some of the main lines of Anselm's thinking are to be found in Simon of Tournai's *Expositio Symboli*, but they have been reduced to a mere skeleton, while Simon has crowded his pages with technicalities.

[24] S, 2.42–3; cf. *AB*, p. 107.

The accretion of detail is noticeable in every area of twelfth-century academic endeavour, but here we can see unusually clearly how the first question 'Why did God become man?' became a question with an ever-growing number of answers. Abelard's account of it brings together the views which had been put forward in the three decades since Anselm had completed the *Cur Deus Homo*.

Anselm's principal theme is that Christ became man in order to put right what had been wrong in the world since the Fall of Adam. Once that was done, things became again as they were intended to be. The human race, that 'precious work' of God, would have perished, he says, if God had not intervened. What God had proposed to do with mankind would not have been possible (*quod deus de homine proposuerat, penitus annihilaretur*).[25] Man could serve his ultimate purpose in the universe, that of filling the places intended for him, together with those left vacant in the heavenly city by the fall of the evil angels,[26] only if God restored him to his former state. (The only significant difference between the state of things before Adam fell and the state of things since the Passion is that men still commit sin as they have done since the Fall. Yet if the faithful became incorruptible as soon as they were baptized there would be no merit in avoiding sin, and no place for the faith and hope without which no one deserves to be saved. For everyone would be able to see the rewards of virtue at once, and no one would be so foolish as to cut himself off from such happiness if he had seen it: *se subtrahere a tanta beatitudine quam videret*.)[27] These are the strictly logical implications of Anselm's view of the reason why God redeemed the world.

Abelard seems to be suggesting something rather different: that the coming of Christ made some change in the world which altered for the better the way things were before Adam sinned. The shift of emphasis is crucial. To the question: 'Why did God become man?' Abelard answers: 'To set an example of the living of a perfect human life'. It is not that Anselm would not have accepted this idea readily enough in itself. But he does not speak of this aspect of the work of Christ in the *Cur Deus Homo*. He certainly did not see it as constituting the principal reason for the Incarnation.

[25] S, 2.52.8–11.   [26] S, 2.74–5.   [27] S, 2.276.7–18, *De Concordia* III, 9.

Few of those who had written about the Incarnation in the years between the completion of Anselm's *Cur Deus Homo* and the Abelardian statement of the *Commentary on Romans* had been content to stop where Anselm stopped. Bruno of Segni had asked himself Anselm's question and answered it along the same lines, but even he had paused to dwell on the fact that Christ 'ate, drank, hungered, wept and did other things which men do', and to meditate upon his burial in intimate detail.[28] Anselm's successors show a new concern for a better understanding of the sheer humanity of Christ, an urge to discuss the details of his ordinary life, to see him perhaps first of all as a man. We have seen how Odo of Cambrai considers the example Christ set. Anselm's account of the Incarnation was philosophically elegant but emotionally unsatisfying perhaps to those who wanted, in some measure, to meet Christ on an ordinary human level.

Much of what Anselm has to say has a place in Abelard's account, although it is a subordinate one. Abelard begins by asking, just as Anselm does, by what necessity (*qua necessitate*) God became man.[29] He goes on to deny (as Anselm does) that the Devil has any right to his power over mankind. This was so common a matter of contemporary controversy that it could scarcely be passed over without comment.[30] 'It is said', claims Abelard, 'that he redeemed us from the power of the Devil.'[31] He argues that the Devil, being himself a creature, could have no right over the man he had seduced unless God allowed it to him.[32] There was therefore no case to be met by God if the Devil laid claim to a right of compensation. And so the debt which was paid was due only to God himself.[33] That is what Anselm maintains and what Bruno of Segni says, and Abelard agrees with them.

It is at this point that Abelard parts company with Anselm. He argues that if the debt was owed to his own honour, God could simply have remitted the debt. There would seem to be no compelling necessity for an act of redemption by sacrifice.[34]

---

[28] *PL* 165.1083.
[29] *Commentary on Romans*, ed. E. M. Buytaert, *CCCM* 11, p. 113.129–114.130, S, 2.48.2.
[30] *AB*, pp. 357–61.   [31] *Comm. Rom.*, ed. cit., p. 114.135.
[32] Ibid., p. 114.151–3.   [33] Ibid., p. 115.174–9.   [34] Ibid., p. 116.202–3.

Yet Anselm regards the honour of God as something so abso-
lute in its sacrosanctity that God would have been denying his
own nature if he had lightly dismissed such an offence against
his honour as Adam had committed. But Abelard asks what we
are to think about the debt we now owe. Surely the anger of God
must be much greater over the killing of his own Son than over
the eating of an apple?[35] This is perhaps rhetorical argument,
not a serious debating point, but it enables Abelard to put
himself in a position where he can argue that God must have
carried out the Redemption as he did, not out of necessity
but from choice. The mere wiping out of a debt will not, in
Abelard's view, provide a sufficiently cogent reason.

Abelard's sparely-argued case has now led him to a point
where he must put forward a hypothesis as to what that additional reason was. He suggests that Christ came to set man an
example by living a perfect human life.[36] As he puts it in a
sermon: *Misit primo Filium suum . . . cuius doctrina nos instrueret, ubi
salutis summa consisteret.*[37] ('He first sent his Son . . . that he might
instruct us in that doctrine in which the whole of salvation
lies.') In the *Commentary on Romans* he asks himself (as Anselm
does not) 'how are we made more just by the death of Christ
than we were before?'[38] Christ, he suggests, bore witness that he
came to introduce men to the true liberty of love: *Ad hanc itaque
veram caritatis libertatem in hominibus propagandam se venisse tes-
tatur.*[39] It seems that straightforward philosophical argument
has led Abelard to the conclusion that the humanity of Christ
and the example he set as a man, must take first place in any
account of the reasons for the Incarnation. In this way, he
draws out of his account of the Incarnation an exhortation to
the imitation of the love of Christ. But we cannot suppose that
Abelard came to these conclusions with an entirely open mind,
any more than Anselm came in this way to his; he has not been
obliged by mere logic to follow through his own conclusions in
his teaching. He places a different emphasis on the reasons why
God became man because he views the matter from a different
perspective. He is looking, above all, for a reason which carries

---

[35] Ibid., p. 116.210–14.
[36] Augustine, *De Catechizandis Rudibus* IV.718, *PL* 40.314.
[37] *PL* 178.423, *Sermo* V.   [38] *Comm. Rom.*, p. 117.226.
[39] Ibid., p. 118.264–5.

force in human terms, rather than for a reason which makes sense primarily in terms of the nature of God.

Anselm does not ignore this aspect altogether. He makes a point of emphasizing that Christ suffered weariness, hunger, thirst, and blows while he was on earth.[40] Yet throughout the greater part of his discussion in the *Cur Deus Homo* he has nothing to say about the manhood of Christ which might make him seem human and approachable. In the *Cur Deus Homo* and the *De Conceptu Virginali* he speaks consistently of the *deus-homo*, of *Deus* rather than *Christus*. Once in the *Cur Deus Homo* he speaks of 'the Lord Jesus Christ' (*dominus Christus Jesus*).[41] But only in a few chapters near the beginning where he discusses Christ's willingness to die does he seem to consider in any direct way how Christ might have felt about the task which he had to carry out.[42] Even here Anselm's emphasis lies almost entirely upon the philosophical problems raised by the action of Christ's free will in a situation where it seems that it was necessary for him to act as he did. He does not allow himself to be drawn by the profoundly affecting character of many of the sayings of Christ he subjects to analysis, into any attempt to see into his mind. He imputes no human feelings to him. In his own devotional writings addressed to the saints and to the Blessed Virgin he began a new fashion for the sympathetic exercise of the emotions. He tried to evoke devotional feeling by encouraging his readers to put themselves in the place of one of the saints in his sufferings, or by talking to the saints as though he could do so face to face. But he always stops short of any attempt to look into the heart or mind of Christ in this way as if it were like his own.

The most important reasons for the absence in the *Cur Deus Homo* of any comment on Christ's personal suffering as a man would again appear to be philosophical at root, and to rest upon Anselm's familiarity with a Neoplatonic view of the divine nature. Anselm points out in the *Proslogion* that God does not suffer when he shows mercy, because God is *impassibilis*. We call God merciful because we feel the effects of his mercy, not because he feels compassion: *sicut misericors es non quia tu sentias affectum, sed quia nos sentimus effectum.*[43] In a not dissimilar pas-

[40] S, 2.53–5.   [41] S, 2.59.21–2.   [42] S, 2.60–7, Book I, 8–10.
[43] S, 1.109.3–4.

sage in the *Cur Deus Homo* Anselm considers why God could not simply have forgiven mankind out of compassion.[44] The taking of so firm a line on the impassibility of God leads Anselm into a position where he is obliged to see the dual nature of Christ firstly in terms of the utter immutability of the divine nature, and only secondly in terms of the susceptibility to suffering and change of his human nature.

Anselm argues that since God cannot be humbled we must suppose that humanity is exalted by being bonded to divinity in the dual nature of Christ: *Non ergo in incarnatione dei ulla eius humilitas intelligitur facta, sed natura hominis creditur exaltata.*[45] 'No humbling is understood, then, to have been brought about in God by the Incarnation, but the nature of man is believed to have been exalted.' When we say that God suffered anything in humility or in weakness, we refer to the *infirmitas* of his human substance, not to any change in the *sublimitas* of his divine nature, which remains *impassibilis.*[46] The important area of discussion in Anselm's view seems to lie here, in the mystery of God's assumption of human nature, not in the actual suffering of the Cross which that assumption made possible. The Passion itself has no place in the *Cur Deus Homo* because Anselm is primarily concerned, not with the nature or degree of the agony involved in the Redemption, but with the way in which that agony was possible at all for an unchanging God.

The direction of Anselm's thought in the *Cur Deus Homo* is, then, quite different from that of Abelard in the *Commentary on Romans*. In a sense, despite Abelard's terser handling of the argument, Anselm's is the harder and more uncompromising way of explaining why God became man. Anselm's hard line of argument was not, as it turned out, what many thinkers of the generation which followed were looking for. There was an increasing tendency to think about Christ rather as Robert Browning does when he puts these words into David's mouth:

'Tis . . . my flesh that I seek
In the Godhead! I seek and I find it.
O Saul, it shall be
A face like my face that receives thee;
a Man like to me,

[44] S, 2.69–71, Book I, 12.
[45] S, 2.59.18–28, Book I.8, and esp. p. 59.27–8.   [46] S, 2.59.23–4.

Thou shalt love and be loved by for ever: a Hand like this
hand
Shall throw open the gates of new life to thee! See the Christ
stand![47]

In something of this spirit Rupert of Deutz tells us how he sees
the Crucifixion as setting an example. When Christ's arms
were spread wide on the Cross, and sin trampled under his feet,
he says, 'he set an example of living which many thousands of
those who come after him must read in him'. (*exempla vivendi
multis milibus sequentium se legenda proposuit.*)[48]

Abelard was asking a question which has been raised by
theologians very recently, and which has posed a problem for
Christians from the earliest centuries:

If Jesus was really the pre-existent Son of God, we should not have expected
his life to be so normal, so free from any hint of his divine status and nature, as
we know it to have been. But since it was in fact such a life, there must have
been some powerful reason for its being such. What was this reason? Why
should there have been a human career—and one so fully human as this one
was—when, granted its background, one would have expected it to be so shot
through with divinity as to be scarcely recognisable as a human career at
all?[49]

Abelard, like John Knox, feels that there must have been not
merely a reason, but a 'powerful reason' for Christ's living of a
human life on earth. He cannot account for it at all unless it
occupies an important place in the scheme of Redemption.

Odo of Soissons asks whether, when Christ ascended to
equality with the Father, redeemed mankind, led captivity
captive, he did so *secundum quod homo*, in that he was a man.[50]
Anselm had answered Odo's question before it was asked when
he said that we cannot think or speak about Christ as man
without referring to his divinity, or about Christ as God without referring to his manhood.[51] Odo's question might well have
seemed to him not worth asking. The kinds of issue suggested to
Odo by the habits of thought he had learned in the schools show
consistently how different was the complexion of discussion in
his day. The new interest in Christ's ordinary humanity was

---

[47] Robert Browning, *Saul*.
[48] *PL* 170.450, *De Victoria Verbi Dei*.
[49] J. Knox, *The Humanity and Divinity of Christ* (Cambridge, 1967), p. 39.
[50] Odo, ed. cit., p. 106, No. 295.   [51] S, 2.29.12–13.

encouraging men to raise questions Anselm would not have entertained for long. Some of them were trivial. Some were likely to divert those who considered them seriously, from what Anselm regarded as the important questions about Christ. If a man has charity, Odo argues, in the way that he is instructed to have it (*ordinata charitas*), he loves God more than himself. Christ had perfect charity. Therefore he loved God more than himself. But he was himself God. And so it seems that either he loved himself more than himself, which is impossible, or he did not have charity.[52] The matter has some interest as a logical curiosity, but a conscientious attempt to resolve the paradox will bring us no closer to understanding what charity is, still less to understanding the humanity of Christ. Curiosity about the manhood of Jesus had a tendency to lead the scholars of the mid-twelfth century into theological by-ways which did not recommend themselves to Anselm.

The attempt to think about Christ as a man—and as an ordinary man, who was like us in everything except in being without sin—gives rise to a range and variety of speculation which the theologian permits himself in few other areas. W. Pannenberg is able to list a dozen or more views as to what Christ was doing when he set mankind an example.[53] Some of the questions which have arisen have troubled thinkers in every age; sometimes they touch on matters which seem urgent only for a generation or two, or which are briefly topical in the way that they are framed. J. A. T. Robinson says that 'previous ages have found it difficult enough to assert that he was genuinely subject to environmental images when he got here—that he really was shaped by these, instead of just passing through them'.[54] No medieval thinker could have seen even the possibility in quite these terms. When Anselm discusses in the *De Conceptu Virginali* why we must conclude that a human infant does not have a rational soul from the moment of its conception, he suggests it is when it looks like a man (*pervenit ad humanam figuram*)[55] that it does so. He has nothing to say about the stages

[52] Odo, ed. cit., p. 114, No. 299.
[53] W. Pannenberg, *Jesus God and Man* (London, 1968), trans., L. L. Wilkins and D. A. Priebe, from *Grundzüge der Christologie* (Gütersloh, 1964), pp. 191ff.
[54] J. A. T. Robinson, *The Human Face of God* (London, 1973), p. 212.
[55] S, 2.148.5–8.

by which the infant Christ developed into a man, and the possibility that he may have been 'formed' by his experiences.

Not far removed from the modern interest in the possibility that Christ was gradually formed as a fully-developed human personality, is a curiosity about what happened in his mind and heart. J. Knox asks whether Jesus' devotional life was different from anything which is possible for us: 'Even if in all other respects Jesus was like us', he suggests, 'surely his relations with God must have been of a different order?'[56] Medieval thinkers are disinclined to intrude so far. They are chiefly preoccupied with preliminary reflections, about Christ's capacity to suffer misery,[57] about whether he had faith, hope, and charity,[58] about whether at the moment of his death the man in him was separated from the God in him.[59] These are the kinds of question which must be answered before we can go much further in thinking about Christ as a man, and they are questions which Anselm's successors had no hesitation in asking.

Some of these questions are of immense importance. It would not be true to say that the effect of the renewed interest of twelfth-century thinkers in the implications of Christ's humanity was altogether to trivialize discussion. But it does appear to have brought theological speculation about Christ down to a level which is sometimes little more than a common curiosity about the life of a fellow man. Its general tendency was almost to diminish Christ in order to understand him better as an ordinary human being.

It might be argued that this was a salutary change of emphasis at first, that when Anselm sees the influence Christ exercised upon man by setting him an example in such uncompromising terms, he is failing to see the manhood of Christ for his divinity. D. Sölle says that Christ 'identifies himself with those who follow after, those who remain behind, those who no longer move forward. He identifies himself with those whose identity is still future.'[60] He stresses the compassion of Christ for the helpless, the failed, and the incompetent, to the point where he sees him as making himself one with them. When

[56] J. Knox, op. cit., p. 42.
[57] Landgraf, ed. cit., pp. 171.29–172.1.
[58] Ibid., p. 172.
[59] Ibid., p. 177.
[60] D. Sölle, Christ the Representative (London, 1967), trans., D. Lewis, from Stellvertretung—Ein Kapitel Theologie nach dem 'Tode Gottes' (Kreux Verlag, 1965), p. 113.

Anselm speaks of the Christ who suffered for us, leaving us an
example so that we might follow in his footsteps (I Peter 2: 21),
he takes another view—arguably almost the opposite view. 'In
this he set us an example of suffering incomparable contempt
and poverty for righteousness' sake',[61] he says. He argues that
our response to this should be to imitate him energetically, and
to strive to live in the same way.[62] Anselm was writing not only
for a monastic readership, but for everyone, when he encouraged his readers to make a deliberate choice of poverty and
hardship so that they might follow Christ's example. In this
view it is the deity in Christ which sets the standard, even if it
is his humanity which gives us a means of understanding in
human terms what it is that we are asked to do. Anselm sees
Christ as setting an example which is also a standard of
spiritual excellence, as elevating humanity Godwards.

Not all twelfth-century thinkers, by any means, disagreed
with his view. Peter Lombard uses the death of Christ as the
starting-point for some reflections about the example Christ
set. He says that God showed his love for us in handing over his
Son to die, 'and we are moved and inspired to the love of God,
who did such a thing for us' (*et nos movemur accendimurque ad
diligendum Deum, qui pro nobis tantum fecit*).[63] The interest of
twelfth-century scholars in the human details of Christ's life did
not by any means blot out their sense of awe and their belief
that, if Christ set an example, a man smould strive to grow
upward by trying to follow it. But it tempered the rigour of
Anselm's emphasis upon the supreme standard Christ had set
and the clear duty of every man to try to reach it, with a
recognition that if he was truly a man, he was a man like us.

In his devotional writing we see another side of Anselm's
Christology; that deeply-felt devotion which Peter Lombard
suggests that the thought of Christ's death should arouse in us
is here, as is a passionate desire to realize, as far as is humanly
possible, the suffering of the Crucifixion. In the *Prayer to Christ*,
Anselm laments the fact that he was not present at the Crucifixion, that he did not share the sufferings of Mary as she watched,
or help Joseph take down the body of Christ from the Cross, or
hear the news of the Resurrection with the happy group of

[61] S, 2.241.17–18.   [62] S, 2.242.1.
[63] Peter, Lombard *Sentences*, Book III, *Dist.* xix,1.

women (*cum beatis mulieribus chorusca*).[64] He tries, as far as he is able by an exercise of sympathetic imagination, to put himself in the position of each of these observers, and to share his or her feelings: 'O most merciful Lady, what shall I say of the flood of tears which flowed from your most pure eyes when you saw your only Son in his innocence, bound, beaten and bruised before you?'[65] Yet even here, Anselm never attempts to enter into the mind of Christ; he longs only to share the pain of those who were present. In his hymns Abelard tries to draw the singers (or the hearers of the hymns) into the scene, as he describes the events of the Crucifixion in detail, hour by hour.[66] The people who were present are not so much in the fore-ground; he does not address himself to them directly, as Anselm does when he speaks to the Virgin and to Christ himself. But both display a desire to re-create what happened dramatically and to involve the sympathetic emotions of the reader—as St. Bernard so characteristically does in his sermons. Anselm is not only a man of his time in writing in this way; he is even ahead of his time, the leader of a new fashion in devotional writing where we are encouraged to experience the Crucifixion's most human aspects as nearly at first hand as we can.

But if we cannot read the Prayers and take the view that Anselm's answer to the question: 'Why did God become man? is a detachedly philosophical one, we can certainly not argue that it is largely inspired or given shape by devotional feeling. It is rather that Anselm's deepest beliefs have been involved in the framing of the arguments. In the *Meditation on Human Redemption* he encapsulates the argument of the *Cur Deus Homo* with a call to the soul to remember that it has been revived from death, redeemed, and set free from bondage (*de gravi morte resuscitata . . . de misera servitute . . . redempta et liberata*).[67] The philosophical principle which underlies the argument of the *Cur Deus Homo* informs this Meditation, too.

As Anselm repeats the substance of his argument in the *Cur Deus Homo* in a condensed form, so he brings out yet more clearly his central preoccupation with the work of Christ in

---

[64] S, 3.8.58–9.   [65] S, 3.8.48–50.

[66] Peter Abelard, *Hymnarius Paraclitensis*, ed. J. Szöverffy, 2 vols. (New York, 1975), II.113.

[67] S, 3.84.3–4.

putting things right. He feels that what Christ has done, above all, is to restore mankind to the freedom for which he was made. The Good Samaritan has cured a sickness.[68] He has done so by living out a great paradox, by showing strength in weakness. Throughout the Meditation Anselm explores the implications of a series of contrasts between the former and the latter state, between darkness and light, helplessness and comfort, servitude and freedom, weakness and strength. When he sets us an example, Christ shows us how we ought to be; he reminds us what we were made for. When we imitate the human life of Christ we are to do so in order that we may behave in accordance with the fact of our Redemption, to be the kind of people we should have been by nature if Adam had not sinned and we had been able to fulfil our proper purposes as men.

The theme of hungering after righteousness is common in Anselm's devotional writings. It reflects another hunger in him: the hunger of his intellect for order. It echoes the thinking about right order (*rectus ordo*),[69] which is such an important element in the argument of the *Cur Deus Homo*. There, he asserts that God cannot allow even the slightest violation of his honour because that would disturb the order and beauty of the universe (*universitatis ordinem et pulchritudinem*).[70] Beneath the tenderness and compassion of the Prayers and Meditations which touch on the work of Christ[71], the substructure of thought remains firm. The example Christ set and the comfort to be drawn from the fact that he was a man like us remain, for Anselm, of secondary importance. The most important thing Christ did was to put things right. Everything else follows from that.

When Anselm tried to answer the question: 'Why did God become man?' he looked from the first for a single answer, to which all other considerations might be regarded as subordinate. Abelard and his successors seem neither to have expected nor to have hoped to find such unity in their explanations of the reasons for the Incarnation. This is scarcely surprising when we consider that, as J. Knox notes, of all the possibilities which may be advanced to explain the life and death of Jesus, 'incarnationism' is the most complex and the most 'diversified in its

[68] S, 3.84.14.   [69] S, 2.48.16, S, 2.73.22–3, for example.
[70] S, 2.73.8, *Cur Deus Homo* I,15.
[71] *Oratio* 10, to Paul, S, 3.41.230–8, describes Christ as a mother-hen.

actual forms'.[72] It has not been easy in any age to construct a single philosophically elegant explanation, and Anselm's confidence that he could do so is unusual. In any case, Abelard, unlike Anselm, had to contend with an ever-widening range of discussion in the schools, and with the contemporary habit of pausing to examine every difficulty seriously and at length, whether it was likely to prove an important stumbling-block or not. Anselm perceived his single central issue by the light of a flame which could not have burned so steadily, or so untroubled by draughts, a generation later. In the difference between Abelard's view of the reason why God became man, and that of Anselm, lies a world of change.

[72] J. Knox, op. cit., p. 14.

3

A THEOLOGY OF CHANGE

If Adam had not Sinned

WHEN God redeemed the world he brought about a change. Wherever there is alteration, or any departure from immutability, the possibility presents itself that the change might have been in some way different, or that it may not be permanent, or that it may lead to further change. While theology concerns itself exclusively with the existence and nature of God it has no need to take account of such matters. But as soon as it considers God's actions in the world—and especially those actions in which he was himself personally involved as a man—it is necessary for theology to consider counter-factual hypotheses. Anselm seems to have discovered the value of a hypothetical method in the discussion of Redemption theology for himself. Traces of the technique are to be found in the work of his contemporaries, but only Anselm made so thoroughgoing a use of it. The method underlies the arguments of the *Cur Deus Homo*, and it gives Anselm a point of departure for everything he has to say there.

The premiss upon which the *Cur Deus Homo* is built is a breathtaking hypothesis. Suppose, says Anselm, that Christ had never been, let us see whether it is possible to prove by necessary reasons that no man could have been saved without him: *remoto Christo, quasi numquam aliquid fuerat de illo*[1] ('setting aside Christ, as though there had never been anything of him'). As he carries out this astonishing exercise, Anselm resorts again and again to hypothesis. The conditional flavour of much of what he has to say in the *Cur Deus Homo* throws many of his verbs into the subjunctive. D. P. Henry has identified in Anselm's works a few hypothetical and disjunctive syllogisms; these are, as he points out, 'employed by Anselm in a quite proficient fashion'.[2] But hypothetical propositions are far more numerous in the *Cur Deus Homo* than is suggested by the single

---

[1] S, 2.42.12.
[2] D. P. Henry, *The Logic of St. Anselm* (Oxford, 1967), pp. 242–3.

example D. P. Henry gives from the work. Even where they do not form part of a sequence of formal syllogistic argument they are recognizably hypothetical propositions framed with technical exactitude according to the rules Boethius outlines.[3] Anselm's hypothetical method in the *Cur Deus Homo* is not, as we shall see, by any means technically unformed by the standards of the day. But it certainly goes beyond the mere borrowing of formal syllogistic procedures in the boldness with which Anselm employs it and in the extent to which it informs his thinking in this treatise.

It is only in the *Cur Deus Homo* that Anselm makes so extended a use of hypothetical methods. It is not difficult to see why this should be so. Only in the *Cur Deus Homo*[4] did Anselm try to work out from first principles what were the possibilities open to God when he wanted to alter the state of affairs which had been brought about by the Fall, and redeem mankind. Contemporary debate had opened up various possibilities for discussion. Could God have made another, sinless, man, as he had once made Adam, and used him as a redeemer?[5] Or could he have used an angel, or any other being but himself?[6] Anselm looks at these and a variety of other alternatives one by one, positing each as a hypothesis and asking himself, 'If God had done that, what would have followed from it?'

We cannot ask, in Anselm's view, what would follow if God were not merciful, or if he were to tell a lie, because these are not real possibilities. When he says that everything God wills is just, he raises for a moment the question: what if God willed to lie? 'It does not follow', he argues, that we may say: 'If God wills to lie it is just to lie', because that is not something it is in God's nature to do; only a corrupt nature which has abandoned the truth can lie. What we should be saying is as absurd as putting together two impossibilities, such as: 'If water is dry, fire is wet.' 'Neither of these is true.'[7] A hypothetical argument has been employed here, but not so as to show the rightness or wrongness of believing that God chose one course of action in preference to another. Anselm has merely shown the absurdity

---

[3] *PL* 64.831–76.

[4] The material in the *Meditation on Human Redemption* is drawn from the *Cur Deus Homo*, and it adds nothing to the arguments there.

[5] S, 2.52.16–18.   [6] S, 2.52.19–24.   [7] S, 2.70.17–27.

of applying the method of hypothesis to the discussion of the unchanging properties of the divine nature. He finds that hypothetical arguments come naturally and helpfully into play only in the discussion of the Redemption and the issues it raises for his contemporaries.

There is a nice irony in his assertion near the beginning of the treatise that he has put forward arguments which may, he feels, be bettered by others.[8] This was a disclaimer which he had used on other occasions; but here his feeling that his solutions are, in a certain sense, hypothetical, and that God may reveal either to him or to others more certain proofs, is particularly pertinent.

Before we look at Anselm's hypotheses in detail it may be helpful to consider the sources of his technical knowledge of the procedures he uses, and the views of his contemporaries on this aspect of dialectic. Boethius' treatise on hypothetical syllogisms was certainly in use in eleventh-century schools. Abbo of Fleury wrote a textbook of his own on the subject a generation before Anselm was born, and his younger contemporary, Peter Abelard, includes a tractate on the hypothetical syllogism in his *Dialectica*.[9] It is far from clear from Anselm's work whether or not he had a working knowledge of the tables of alternative patterns for affirmative and negative hypothetical and disjunctive arguments which Boethius gives.[10] But like Boethius and Abelard Anselm seems to have been familiar with the various types of hypothetical and disjunctive propositions. Abelard distinguishes the propositions which begin with *si* ('If Socrates is a man he is an animal') from those which begin with *cum* and have some temporal significance.[11] Disjunctive propositions in their simplest form are introduced by: *aut . . . aut*, 'either . . . or'.[12] Each of these types may be negated. More complex structures may be built up. To take two examples from Boethius:

cum sit a, est b, cum sit c, est d,

or:

si est a, cum b et si est b, est c.[13]

---

[8] S, 2.50.3–13.
[9] *Abbonis Floriacensis Opera Inedita*, ed. A. van de Vyver (Bruges 1966) and *Abelard, Dialectica*, ed. L. M. de Rijk (Assen 1956, pp. 498–532.)
[10] *PL* 64.849, 852, 853, 855–6, 863, 867, 868, 873–4.
[11] *PL* 64.834, Abelard, op. cit., pp. 471 ff., pp. 481 ff.
[12] *PL* 64.834, Abelard, op. cit., pp. 488, 495.   [13] *PL* 64.838.

All these variants occur in the *Cur Deus Homo*, and they do so sufficiently frequently to indicate that Anselm is doing rather more than allowing himself to fall into the syntactical patterns which the framing of a hypothesis would naturally suggest. There is, as so often in Anselm's arguments, an air of technical skill fully mastered and allowed to serve just such purposes as he chooses without making itself obtrusive at a mechanical level.

Si Adam non peccasset,[14] 'If Adam had not sinned', Anselm postulates, God would have put off the perfecting of the heavenly city until the foreordained number of men was available to complete it. If Adam and Eve had overcome temptation and not sinned (*si vicissent, ut tentati non peccarent*), they would have been confirmed, with all their progeny, in a state where they could not sin. But since they were overcome by sin, they have become so weak (*sic infirmati sunt*) that they cannot of themselves be free of sin.[15] Here Anselm is using straight-forward hypothetical propositions of the *si* type. He shows, in the first case, the possible consequence of an eventuality which did not come about, but he sees it as more than a possible outcome; had Adam not sinned, then this is what would certainly have happened. In the second case we are given not only a statement of how things would have been, but an explicit account of how they are. Like many of the hypothetical propositions he puts forward in the *Cur Deus Homo* these imply the existence of a settled chain of cause and effect; if we are prepared to accept that a given effect must follow, it becomes relatively easy to choose between hypotheses (where we are given alternatives) or to see the implications of a state of affairs which now exists by contrast with a state of things which might have been.[16] It is upon the underpinning of *inevitabilia* that Anselm's hypotheses rest. Anselm asserts, for example, that God's anger is nothing but a will to punish (*voluntas puniendi*). On that assumption, he puts forward a hypothesis whose untenability is immediately apparent: *Si ergo non vult puniri peccata hominum*,[17] 'if therefore he does not wish to punish the sins of men'; in that case, man is free of sin and of the anger of God. To suggest that God does not wish to punish the sins of

---

[14] S, 2.80.10–13.   [15] S, 2.81.17–19.   [16] S, 2.60.6–10.
[17] S, 2.54.6–9.

men is to deny the nature of God's anger. It is frequently the case that arguments beginning with *si* in the *Cur Deus Homo* deal in this way with questions whose answers can quickly be determined, by reference to those things which are immutable in God himself or in the way he has ordained creation.

Occasionally Anselm introduces a *cum* into his argument. It was sometimes suggested that it was difficult to understand why God should have chosen to redeem mankind at such a cost to himself and in such a difficult way, when he could have done so by an act of will alone. It seemed to the holders of this opinion that if he did the hard way what he could have done easily he did not act wisely.[18] Anselm discusses whether it was truly an act of little wisdom not to save mankind by an act of will 'when' God could have done so (*si humanum genus salvare noluit . . . cum sola voluntate potuit*).[19] He has used the *cum* type of hypothesis to pose a question over which he knows that there is heated argument. Similarly, in Book II of the *Cur Deus Homo* he considers why man could not have been made like the angels, unable to sin, and yet worthy of praise because they did not sin. The angels, he has pointed out, have deserved to be able not to sin, and they are to be praised for this because they have in themselves, as God himself has, that which makes them refuse to sin. In this, they are a little like God (*in quo aliquatenus similes sunt deo*).[20] On the same grounds, although in an incomparably greater manner, Christ was both unable to sin and worthy of praise because he did not sin.[21] 'Since God could make such a man', asks Boso,

Why did he not make the angels and the two first men so that in the same way they could not sin and yet were worthy of praise because of their righteousness?

cum deus talem possit facere hominem, cur non tales fecit angelos et duos primos homines, ut similiter et peccare non possent et de iustitia sua laudandi essent?[22]

Again, Anselm employs a *cum* type of proposition. 'Since God could do this . . .' or 'When God could do this . . .' poses a different kind of difficulty from that of the *si* hypothesis, because God's power to arrange things in such and such a way must be admitted and some other explanation for his choice not

---

[18] S, 2.54.14–16.   [19] S, 2.54.12–13.   [20] S, 2.107.19–20, 27–9.
[21] S, 2.108.8–12.   [22] S, 2.108.15–17.

to do so must be found than the simple demonstration that it is against his nature to do it. We cannot say, 'If God lies', because God cannot lie. We cannot see any other consequence but the known consequence of Adam's sin. But if we know that God can make a man without sin, who cannot sin, and who is to be praised for not sinning, it is less easy to see why he did not make men and angels like that in the first place. (Anselm says that he did not do so because such beings would have been *idem ipse qui deus*, like God themselves.)[23]

With disjunctive arguments we move into an area of still greater difficulty. Here Anselm is putting forward two or more alternative courses of action, neither of which is immediately obvious as the only one possible to God. God could either have assumed human nature from Adam, or made a new man as he made Adam (*Aut enim assumet eam de Adam, aut faciet novum hominem.*)[24] In Book I, 7 where the Devil's rights over man are discussed, Anselm introduces a threefold series: *Namque si diabolus aut homo suus esset aut alterius quam dei, aut in alia quam in dei potestate maneret . . .*[25] If the Devil or man had been his own master, or the subject of anyone but God, or had been in the power of anyone other than God, then perhaps the Devil might have had some rights over man; but since both belong to God, that cannot be the case. Here he is suggesting that none of these three alternatives is tenable; in the first example he goes on to explain that if God had made a new man as he made Adam, that new man would not have been of Adam's race (the *genus humanum*) and he would have had no power to pay Adam's debt because he would have had no responsibility to do so.[26] It is not that Anselm is not able to furnish solutions to these difficulties quickly and economically. But he is obliged to cast his initial proposition in this disjunctive form because two or more distinct possibilities seem at first glance to have equal claims to attention.

Several of the variant forms Boethius outlines appear elsewhere in the *Cur Deus Homo*: the double negative disjunctive form: *nec . . . nec*,[27] the string of 'ifs',[28] a *sive . . . sive*.[29] But perhaps enough has been said to indicate how technically

---

[23] S, 2.108.20–1. [24] S, 2.102.27. [25] S, 2.56.3–4.
[26] S, 2.102.30–103.1. [27] S, 2.28.29–30. [28] S, 2.85.
[29] S, 2.52.14–15.

varied and thoroughgoing a use Anselm makes of hypothetical
and disjunctive propositions—and occasionally complete syllogisms—in the *Cur Deus Homo*, and how forcibly his approach
suggests that he was familiar with the technical procedures
taught by Boethius, at least in outline.

The *Cur Deus Homo*, then, contains a number of counter-
factual hypotheses of various types which may be loosely identified with the types which contemporary dialecticians distinguished. But its hypothetical character goes far deeper than
that. Anselm builds up a complete hypothetical theology[30] of
the Redemption in the course of the treatise, beginning with the
question: What would have happened if Satan had not fallen?
He does not introduce his hypotheses in chronological order,
partly perhaps because his declared intention is to ask whether,
if Christ had not existed, we should have had to postulate his
existence in order to see how redemption could be carried out.
He has therefore not placed in the forefront of his mind the
preliminary questions: What if Satan had not fallen? What if
Adam had not fallen? Nevertheless, these questions are raised
during the course of the treatise, and they are answered in such
a way that the solution Anselm proposes forms an integrated
account of the Redemption which makes it of a piece with the
events which went before it.

It is of some significance that in almost every case we find
that the hypothesis Anselm puts before his readers was being
discussed by his immediate contemporaries, too. His achievement was not only to construct a systematic hypothetical theology of the Redemption, but also to work into it replies to
difficulties which were topical and pressing in his own day, and
which continued, in many instances, to trouble theologians for
some time afterwards. Some of these were relatively ephemeral
in their interest; others pose perennially important doctrinal
issues. But all of them seemed to Anselm matters which could
not be left without comment if he was to satisfy both *fideles* and
infideles as he says he wanted to do.[31] But instead of simply

---

[30] Hypothetical theology is used as a technical term later in the twelfth century to
refer to those branches of theology which deal with created spirits, as distinct from the
theology which is concerned solely with God himself. But this usage of the term is
unlikely to have been known to Anselm.

[31] S, 2.50.15.

answering a question, Anselm leads his readers to see what would follow if a given circumstance were true, and thus to see for themselves what the answer to the question must be.

The first question of a hypothetical kind we can ask, chronologically speaking, is: What would have happened if Satan had not fallen? As Anselm of Laon points out, if we ask what would have happened if God had not made any created thing we cannot suppose that he himself would have been different in any way: *in seipso plene beatus esse potuisset, quippe nullo indigens.*[32] ('He would have been able to be wholly blessed in himself, for he needs nothing.') It is only in connection with created things which are subject to change that we can usefully ask what would have resulted from a given course of action. The question of the day with which Anselm was clearly familiar, was whether if Satan had not fallen, man would ever have been created. In Chapters 16–18 of Book I he takes up an aspect of the question again raised in a Sentence of the Laon school, *De numero electorum.* The Sentence pronounces that those who say that as many men are to enter into eternal life as angels fell are wrong, for as many men are to be saved as angels remain unfallen. *Et si plures salventur a nullo diffinitur.*[33] ('No one determines whether more are to be saved.') Anselm asks whether we can in fact decide at least this last aspect of the question.[34] Either we must postulate that the angels as they were originally created were exactly as many as the heavenly city required, or we must assume that from the first some men were intended to occupy places in the city. If man was created only to fill the gaps left by the fallen angels, he points out, the elect among men would be obliged to rejoice at the fall of the angels, since that was the reason for their being in heaven, and the blessed cannot rejoice at the misfortunes of others.[35] It would seem, then, that man must have been intended to be created from the first. The elect among men will therefore be more in number than the fallen angels.[36]

Within this complex of problems, Anselm and his contemporaries saw further hypothetical propositions which might be

---

[32] Lottin, p. 50, No. 54.3. [33] Lottin, p. 125, No. 173.
[34] Exactly this question is raised S, 2.76.9–15.
[35] S, 2.78.18–26. [36] S, 2.76.13–14.

put forward. Anselm remarks that some understand in Genesis (*quidam intelligunt in Genesi*) that man was made after the fall of the angels.[37] An alternative view is that all creation was made at once (*tota creatura simul facta est*).[38] Anselm works out at some length the implications of each of these hypotheses for the completing of the heavenly city. His underlying assumption is that, whatever had happened, and whether the angels had fallen or not, God's purpose would inevitably have been worked out, and the heavenly city would have been perfected. It is against this certainty that he tests each hypothesis. The drift of his argument is that even if Satan had not fallen, the ultimate outcome would have been the same; good angels and good men would have taken their places in the heavenly city.

The same guiding principle has been applied in the discussion of the next hypothesis: What would have happened if Adam had not fallen? We have already seen how Anselm argues that in that case, Adam and all his progeny would have been confirmed in their power to resist sin.[39] God would also have put off the perfecting of the heavenly city until sufficient men were ready, and they would have had their mortal bodies transmuted into immortality.[40] This is the view put forward by Anselm of Laon, who says that, if he had not sinned, Adam and his posterity would have remained in Paradise until it was time for them to be received into the heavenly city.[41] But Anselm of Canterbury has more obviously in view his ultimate test of any hypothesis: if a given possibility had occurred, would it have frustrated the purposes of God? He seems to conclude that whatever the rational creation had done, whether all angels and all men had remained righteous or not, the city would have been perfectly furnished according to the divine purpose.

But Adam did sin, and Anselm moves on to consider what possibilities were open to God next. The question of most pressing interest to his contemporaries was whether in committing sin and giving himself into the power of the Devil Adam had conferred on the Devil any rights over himself for which God must recompense him if he wanted to reclaim mankind. Hermann of Tournai singles out the point.[42] More tellingly,

[37] S, 2.76.20–1.   [38] S, 2.76.27.   [39] S, 2.81.17–19.

[40] S, 2.80.10–13.   [41] Lottin, p. 36, No. 38.   [42] PL 180.11–12.

Abelard lists it among the issues commonly raised in his day in discussing Redemption theology.[43] Anselm's view is that the Devil can have no rights over man because both he and man are subjects of God, and as Satan's lord, God is under no obligation to make him any recompense for taking back what belongs to him.[44] The payment which was due in recompense was due from man to God, and the hypothesis that the Devil had a claim is dismissed.

Two possibilities are advanced as alternatives to the events of the Redemption as the Bible describes them. Could God simply have forgiven the sin of Adam? (Abelard asks this question, too.)[45] Anselm's reply is that to do so would have been to allow himself to be dishonoured, because it would have meant taking no account of the flaunting of his commands. That would, in Anselm's eyes, be inconceivable.[46] Could God have allowed man to be lost for ever, to take the ultimate consequences of his sin, without interfering? Anselm's argument is that man is God's precious work (*pretiosum opus*)[47] and that he could not allow him to be wasted,[48] or his own plan for him frustrated.

We have arrived at a position where it seems that God must both save mankind and receive payment for the debt: *Aut enim peccator sponte solvit quod debet, aut deus ab invito accipit.*[49] ('For either the sinner spontaneously pays what he owes, or God receives it from him against his will.') In either case, man will pay the debt. Anselm's contemporaries were much concerned with the question: Who or what could or ought to pay the debt? Bruno of Segni's first hypothesis is that an inanimate object could have done so, and dismisses first that, and then the possibility that a brute beast, an angel or a member of the human race could have done so.[50] His objection to an angel making the sacrifice is very much Anselm's objection. If an angel had saved mankind: *eumdem angelum pro deo veneraretur*[51] ('the same angel would be venerated in God's place'). Anselm

---

[43] Peter Abelard, *Commentary on Romans*, ed. M. Buytaert, *CCCM* 11 (Turnholt, 1969), p. 114.151–2.

[44] S, 2.55.11–12.   [45] Abelard, op. cit., p. 115.179–91.

[46] S, 2.72–4, Book I.15.   [47] S, 2.52.8, Book I.5.   [48] S, 2.85, Book I.19.

[49] S, 2.72.8–9.

[50] *PL* 165.1080–1, *De Incarnatione Domini.*   [51] *PL* 165.1081.

says much the same in Book I,5 of the *Cur Deus Homo*.[52] This serves as an objection to any other redeemer but Christ, that is, God himself. It is not the only objection put forward by Anselm or by Bruno, but, along with other points which are raised, it brings both to the stage where it is clear to them that only a being who is himself man and God at once will do, since no one but God is able to pay the debt and no one but man has an obligation to do so.[53] Thus by systematic elimination of alternative hypotheses and by testing each one against the immovable fact that God must both save mankind and have the debt to his honour discharged, Anselm constructs an account of the reason for the Incarnation itself.

He had already dealt, in the *De Incarnatione Verbi*, with another set of popular contemporary hypotheses: the suggestion that the Father or the Holy Spirit, or all three Persons of the Trinity were, or might have been, incarnate. This was an issue which had been raised by Roscelin. Anselm does not name his opponent in the *De Incarnatione Verbi*, but he explains that he claims that if the three Persons are truly one God, then the Father and the Spirit were incarnate with the Son.[54] Anselm argues in reply (and repeats briefly in the *Cur Deus Homo*) that if the Father were incarnate he would be the Virgin's son, and there would be two unequal sons in the Trinity, one the Son of God, the other the son of a human mother. And the Father would be the grandson of the Virgin's parents and the Son would be her grandson, although he would have no inheritance from her. If the Holy Spirit were incarnate there would again be two sons in the Trinity of unequal standing. For all these reasons only the Son could have been incarnate.[55] A very similar chain of reasoning leads Bruno of Segni to the same conclusions.[56]

We must ask next why the Son was born, not of two human parents or of a man, but of a woman, and a virgin at that. Anselm tries out a series of hypotheses. He eliminates them one by one. He suggests that if he had been born of a union of man and woman (*commixtione utriusque*) that would have been less *mundus* and *honestus*, less clean and wholesome, than if he was born of one sex only. To be born of a woman alone showed forth

[52] S, 2.52.19–24.   [53] PL 165.1082–3; cf. S, 2.101.3–21.
[54] S, 2.11.1.   [55] S, 2.25–6; cf. S, 2. 105.16–22.   [56] PL 165.1082.

his power best, and there is, in Anselm's eyes, no need to demonstate why a virgin is to be preferred to a non-virgin.[57]

Anselm's hypothetical theology of the Redemption has served its purpose when he has reached this stage in his argument. There if no discussion of the reasons why the sacrifice was made by crucifixion, because for Anselm the only matter of importance is the fact that it had to be made at all, and by the Person of Christ incarnate. Nor does Anselm pause to speculate as Abelard does, about the reasons why Christ spent so long on earth before his death.[58] He asks whether, if the Jews had believed the Gentiles would still have been called,[59] but his only purpose in raising this hypothetical question about an event which took place after the death of Christ is to provide a convenient parallel with the case of angels and mankind. Otherwise, he concentrates exclusively upon the arguments which arise from his first hypothesis, the *remoto Christo* principle.

It is clear, then, that Anselm is not really presenting us with alternative viewpoints in the series of hypotheses he postulates in the *Cur Deus Homo*; he is intent, rather, on getting out of the way all the possibilities which he knew to be in the minds of his contemporaries, and which he envisaged as leading to conclusions at variance with established doctrine. The drift of his thought is like this: If God had done this, but he did not . . . ' or: 'If this had happened, but it did not . . .' At each hypothesis he pauses only to show why it was not a possible choice or why, even if what it outlines had happened, God's purpose would not have been frustrated.

Some of his contemporaries tried to apply the hypothetical method to other topics. A Sentence of the school of Laon puts the case: 'If man had been established in immortality (*immortalis conditus*), as he would have been if he had not sinned, he would have got to heaven by the merit of his free will.'[60] If Adam had not sinned, there would still have been night and day,[61] postulates another. 'If the whole world disappeared and returned to nothing', says Hermann of Tournai, 'God would not be the poorer.'[62] But by far the bulk of the occasions on

[57] S, 2.102–4, Book II.8.   [58] Abelard, op. cit., pp. 118–19.

[59] S, 2.78.29–30.   [60] Lottin, pp. 254–5, No. 325.

[61] Lottin, p. 256, No. 327.   [62] *PL* 180, 12.

which they resort to hypothetical methods involve considerations which fall within the scope of Redemption theology. Even
if many of them did not perceive so clearly as Anselm did that it
was in this area that the hypothetical method was likely to
prove particularly fruitful, they found by practical experiment
that this was where it was most useful. The *Quaestio* method lent
itself to the resolution of theological problems of every kind,
and not only to those where we may ask what would have
happened if things had gone a different way at certain crucial
points in sacred history. Even Honorius Augustodunensis,
much as he admired Anselm's works, and heavily as he drew
upon them, has preferred to pose Anselm's hypotheses in the
form of questions: *Cur non angelus vel homo pro redimendo homine est
missus, sed Dei filius?*[63] ('Why was an angel or a man not sent to
redeem mankind, but the Son of God?') *Cur nec pater nec spiritus
sanctus; sed solus filius est incarnatus?*[64] ('Why was neither the
Father, nor the Holy Spirit, but only the Son incarnate?') The
hypothesis lends itself satisfactorily to only a limited number of
purposes in speculative theology and the theologians who came
after Anselm were increasingly inclined to prefer procedures of
wider application as they strove to produce a workable system
for teaching theology in the schools.

Anselm has, characteristically, made a use of a technically
recognizable method of argument which was available to the
dialecticians among his contemporaries, without allowing the
technical expertise he possesses to obtrude. He has veiled his
technical skill so successfully that it is impossible to determine
exactly how far it extended. But that it has been of assistance to
him in framing the arguments of the *Cur Deus Homo* is beyond
dispute; perhaps it has had a rather more profound effect than
that, in enabling him to organize the considerable body of
contemporary opinions with which he was familiar and to show
how no alternative hypothesis is tenable. By means of his
hypothetical method he demonstrates the inevitable unfolding
of what he sees as the divine purpose.

Forces of Change

'Who will believe this of God?' asks the Jew in one of the

---

[63] *PL* 172.1207, *Inevitabile.*   [64] Ibid.

dialogues between Jews and Christians.[1] He has been holding up for ridicule what Christians believe: that God himself became man and was crucified in order to save mankind from sin and death. Like other Jews of his day he found a great stumbling-block in a doctrine which seemed to imply that God must have undergone change in order to become man. The problems posed by Incarnation and Redemption were of another order altogether from the matters connected with unity and Trinity which Greek metaphysics was so admirably suited to handling: those aspects of the divine nature which Boethius defines as the proper subject-matter of theology.[2] Indeed, it was designed for exactly such purposes; it is a philosophy of the immutable. The new difficulties which arose for twelfth-century thinkers came to the fore—at least in part—because the old schemes of explanation did not meet the requirements of a philosophy of 'change'.

Anselm says early in the *Cur Deus Homo* that he sees that the issues raised by the doctrines of Incarnation and Redemption cannot be satisfactorily resolved without a discussion of will, power, and necessity.[3] He thus identifies three 'forces of change' which, as he shows, must be considered in their relation to the fact of the immutability of God if we are to come to any understanding of the way in which the world could be redeemed. He acknowledges that he will not be able to discuss these matters fully in the space available to him. But in putting his finger on the problem at all he shows that he had seen that there are difficulties here which lie outside the scope of the existing procedures. Anselm's particular insight was not to win the attention it deserved. Twelfth-century discussions were not concerned primarily with will, power, and necessity in this connection. But it was undoubtedly he who first fully perceived the additional dimension of philosophical difficulty which such matters involved, and who attempted to adapt the old metaphysics to new purposes.

We find Anselm discussing his three forces, together or individually, only where changes and events are under consideration. In the *Monologion* and the *Proslogion* he had dealt with the

---

[1] BL MS. Royal E. XIV, fo. 70, Bod. MS Laud. Misc. 264, fo. 122.
[2] *Theol. Tractates*, p. 8; cf. E. J. Fortman, *The Triune God* (London, 1972), p. xxiv.
[3] S, 2.49.7–13.

existence and with the unchanging attributes of God: 'For that same Spirit, because of his changeless eternity, cannot be spoken of in terms of any kind of *motus*, as if he "was" or "will be"; but he simply "is".'[4] In discussing such eternally consistent matters, it is, as Anselm claims, not only unnecessary but even impossible to say anything about the operation of forces of change. No force acts upon God.[5] It is only in the *Cur Deus Homo*, the *De Conceptu Virginali*, the *De Concordia* (and the *De Casu Diaboli* where Anselm asks how the forces of change may operate upon a created being) that he considers the way such forces work. He found that it is only problems raised by events: the Fall of Satan, God's becoming man, the interaction of man's free will and God's foreknowledge, foreordaining, and grace in individual human lives, which make different philosophical procedures appropriate.

In Chapter ix of the *Cur Deus Homo*, Book I, Anselm looks first at the question of Christ's power to choose to die of his own free will. He settles at once upon the fact that God is a special case, and that while a man may be compelled by necessity, or feel the force of someone else's power, God cannot himself be affected by any force. If a man exercises his will, he must in every case make a moral choice between a right and a wrong use of it, while God's will can never be wrong. We must conclude that Christ died of his own free will (*quod sponte mortuus sit*),[6] because no force could have compelled him to die.

But the words of Scripture sometimes seem to contradict this view. The Bible says, 'He was made obedient even unto death';[7] 'I have come not to do my own will',[8] and so on. Anselm therefore has to show how the biblical expressions may be interpreted so as to demonstrate that Christ was indeed under no compulsion. He takes it as a first principle that God did not force Christ to die, but that of his own free will he underwent death: *non ergo coegit Deus Christum mori*.[9] The association of constraint (*coactio*) with necessity, is a common one in Anselm's thought, as D. P. Henry has pointed out.[10] It is therefore in terms of a discussion of necessity that Anselm tries to work out his explanation. 'Every necessity is either a con-

---

[4] S, 1.46.3–5. [5] S, 1.106.11–12. [6] S, 2.61.4.
[7] S, 2.61.4–6. [8] Ibid. [9] S, 2.62.5.
[10] D. P. Henry, *The Logic of St. Anselm* (Oxford, 1967), p. 172.

straint or a prohibition' (*omnis quippe necessitas est aut coactio aut prohibitio*),[11] but words such as *trahere* and *impellere* cannot normally be properly used of God.[12] They are mere conveniences, used *faute de mieux* when we talk of God. For purposes of argument, Anselm needs to show again and again that the permutation of will, power, and necessity in God and in created beings will lead to different results. By setting one force against another in its special sense in connection with God, and in its ordinary sense in connection with man, Anselm is able to show that Christ's will to die was a free choice, even though, for lack of suitable language, the Bible speaks in terms which imply obedience and constraint of the will.

Anselm is able to support his case directly from Scripture, too. God is all-powerful, and Christ has explicitly said: 'I lay down my life.' (*Erat namque omnipotens; et . . . ipse dicat: Ego pono animam meam.*)[13] He cannot have said that out of a lack of power. Therefore he died, 'By no necessity, but of his own free will' (*nulla necessitate sed libera voluntate*).[14] Will, power, and necessity are all taken into consideration here, and Anselm has been able to test the operation of all three forces in the special case of God in order to construct his argument.

A typically Anselmian method of circumventing paradoxes is to separate several senses of a term.[15] In the *De Libertate Arbitrii* he defines the will, and divides it into parts. The will is *ipsum instrumentum volendi*, the single instrument of willing, which is always present in the soul, whether it is in operation or not (*semper est in anima*); it is also whatever we will, and that may include a wide variety of things (*tam multiplex est*).[16] The will is therefore twofold—or perhaps it is simply that we use the word *voluntas* equivocally, as we do the word 'sight'. (*sicut visus aequivoce dicitur, ita et voluntas.*)[17] In any case, from the first, Anselm separates the instrument of the will from its action. The same division is to be found in the *De Conceptu Virginali*, where Anselm says quite clearly that he sees the will as a 'force'; *Aliud enim est vis illa animae qua ipsa anima vult aliquid.*[18] ('The force of

---

[11] S, 2.123.23–4.   [12] S, 2.65.5.   [13] S, 2.66.8–10.
[14] S, 2.66.6–8.
[15] I have looked at some of the ways in which Anselm does this in 'The "Secure Technician": Varieties of Paradox in the Writings of St. Anselm', *Vivarium*, XIII, i (1975), 1–21.
[16] S, 1.219.1–16.   [17] S, 1.218.26.   [18] S, 2.143.27–8.

the soul with which the soul itself wills something is another matter.') The theory of the will is more fully developed still in the *De Concordia*. 'Each instrument has its own powers and its own uses. In the will we call these powers "desires"': (*Quoniam ergo singula instrumenta habent et hoc quod sunt, et aptitudines suas, et suos usus . . . Quas aptitudines in voluntate possumus nominare affectiones.*)[19] The will is therefore a force, and the power which gives impetus to that force, and a force in action. Only at times when the instrument lies unused in the soul can it be said to be passive. In the *De Concordia* Anselm employs a similar device for 'necessity', separating the possibility-of-sinning-in-the-future from the-necessity-of-sinning-in-the-future to which every son of Adam is heir.[20] He demonstrates the working of necessity in action by examining carefully the different modes of its operation, just as he has demonstrated the working of the will in action by examining different senses of the term *voluntas*. At every stage he has looked for points of difference, so that even where he cannot work by setting one force against another in its special relation to God, he is able to show how a single force may be regarded as two or more separate entities for purposes of argument.

The element of natural changeableness which the importing of such forces into the discussion introduces, can be made to serve the purposes of a 'theology of change' in various ways. There are powers which a man ought to have and powers which are not proper to him.[21] Some powers are integral to his very being as a man, while others are not. In the case of God himself, omnipotence is an attribute of all three Persons of the Trinity, although no single power can be identified with one Person of the Trinity as Augustine had tried to identify will or *voluntas* with the Holy Spirit.[22] God always has the power to put his will into effect, but a man has not. God cannot be compelled by necessity as a man may be. In the respects in which God differs from man, Christ also differs from ordinary men, and yet we can speak of his will and his power and his voluntary submission to necessity using the same words as we should employ if we were talking about an ordinary man, provided we bear in mind their special signification in connection with Christ. For

---

[19] S, 2.279.6–10.   [20] S, 2.149.21–9.   [21] S, 2.92.31–2.
[22] *De Trinitate* X.x.13–xii.19.

working purposes this gives us the language in which to discuss
a theology of change, if a limited one.

Anselm demonstrates something of the flexibility this allows
him. He gives this example: If I propose to cross a river by boat,
when it is possible for me to cross it either by boat or on
horseback (*possum*), in deciding to go by boat (*propono mihi*) I put
off crossing the river until a boat is available. If I then say that I
have crossed the river because there was a boat, it is only my act
of will in deciding not to cross on horseback which has made the
word 'because' appropriate. I have selected one power and
submitted myself to its consequent necessity.[23] It is clear
enough how much scope such a device can be made to yield for
purposes of argument, whether it is the will, power, and necessity of man or the same three forces in connection with God
which are under discussion.

In the *Cur Deus Homo* Anselm provides a most elegant
example of the ways in which such a balancing of the three
forces may be used to explain how what seems to be change in
God is no such thing. He wants to show how Christ both could
and could not sin:

> Every power is dependent on will. When I say that I can speak or walk, it is
> understood that I mean 'If I wish'. For if 'will' is not understood, we are
> dealing not with power but with necessity . . . And so we can say of Christ
> that he could lie, if we understand, 'If he wished'. Since he cannot lie without
> willing to do so, we can also say that he refused to lie. And so he both could
> and could not lie.[24]

Anselm has here arranged his three forces, of will and necessity
and power, in such a way that each provides a check upon the
others, and he has been able to accommodate his paradox
without implying that Christ was subject to any necessity.

Anselm exploits the possibilities of his three forces to some
effect when he searches for arguments to show how God willed
to redeem the world, how he was able to do so, and how it was
(in a special sense) necessary for him to do so. Few of his
contemporaries chose the same principles in their own arguments; although God's will, God's power and necessity are
commonly discussed they are not systematically brought

---

[23] S, 2.63.4.   [24] S, 2.107.1–9.

together so as to show how they work together, (and how they interact with the same forces in man) except by Anselm himself. As yet, only he saw their larger philosophical uses, and only he can be said to have worked out at all fully a new approach to the theology of change. In the Sentences of the school of Laon discussions of the will of God concern its operation in the world and the different views of it which the Bible gives us. It is never envisaged as a force of change in the way that Anselm sees it. In the little treatise *On the Power and Will of God* which is printed in Migne among the works of Hugh of St. Victor, will, power, and necessity are examined together, but merely with the intention of deciding whether the power or the will of God is the greater. If the will of God is the greater and he wills things he cannot do, we cannot call him omnipotent; but if his power is greater, he must be able to do things which he cannot will, and thus to act against his own will.[25] The paradox is of some philosophical interest, but its resolution does not involve the exploration of a means of talking about change; the treatise lacks the scope of Anselm's attempt to find a set of principles which will encompass those theological problems where change has to be accounted for.

[25] *PL*, 176.539–40.

CONCLUSION

WE began with a quotation from a sermon of Karl Barth's. Perhaps we might end with another. Of the liberal theologians of the nineteenth century he remarked: 'For this theology, to think of God meant to think, in a scarcely-veiled fashion, about man.'[1] The theologians of the generation after Anselm were beginning to think like this, about a God whom they strove increasingly to understand in human terms. It was the element of change and move-ment—what we might call the historical element—in the topics which were attracting interest among contemporaries which gave the new theology its character and its immediate human appeal. The enlarged perception of the possibilities of human reason as an instrument of argument supported this interest and gave it vigour and direction.

There is a positive side to this development and a negative one. As R. W. Southern has put it, 'these religious develop-ments conquered the universe for humanity, and made God so much man's friend that his actions became almost undistin-guishable from our own'.[2] At its best, the effort to understand God in human terms made those terms themselves expand under the pressure of accommodating so great a guest. The aids to understanding which secular studies provided in speculative theology enlarged the compass of the human intellect. At its worst, the attempt to know God as if there were nothing to be understood about him which could not be fully encompassed by human reason was bound to limit intellectual aspiration to what was readily within reach. When Anselm wrote about the *homo assumptus* he took the term to refer to 'man elevated' to the ultimate height of union with God. Some of the theologians of the mid-twelfth century had, as we have seen, more of an eye to the man who was assumed, to the means by which God humbled himself.

[1] E. Busch, *Karl Barth*, p. 119.
[2] R. W. Southern, *Mediaeval Humanism* (Oxford, 1970), p. 37.

Anselm's writing is pervaded by an overwhelming sense that the glory of God is inaccessible to human understanding, and a concomitant belief that it is that very inaccessibility which ought to cause us to stretch our minds upwards in search of him. In Anselm himself, this view of things imposes a philosophical direction upon his thinking as well as a direction of spiritual aspiration. Anselm felt equally strongly the double imperatives of obligation and inability which he expresses so fervently in the first chapter of the *Proslogion*; '[Your exile] longs to reach you, and your dwelling-place is beyond reach.'[3] By comparison, Abelard perhaps resembles the fallen angel of St. Bernard's sermon in having his wings as a thinker unbalanced.[4] In him the sense of obligation to learn about God sometimes has an air of sheer intellectual curiosity. His feelings of inadequacy are less often in evidence than a solid confidence in his own powers of mind. He flies, by choice, a less uniformly upward course than Anselm attempted to fly on his own 'spiritual wings'.[5] If few of Abelard's contemporaries matched him in intellectual self-confidence, many of them shared with him a readiness to consider intellectual curiosity valuable which is perhaps the most significant new attitude of twelfth-century scholars. It sometimes seems that Abelard is inclined to look God in the eye more boldly than Anselm does. He is, as we have seen, ready to question points of doctrine which Anselm thought were settled for ever. Twelfth-century scholars like him were beginning to think about God with curiosity as well as awe.

Anselm's uncompromising firmness of view was the only response he found himself able to make to a God who could not change, in whom there could be no inconsistency. It was, philosophically speaking, a hard line. It also made great demands of an emotional and spiritual kind on anyone who was prepared to follow through its implications. Anselm was made of exceptionally tough stuff not only intellectually, but also spiritually and emotionally. He set a standard with which other men would in any case have found it hard to match themselves.

---

[3] S, 1.98.10–11.
[4] *Sancti Bernardi Opera*, ed. J. Leclercq and H. Rochais (Rome, 1968), V, 311–14, Sermon for the first Sunday in November.
[5] S, 2.7.9–10.

Those who loved and admired him emulated him while he lived, but it is not to be expected that anyone should have found it easy to follow his lead in the next generation. An entirely God-centred theology is not so readily assimilable as a theology in which the emphasis rests upon the fact that God became a man like us. A policy of no compromise can scarcely be expected to have so ready a popular appeal as a system of thought where there is room for reservations to be accommodated.

Besides, Abelard and his fellows had something to offer at once more palatable and more obviously exciting, easier to understand, and more quickly rewarding. They encouraged the asking of questions, whether those questions were prompted by a genuine desire to have a difficulty of conscience resolved, or a misunderstanding cleared up, or whether they were suggested merely by a moment's curiosity. The change of direction in theological studies which took place between Anselm's day and Abelard's shows clearly enough the early effects of a new readiness to allow scope to the natural curiosity of the human mind.

This general willingness to allow comparatively free range to those human qualities of restlessness and love of change, curiosity and uncertainty, willingness to respond to challenge, and competitiveness, which monastic life is designed to discipline, runs against the direction of Anselm's striving. These are also exactly the respects in which, in medieval eyes, a man is least like God. It was by giving room to such qualities of mind that twelfth-century theological thought developed its peculiar character. In this way it became perhaps more human and less God-like in its aspirations.

It is probably true, too, that if we go about things in this way, the first principles to which we must go back in theology will be very fundamental indeed. It is possible to go back to first principles in one sense, by setting aside all the accretions of later scholarship and basing one's Christianity upon a plain man's reading of the Bible. But if we go further and question whether what the writers of Scripture themselves have to say can be taken at its face value, if, in order to allow reason a clear run, we deliberately set aside or bring into question all the written aids provided by writers of previous centuries too, then we must start again from the beginning indeed. Anselm did not set those aids aside when he tried to reason things out from first principles. Although, when he had mastered them thoroughly, he worked independently of them, he referred back to them constantly. He tested his conclusions against them. Some of his successors constructed new theologies by asking preliminary questions with open minds (even if their answers did not accord with older authority) by giving rein to their natural curiosity and coming to terms in themselves with an entirely human desire for change.

It is thus the inconsistency of man, the rogue element in him, which set the *rectus ordo* at naught and provided the conditions of an intellectual climate in which the character of theology could change. Paradoxically, but perhaps understandably enough, the asking of awkward and sometimes damaging questions went hand in hand with the fashioning of a new system, a desire to organize the new material, to set out the questions which were being asked with their answers in an orderly manner. A new *rectus ordo* of thought rapidly emerged out of the old. But the direction of change persisted. Where Anselm had tried to model his theology on the simplicity of God, his twelfth-century successors allowed themselves to enjoy to the full the multiplicity of possibilities with which human reason presented them. In theology at least, the new interest in man made itself felt in a realization of the full range of powers of the human mind; the desire for order was balanced by an urge to explore beyond the bounds of order. The desire to construct systems was matched by a willingness to destroy them.

It is hard to believe that Anselm's self-imposed restrictions in any way hampered the movement of his thought. His intellect never seems to have chafed in its harness. Indeed, he enjoyed a freedom from peripheral considerations which enabled him to see a straight road clearly before him. Perhaps that was necessary to him. Later thinkers offered something much more manageable to the majority of readers by allowing for the influence of perhaps more ordinary human qualities of mind. Anselm's intellectual power made it relatively easy to subordinate these to his over-all purposes, but other men were glad to give them some rein—as they were able to do in Abelard's day. The intellectual anxieties of Anselm's friends and pupils, and of the theologians of the next generation, are, for the most part, the universal anxieties of educated men. *Mutatis mutandis*, the moral and philosophical and methodological choices they made still have to be made.

APPENDIX: GILBERT CRISPIN

GILBERT Crispin has been much overshadowed by his friend and master Anselm of Canterbury.[1] A general study of Gilbert's life and works was published nearly seventy years ago by J. Armitage Robinson.[2] His work has attracted attention since largely as a result of his connection with Anselm, and its importance in its own right has been recognized only in the case of the *Dispute between a Christian and a Jew*, which was one of the most influential of the dialogues of this kind which proliferated between the end of the eleventh and the middle of the twelfth century.[3] Gilbert is unlikely ever to hold a place in the development of speculative theology entirely on his own merits, if only because his writings have almost as much to tell us about Anselm's teaching and writing as they do about his own. Gilbert shows us, as perhaps no one else does, how Anselm's ideas worked on the mind of an able pupil—not because he had no other disciples, but because no one else's work has quite so intimate an air of the Anselmian schoolroom about it. Gilbert's *De Casu Diaboli* and, to a lesser extent, his treatise on the Holy Spirit, breathe the air of Bec.

Gilbert had entered Bec as a boy and he had grown up there during the years when Anselm was Prior. In his early thirties, about 1078 or 1079, he was brought to Canterbury by Lanfranc, and within a few years he was made Abbot of Westminster (probably in 1085). It seems likely that Anselm took refuge with Gilbert at Westminster in the winter of 1092 to 1093, when the See of Canterbury had been left vacant by the death of Lanfranc, and political pressures were building up. Anselm

---

[1] See R. W. Southern, 'St. Anselm and his English Pupils', *MARS* 1 (1941), 3–43, and 'St. Anselm and Gilbert Crispin, Abbot of Westminster', *MARS* 3 (1954), 78–115, and *St. Anselm and his Biographer* (Cambridge, 1963), pp. 205–6, 208–9, 246–7.

[2] J. Armitage Robinson. *Gilbert Crispin, Abbot of Westminster* (Cambridge, 1911).

[3] Gilbert's *Disputatio Iudei et Christiani* is edited by B. Blumenkranz (Antwerp, 1956), where a full bibliography is given. To this might be added my article, 'Gilbert Crispin, Abbot of Westminster: the forming of a monastic Scholar', *Studia Monastica* (forthcoming).

was still working on the *De Incarnatione Verbi* at this time, and he was beginning to think out the *Cur Deus Homo*. No doubt he and Anselm talked theology as they had done at Bec. Perhaps their conversations refreshed Gilbert's memories of his schooldays; certainly some elements of Anselm's discourses remained in his mind when he came to write on similar subjects for his own monks at Westminster.

Gilbert was a scholar of good general ability, able to turn his hand to the writing of biography (the *Vita Herluini*), sermons, a treatise on the three Maries of the Gospels, a treatise on monastic life,[4] as well as to the composition of the influential *Disputation between a Christian and a Jew*,[5] and to topics of speculative theology: the Fall of Satan, grace and predestination,[6] the origin of the soul,[7] and the doctrine of the Trinity in relation to the Holy Spirit. If he did not possess a profoundly original mind, he had an enduring interest in such matters, which Anselm does not appear to have succeeded in awakening in Gundolf, another monk of Bec and more nearly Anselm's contemporary. He became Bishop of Rochester in 1078, and although he was both astute in business matters and deeply pious,[8] he was no theologian. The *Vita Gundulfi* relates that he was often moved to tears by Anselm's words,[9] but his spiritual gifts were evidently not of the intellect, and he appears to have written nothing but the letters to which Anselm's replies survive. Even Boso, Anselm's companion in the dialogue of the *Cur Deus Homo* and later Abbot of Bec, wrote no theological works of his own, although Anselm evidently found him a stimulating companion and there can be no doubt of his ability to handle theological and philosophical problems. Few of the monks of Bec, who seemed to contemporaries like philosophers (according to Orderic Vitalis)[10] imitated their master in the writing of works of theology. Certainly it would have taken some courage

[4] Texts in 'St. Anselm and Gilbert Crispin', pp. 91–115.
[5] *Gisleberti Crispini Disputatio ludei et Christiani*, ed. B. Blumenkranz (Antwerp, 1956). Blumenkranz gives full details of MSS and edns. of Gilbert's work.
[6] BL MS Add. 8166, fos. 18ᵛ–22ᵛ.
[7] Ibid., fos. 37–9.
[8] M. Gibson, *Lanfranc of Bec* (Oxford, 1978), pp. 175–6.
[9] *PL* 159.817A.
[10] Orderic Vitalis, *Historia Ecclesiastica*, ed. M. Chibnall, II (Oxford, 1969), Book iv, ii, 146.

to make the attempt, and it is unlikely that Anselm would have thought it advisable for young men to write speculative theology. Gilbert is an exception. It may be that his removal to England enabled him to achieve a certain independence of mind and to mature in his own way. If his mind had been formed by Anselm before he left Bec and his ideas developed by conversation with him in later years, Anselm's influence had not stifled him. It had developed in him the power to use the abilities he had.

Gilbert has some claim to respect as a scholar and theologian in his own right. If his work is set beside that of contemporaries other than Anselm it becomes plain that he possessed an unusual competence in handling theological arguments, a good sense of sound doctrine, and considerable skill in making himself understood to beginners in such studies. His writings are of interest, too, because they are the product of the period of transition with which we have been concerned, between a kind of scholarship which is largely monastic in inspiration, and which owes a large debt to Augustine, and a method of approach which we may loosely call scholastic. Like Anselm's works, Gilbert's treatises incorporate something of both traditions.

They stand at another crossroads, too. Theology was still primarily the *studium sacrae scripturae*. Gilbert's treatises are concerned with matters of speculative theology, and yet the author identifies them as questions which arise out of the study of the Bible (*de sacris paginis*).[11] In the *De Spiritu Sancto* Gilbert proposes to deal with questions of this kind by means of a formal disputation—an *altercatio*[12] which lies somewhere between an Augustinian dialogue and the *disputatio* of the later twelfth-century schools. Yet he never loses sight of the importance of grounding everything he says in the text of the Bible: 'Let us lodge the anchor of our disputation in Holy Scripture', he says at one point in the *De Casu Diaboli*, as he and his pupil embark on a fresh topic.[13] Throughout the treatises Scriptural texts are used for corroboration, for illustration, and, above all—and here Gilbert's approach most closely matches

---

[11] BL MS Cotton Vespasian A xiv [=V], fo. 109; cf. S, 1.173.1.
[12] V, fo. 109.   [13] BL MS Add. 8166 [=A], fo. 20.

Anselm's—as starting-points for discussion. This was where the new work of the twelfth century began. Gilbert's treatises are a little like the *quaestiones* with which Peter Abelard interrupts his *Commentary on Romans*;[14] they arise from the study of the Bible, but within the context of that study, some treatment of separate questions has become necessary. If Gilbert's *quaestio* arises from a particular text in each case, it also constitutes a distinct philosophical or theological problem.

Anselm's *De Casu Diaboli* was the last to be written of the three treatises which form a group designed to help in the study of Holy Scripture: the *De Veritate*, the *De Libertate Arbitrii*, the *De Casu Diaboli*. Gilbert Crispin left Bec for Canterbury in 1078 or 1079, before it was finished.[15] But there is no reason to suppose that he was not present on occasions when the subject-matter of all three was discussed. Anselm touches upon the problem of reconciling human and angelic free will with the foreknowledge, predestination, and grace of God, in the *De Libertate Arbitrii*. His chief concern there is with the nature of the freedom of the will. He returned to other aspects in the *De Concordia*, but the *De Concordia* has all the marks of a treatise for which much of the thinking had been done long before, and it is evident from its continuity with his thoughts in the *De Libertate Arbitrii* that he did not begin to work on its subject-matter only at the end of his life. In his treatise Gilbert deals with the same subject, and it is very likely that when Gilbert wrote on this topic he was able to draw on memories of Anselm's conversation and teaching during his years at Bec. There is no reason to date the composition of Gilbert's *De Angelo Perdito* after the publication of the *De Concordia*. The group of problems with which it is concerned were all seen by Anselm as germane to the subject-matter of his own 'three treatises'. Gilbert could have written the work at any time after he left Bec, with or without the benefit of reading Anselm's finished *De Casu Diaboli*. He has, in any case, not simply repeated Anselm, but made a new unity of his explanations and produced a treatise which stands on its own merits.

[14] *Petri Abaelardi Opera Theologica*, ed. M. Buytaert, *CCCM* 11 (Turnholt, 1969), pp. 113–18.

[15] See 'St. Anselm and Gilbert Crispin', pp. 78–9. On the chronology of Anselm's works see the *ratio editionis* to S.

There is material here, too, which has a place in the *Cur Deus Homo*. Gilbert, like Anselm, asks whether men were made to fill the places left vacant by the fallen angels, and whether the number of men and angels can be determined.[16] This was a topic of some general contemporary interest, as the surviving Sentences of the school of Laon demonstrate.[17] Perhaps it was among the matters Gilbert Crispin discussed with Anselm when they met again in England in 1092 to 1093, at the time when Anselm was beginning to think out his approach to the problems considered in the *Cur Deus Homo*.[18]

We cannot date Gilbert's *De Angelo Perdito*, then. But its air of mature consideration points to Gilbert's having mastered its subject-matter in early years, and written his treatise after some years of reflection. He sought neither to imitate Anselm, nor to outdo him, but to meet the needs of ordinary monks like those at Westminster, who were not quite the 'seeming philosophers' of Bec.[19]

I *On the Fall of Satan*

1. *Note on the Manuscript*

The *De Casu Diaboli* is to be found in only one manuscript, British Library MS Add.8166, which is described by J. Armitage Robinson (pp. 54–5, 72–3). It is a twelfth-century manuscript, compiled, Robinson suggests, by someone who had access to 'various literary remains' of Gilbert's, and who tried to bring them together in a single collection. But, as he notes, there is 'foreign matter' and some confusion. The text of the *Disputatio Gisleberti Abbatis Westmonasterii Contra Judaeos* (fo. 3ᵛ–17ᵛ) is of especial interest, because it differs in a number of features from what appears to have been the final text. It may represent an early draft. The manuscript also contains Gilbert's Palm Sunday sermon (fo. 17ᵛ–18ᵛ), a piece on the Eucharist (fo. 22ᵛ), and the *Disputatio cum Gentile*.

2. *On the Fall of Satan: some Anselmian parallels*

(a) 'Being in the truth; the happiness of Satan; will, perseverance, and the source of Satan's sin'. (Cf. Anselm: Preface to *De*

---

[16] A. fo. 21; cf. S, 2.74–84.
[17] Cf. Lottin.
[18] 'St. Anselm and Gilbert Crispin', pp. 87–8.
[19] Orderic Vitalis, op. cit.

Veritate, S, 1.173.15–16, *De Veritate*, Chs. iv–v, S, 1.180–2; *De Casu Diaboli*, Chs. i–iii, S, 1.233–40, Chs. xii–xiii, S, 1.251–8.) MS Add. 8166, fos. 18ᵛ–19ᵛ.

Question: Truth says in the Gospel that the fallen angel 'Did not remain in the truth' (John 8:44). I ask, therefore, how this is to be understood. For if he had never been in the truth, the Lord could not blame him for not remaining in the truth. Therefore he was at some time in the truth. But to be in the truth is to know that what exists exists, and that what does not exist does not exist. For to think that what does not exist exists, or that what exists does not exist, is not to be in the truth but to be in falsehood. Therefore the fallen angel was in the truth as long as he knew happiness. Why, then, did he not remain? Either he did not remain because he did not will to remain, or he did not remain because he was not able to remain. But he who did not will to remain in happiness certainly did not know what happiness was . . . He was not then created happy, but wretched and miserable, he who was created not knowing and ignorant of happiness. But if he willed to remain, and was not able to remain, why was he to blame? . . .

The Apostle . . . says: 'What do you have that you have not received? But if you have received, why do you glory as though you had not received?' (I Corinthians 4:7.) The fallen angel did not have perseverance in good because God did not give it. Why therefore did God demand from him what he had not received? . . . The fall of Satan seems in this way to be capable of being turned back upon God, which it is wicked for anyone to believe. So (fo. 19) either Satan did not have freedom of will because he was not able to will what it was necessary to will (that is, that he should will to remain in the truth) or some violence was done against free choice . . . Whichever of these we accept, we remove the blame far from Satan.

Reply: You express things confusedly . . . and so you confound their consequences. Let us take the example of the Apostle which you gave, and work it out in proper order: 'What do you have that you have not received?' . . . We concede that man has no good, angel has no good, which he has not received, for every good is from God. And because Satan had no good from himself, he had no good which he did not receive . . . Satan . . . did not have perseverance in good, not because he was not able to have it, but because he did not will to have it . . .

It is one thing to make use of reason, another to be able to make use of reason. So, too, it is one thing to persevere, another to be able to persevere. Everyone who makes use of reason is able to make use of reason, and everyone who perseveres is able to persevere. But not everyone who is able to make use of reason makes use of reason, for sometimes he misuses it; and not everyone who is able to persevere perseveres; for many a man fails to complete what he has begun. And it is one thing to be able, or not to be able, to make use of reason, and another to be able to make use, or not to make use, of reason. For that which cannot make use of reason is irrational or non-rational; [that which is able to make use of reason] can be reasonable, even if it sometimes misuses reason. So therefore it is one thing to be able or not to be able to persevere, and another to be able to persevere or not to persevere. Satan, because he was able to persevere and did not persevere . . . had either possibility open to him. Since, as I say, he was able and did not will [to persevere], he sinned, and was rightly condemned.

(b) (fo. 19ᵛ) *Posse* (cf. *Memorials*, p. 346, *Proslogion*, Ch. vii, S, 1.105.9–16.)

We must first consider what it is 'to be able'. For we often misuse this word or name, that is 'to be able'. For if we do not pay attention to what it is 'to be able', either we shall say that God cannot do everything, or we shall confess that God can die.

(c) 'That than which nothing better can be thought'. MS Add. 8166, fo. 19ᵛ, cf. *Proslogion*, Chs. xiv, xviii, S, 1.111–19; S, 1.114.21.

Question: Until a stronger reason or a clearer authority of Holy Scripture occurs to me, I concede what you say. But since God is the greatest good (for God is that than which nothing better can be thought) . . . I ask why God made Satan such that he could sin. For it would have been better even that he should not have been created than that he should have been created such that he could sin, just as the Lord says in the Gospel, of Judas the betrayer: 'It would have been better for that man if he had not been born.' (Matthew 26:24.) Why, therefore, did God not bring about that which was better, that is, that there should be no Satan, and bring about what was worse, that is, that he should exist?
Reply: . . . 'If . . . a rational creature is better than an irrational, it is better that the most good Creator should begin his creation with that which is better in the order of things, that is, that he should make the angel rational, because this nature is better than the irrational. . . . Therefore the good Creator did what he ought to do, for he did that which was better; nor was it right that he should make first that which was worse . . . Therefore the Creator made Satan such as he ought to have been made by the most good Creator . . . but Satan ought to have done what he did not do, not because he was not able, but because he did not will, (nor [strictly] because he did not will, but because he willed against right order and against God). Indeed it would have been better for Satan not to have been at all, than that he should have been such as he made himself; but with regard to the dignity of his creation, it was altogether better that he should have been created rational than not rational.

II *On the Holy Spirit*

1. *Note on the Manuscript*

Gilbert's treatise on the Holy Spirit is to be found in British Library MS Cotton Vespasian A xiv, fos. 109–110ᵛ. The manuscript is described by J. Armitage Robinson (p. 55, pp. 70–2).

Three manuscripts have been bound together: the first (fos. 1–105) contains a calendar, with a number of Welsh saints and some saints' lives. The second has (fos. 106–108ᵛ) Bede's account of the correspondence between Gregory the Great and Augustine of Canterbury, Gilbert's treatise, and further extracts from Bede (fos. 111–113ᵛ). The last part contains letters of Alcuin and other material (fos. 114–179).

2. *Relation to Anselm's Works*

Anselm's *De Processione Spiritus Sancti* was written about 1102, four years after he had delivered, at the Council of Bari, the speech on which it is based. At some time after he had been made Archbishop, Gilbert sent him a treatise of his own on the Holy Spirit, with a request that he should resolve the final question which the pupil raises in the dialogue. It is not impossible that this little work was written after 1102, but it may well belong to the previous decade. It owes something to Anselm, but a great deal to Gilbert's own reading of Augustine, and it represents, in many respects, an independent work.

The most striking Anselmian echo in the treatise is the use of the image of the river Nile, which Gilbert almost certainly borrowed from Anselm. This image of Trinity is to be found in Augustine only in a rather different form.[20] Anselm employs it twice, once in the *De Incarnatione Verbi* and once in the *De Processione Spiritus Sancti*,[21] and it is possible that it was a favourite of his in discussion with his monks. Gilbert's *magister* says that when we speak of the spring, river, and pool which make up a watercourse, there is no danger of our confusing the names and calling the river a pool, and yet the spring, river, and pool are one and the same substance. To take the example of a specific river: the word 'Nile' may be predicated of spring, river or pool, and yet there will be not three Niles but one. The words we use for the Trinity and for the Persons behave in this way. More: the river comes from the spring and the pool from both spring and river, but the spring is not from the river, nor the river from the pool. Again, the parallel with the Trinity holds. Gilbert envisaged no problems arising out of the use of this

---

[20] On this image see my article, 'St. Anselm's Images of Trinity', *JTS* xxvii (1976), 47–56.

[21] S, 2.31–2 and S, 2.203–5.

image for his readers; he thought it straightforwardly helpful, as no doubt Anselm did, too, when he first used it. In the *De Processione Spiritus Sancti* he was obliged to meet a number of objections on the part of the 'Greeks', who perceived various anomalies in it by extending it to cover further aspects of the doctrine of the Trinity. It implies, for example, that the Holy Spirit proceeds from the Father through the Son.[22] Gilbert's use of the image is entirely in keeping with his purposes in the treatise. There is nothing contentious or controversial here.

The pupil expresses his satisfaction that it is reasonable to believe in one God. He asks what *rationis necessitas*, what compelling reason, obliges us to believe in the Trinity. Here again there is an Anselmian echo. In the *Cur Deus Homo* Anselm asks what *ratio* and *necessitas* caused God to become man,[23] and looks for *rationes necessariae* to explain the Redemption. Gilbert's pupil accepts that we believe that God exists because we were made by him and we are in him, and we cannot escape from his power. But he does not understand what reason should lead us to believe that there are three Persons. In other words, he asks to be provided with grounds other than those of textual authority for faith in the doctrine of the Trinity. This again is very much an Anselmian exercise in its conception. He had sought from the time when he composed his first published treatise, the *Monologion*, to provide an account of the *rationis necessitas*[24] which underlies orthodox doctrine, and to fill the gaps which Scripture leaves in explaining such matters.

In particular, Gilbert's pupil asks, how was it possible for Christ to be incarnate without the Father and the Holy Spirit being incarnate, too, if the Trinity is one in essence? Gilbert does not answer this last question. He brings the discussion to an end at this point with the comment that his pupil is allowing his curiosity too much rein. He tells him that he must learn to restrict himself to matters within reach of his understanding. His caution is typical. But there is matter in the final question for another treatise; certainly it constitutes a separate *quaestio*, and in his dedication Gilbert hands it to Anselm to be settled. It is curious that Gilbert makes no use of Anselm's arguments on exactly this point in the *De Incarnatione Verbi*. His treatise must have been written after the publication of the *De Incarnatione*

---

[22] S, 2.203–5. [23] S, 2.48.2. [24] S, 1.7.10.

Verbi in 1093 or 1094 because it is addressed to Anselm as Archbishop, and it is likely that he drew his Nile image from the work. His refusal to be drawn into further discussion suggests rather that he did not wish to enter upon a further area of inquiry. He had already covered the essential points in the doctrine of the Trinity in so far as it relates to the Holy Spirit.

His willingness to pause at this point bears out a suggestion of R. W. Southern's in another connection, that 'Gilbert would gladly have remained on the humbler level of Biblical exegesis and not ventured on the heights of speculation'.[25] Gilbert was cautious and sensible; he was also a man who recognized his own limitations and who was able, as a scholar, to work within them very satisfactorily. As an early English theologian he would win few marks for pioneering spirit. Apart from the *Disputation between a Christian and a Jew* his treatises were not, it seems, much copied and his influence was probably confined to a small circle of friends. His achievement was modest, but his works have a solidity and a finish which give them some claim to respect. It is not easy to explain doctrinal profundities simply and clearly, and it is not easy to know when to stop in pursuing a line of philosophical or theological investigation. Compared with Anselm, Gilbert is a humble and pedestrian thinker, but he wrote well, he met a need within the England of the day, and he deserves a place in the history of English learning in the eleventh and twelfth centuries.

3. *Gilbert Crispin's Nile Image*
MS Cotton Vespasian A XIV, fo. 110ᵛ.

Master: A river comes from a spring; a pool is collected from both spring and river. The spring, the river and the pool are three different things, and cannot be called by one another's names, yet the substance of the spring, the river and the pool is not different, but one and the same. Let 'Nile', for example, be predicated of the spring, the river and the pool; yet there are not three Niles but one Nile . . . It is not, therefore, surprising if the Father is God, the Son God and the Holy Spirit God, yet there are not three Gods but one God. Again, if the river is from the spring, and the pool from the spring and the river, it does not follow that the spring is from the river or the river from the pool. It is not surprising that the Son is from the Father, the Holy Spirit is from the Father and the Son, yet the Father is not from the Son or the Son from the Holy Spirit, and that the Son proceeds from the Father and not from

[25] 'St. Anselm and Gilbert Crispin', p. 98.

the Holy Spirit, although the Spirit proceeds equally and inseparably from the Father and the Son.

This name 'Nile' is given to the Nile to specify what is the Nile. But those three names of forms [*habitudines*], 'spring', 'river', 'pool', do not refer to the Nile as a whole, but they tell us that the Nile is such, and may be thought of as such, that here it is a spring, here it is flowing, here, where it is not flowing, it is a pool. This word 'God' signifies the substance of God, and because he is one individually, he cannot be spoken of in the plural. These three names of relations ('Father', 'Son', 'Holy Spirit') do not refer to God as a whole, but in some way they tell us that God is such, and may be thought of as such, that he is one in divinity of substance, but three in Persons. For this name 'Person' is used to refer to those three; and the one word can be used in the singular of the individual Persons, and in the plural of the three Persons. For 'Person' can be said of the Father and 'Person' can be said of the Son, and 'Person' can be said of the Holy Spirit, and Father, Son and Holy Spirit are three 'Persons', not one 'Person'. Therefore, although a similar name which is common to both the single thing and the three—that is spring, river and pool—is missing in the example of the Nile we have given, if there may be any appropriate comparison between human and divine matters, that analogy (*proportio*) does not seem unsuitable.

SELECT BIBLIOGRAPHY

Anselmi Opera Omnia, ed. F. S. Schmitt (Rome/Edinburgh, 1938–68).
Translations: Anselm of Canterbury, trans. J. Hopkins (New York, 1974–5), 4 vols. includes all the treatises.
—— *St. Anselm's Proslogion* trans. M. J. Charlesworth (Oxford, 1965), includes a philosophical commentary.
—— *The Prayers and Meditations of St. Anselm* trans. B. Ward (London, 1973).
Eadmer, *The Life of St. Anselm*, ed. R. W. Southern (London, 1962).
R. W. Southern, *St. Anselm and his Biographer* (Cambridge, 1963).
D. P. Henry, *The Logic of St. Anselm* (Oxford, 1967).
J. Hopkins, *A Companion to the Study of St. Anselm* (Minneapolis 1972) contains a full bibliography brought up to date in *Anselm of Canterbury*, vol. IV.
G. R. Evans, *Anselm and Talking about God* (Oxford, 1978).
Anselm's contemporaries and the new generation
Some texts available in modern editions:
Peter Abelard, *Dialectica*, ed. L. M. de Rijk (Assen, 1956).
—— *Dialogus inter Philosophum, Judaeum et Christianum*, ed. R. Thomas (Stuttgart, 1966).
—— *Historia Calamitatum*, ed. J. Monfrin (Paris, 1967).
—— *Opera Theologica*, ed. M. Buytaert, *CCCM* XI, XII (1969).
—— *Ethics*, ed. D. E. Luscombe (Oxford, 1971).
Alan of Lille, *Textes inédits*, ed. M. T. D'Alverny (Paris, 1965).
Anselm of Havelberg, *Dialogus* I, ed. G. Salet (Paris, 1966).
Clarembald of Arras, *Life and Works*, ed. N. M. Häring (Toronto, 1965).
Garlandus, *Dialectica*, ed. L. M. de Rijk (Assen, 1959).
Gerhoch of Reiehersberg, *Letter to Pope Hadrian about the Novelties of the Day*, ed. N. M. Häring (Toronto, 1974).
Gilbert Crispin, *Disputatio Judei et Christiani*, ed. B. Blumenkranz (Antwerp, 1956).
Gilbert of Poitiers, *Commentaries on Boethius*, ed. N. M. Häring (Toronto, 1966).
Hugh of St. Victor, *Didascalicon*, ed. C. Buttimer (Washington, 1939).
Thierry of Chartes and his school, *Commentaries on Boethius*, ed. N. M. Häring (Toronto, 1971).
William of Conches, *Glosa super Platonem*, ed. E. Jeauneau (Paris, 1965).

Accessus ad Auctores, ed. R. B. C. Huygens (Leiden, 1970).

Logica Modernorum, ed. L. M. de Rijk (Assen, 1967), 2 vols.

Additional texts, apart from those still available only in Migne's *Patrologia Latina*, may be found in *Recherches de théologie ancienne et médiévale, Archives d'histoire doctrinale et littéraire du mogen âge, Beiträge zur Geschichte der Philosophie und Theologie des Mittelaiters. Cahiers de l'institut du moyen-âge grec et latin, Copenhagen.*

General Studies

J. W. Baldwin, *Masters, Princes and Merchants* (Princeton, 1970), 2 vols.

C. N. L. Brooke, *The Twelfth Century Renaissance* (London, 1969).

M. D. Chenu, *La Théologie au xiie siècle* (Paris, 1966).

E. Curtius, *European Literature in the Latin Middle Ages* (London, 1953).

M. Claggett (ed.), *Twelfth Century Europe and the Foundations of Modern Society* (Madison, 1967).

J. de Ghellinck, *Le Mouvement theologique du xiie siècle* (Bruges, 1948).

—— *L'Essor de la littérature latine au xiie siècle* (Brussels, 1955).

C. Haskins, *The Renaissance of the Twelfth Century* (Cambridge, Mass., 1927).

—— *Studies in Mediaeval Culture* (Cambridge Mass., 1929).

D. E. Luscombe, *The School of Peter Abelard* (Cambridge, 1969).

G. Paré, A. Brunet, P. Tremblay, *La Renaissance du xiie siècle* (Paris, 1933).

B. Smalley, *The Study of the Bible in the Middle Ages* (Oxford, 1953).

R. W. Southern, *Mediaeval Humanism* (Oxford, 1970).

INDEX